ON THE ROAD TO REBELLION:
THE UNITED IRISHMEN AND HAMBURG, 1796–1803

On the Road to Rebellion

THE UNITED IRISHMEN
AND HAMBURG
1796–1803

Paul Weber

FOUR COURTS PRESS

Set in 11 on 13 point Ehrhardt
by Carrigboy Typesetting Services for
FOUR COURTS PRESS
55 Prussia Street, Dublin 7
e-mail: fcp@indigo.ie
and in North America for
FOUR COURTS PRESS
c/o ISBS, 5804 N.E. Hassalo Street, Portland, OR 97213

A catalogue record for this title
is available from the British Library.

ISBN 1-85182-311-5

Printed in Great Britain
by Hartnolls Ltd, Bodmin, Cornwall

TO MY PARENTS

Since they do not speak English,
this study is a closed book to them, and yet
to their help I owe more than I can say.

Contents

Preface

When I arrived in Dublin in October 1991, the United Irishmen and Hamburg were nothing but an *idée fixe*. Although I had a rough notion of how to proceed, taking up my studies at Trinity College was still a leap into the unknown. After entering Professor Cullen's room for the first time, I soon realised that working on the 'Hamburg connection' was more than going into raptures over Irish freedom fighters in faraway places. Without the help of many friends in Ireland, Britain and Germany, the *United Irishmen and Hamburg* would hardly have been brought to light.

On the academic side, I am indebted to Prof. Dr Peter Alter, the late Prof. Dr Erich Angermann and Dr Thomas Bartlett who kept me on track during my student days in Köln (Cologne) and Galway, but most of all I am grateful to my supervisor Prof. L.M. Cullen for channelling my efforts properly. Without his criticism and encouragement, I could easily have been thrown off track. Since intellectual stimulation is not confined to the venerable walls of Trinity College, I would also like to thank Senia Paseta and Ruan O'Donnell for academic help and friendship.

I am greatly indebted to numerous helping hands in the archives and libraries in Ireland, England and Germany. In particular, I wish to thank Dr Lorenzen-Schmidt and Gisela Fabian for standing by my side during my stay in Hamburg.

Various authorities gave financial assistance to me and my project. I owe a particular debt to the Irish Department of Education as well as to those responsible for administering Trinity monies, especially to Dr Robinson-Hammerstein whose benevolent support was vital to the progress of my studies.

A friend in need is a friend indeed. Thank God I have many of them. Without my friends, I would have been cut off from the real world and stuck in the ivory tower. Therefore, thank you very much for being there when I needed you: Peter, Stefan, Jörg, Gisela, Marie, Frank, Kate, Holger, Eva, Bettina, Judith, Gail, Eleanor, Ann, Pete, Frank (Hamburg), Nils, and many others. Most of all, I am grateful to my parents, Katharina and Peter, and my brothers for being the most wonderful family one can hope for. I will never be able to thank them enough for what they have done. Shortly before closing the matter, my wife Gabriele and little Paula have interfered in *United* affairs. Their 'audible' support has helped to bring this study to fruition.

Abbreviations

Ham. Staats.	Hamburger Staatsarchiv
Nat. Arch.	National Archives, Dublin
NLI	National Library of Ireland, Dublin
PRO	Public Record Office, London
PRONI	Public Record Office of Northern Ireland, Belfast
TCD	Trinity College, Dublin

The Exile of Erin

There came to the beach a poor exile of Erin,
The dew on his thin robe hung heavy and chill,
For his country he sighed when at twilight repairing
To wander alone by the wind-beaten hill.

But the day-star attracted his eyes' sad devotion,
For it rose o'er his own native isle of the ocean,
Where once in the pride of his youthful emotion
He sang the bold anthem of Erin go Bragh.

Poem by Thomas Campbell, written in Hamburg some time after the Irishman's arrival in the city at the turn of 1798–9, reproduced in *Correspondence of Charles, First marquis Cornwallis*, ed. Charles Ross, II (London, 1859), 362.

Introduction

After covering some thousand kilometres, the United Irish poet, Thomas Campbell, reached Hamburg around the close of 1798. He had left Ireland in the wake of the disastrous failure of the rebellion and had subsequently headed for Hamburg, the biggest port on the north German coast. There, he met an 'Exile of Erin' who had turned his back on his 'native isle of the ocean'. Campbell's fate is no isolated case, since, at the end of the eighteenth century, Hamburg had become the second home to many a United Irishman. But what was the Irishmen's business in that strange place far away from Ireland? To answer this question is the main concern of this book.

Quite different strands of development led up to the birth of Irish republicanism and the creation of a national movement interacting with forces outside the narrow confines of the British Isles. After many years of remarkable tranquillity, Ireland was thrown into a whirl of events towards the end of the eighteenth century. The foundation of the Society of United Irishmen in the autumn of 1791 did not mark the beginning of Irish nationalism, but the United men certainly helped a true independence movement see the light of day. Their sources of inspiration were diverse. While the American war of independence had attracted widespread admiration and attention, it was above all the French Revolution that lent wings to the ideas of thinking men in Ireland and all over Europe. The breathtaking changes in France made them believe that a new age had begun for the whole of mankind and that also the Irish would participate in that universal struggle for liberation.[1] Animated by the French example, the United Irishmen set their sights on a juster society. Inspired by the notion of a 'United Society of the Irish nation', they demanded 'a complete reform in the legislature founded on the principles of civil, political, and religious liberty.'[2] While their demands were constitutional until

---

1 See Gough, Hugh, 'The French Revolution and Europe 1789–99', in Gough, Hugh and Dickson, David, eds, *Ireland and the French Revolution* (Dublin, 1990), 1–13 on the impact of the French Revolution on Europe.
2 Reproduced in Cronin, Sean, *Irish Nationalism. A History of its Roots and Ideology* (Dublin, 1980), 23.

1794–5, they subsequently conspired to remove by force English rule in Ireland. Government suppression had put an end to United efforts to achieve reform by peaceful means, thus forcing Irish radicals to create a different basis for their political activities. After flirting with French ideas for a number of years, the United Irishmen's approach to revolutionary France was only a matter of time. In concert with their disaffected comrades on the British mainland, they wanted to emulate their French brethren in recovering their liberty. From 1795–6 onwards, the Irish radicals turned towards France for military aid in order to carry through their plans of establishing an Irish republic. For the greater part of some ten following years, they were governed by the notion of a French–assisted revolution in Ireland. The United Irishmen had changed from a national to an international phenomenon.

The United Irishmen's attachment to the cause of the French fell on fertile ground in France. Irish overtures seemed to offer a chance to secure victory in the bitter war against Europe's major monarchies in general and against England in particular. England had been the driving force behind a coalition of powers, including among others Austria, Prussia, Spain and Portugal and attacking France on all fronts since 1792–3. As Britain's oldest dependency, Ireland was seen as the vulnerable backdoor to the arch-enemy in the north and a trump-card of decisive importance. Moreover, in supporting the Irish fight for freedom, France could take revenge on its arch-enemy in the north for its involvement in the bloody counter-revolutionary war in the Vendée. Accordingly, the United Irishmen stood out from the numerous republicans from all over Europe who were courting successive French governments in order to draw attention to their subversive plans. The Irishmen's diplomatic achievements make manifest the crucial importance of the Franco–Irish alliance for both sides. Irish agents not only gained easy access to the French authorities after first arriving on the Continent in 1796, but also induced them to send thousands of men, ships and arms in support of the Irish republican movement in the course of the following two years. After the failure of the uprising of 1798, the United Irishmen ceased to be a 'mass-based, secret society' in Ireland.[3] With no powerful organization at home, the Society fell out of favour with the French authorities. Its exiled leaders on the Continent tried hard to reanimate French interests in Irish affairs, but were fobbed off with promises in the years subsequent to the rebellion. The Irish comrades-in-arms of the 1790s had become a set of disillusioned refugees by the beginning of the nineteenth century.

In the heyday of the Franco–Irish alliance (1796–8), the scale of United migration to and from France is impressive. It is indicative of the development

3   Curtin, Nancy J., *The United Irishmen. Popular Politics in Ulster and Dublin 1791–8* (Oxford, 1994), 115.

of the Irish–French liaison. Moreover, it helps to gain an insight into the Society's fortunes at home. Thus, the rebellion of 1798 had an enormous effect on radical migration from the British Isles, initially because of United efforts to secure French assistance in a rising against English rule in Ireland and finally because the rising really materialized – and failed. Although the home movement they claimed to represent had become a mere sham, the United leaders in exile on the Continent remained active after 1798. Their years of travel and flight continued until well into the nineteenth century; and it is this aspect of United to-ing and fro-ing which occupies an important place in this book.

For many years it would seem that the United Irishmen had sunk into oblivion. Recently, an increasing number of historians have started to direct our attention to the United Irish movement. Extensive research has been done on many aspects of Irish radicalism of the 1790s and 1800s. Apart from more general works, like McDowell's *Ireland in the Age of Imperialism and Revolution*, Whelan's *The Tree of Liberty* and Bartlett's *The Fall and Rise of the Irish Nation*, numerous historians, mostly arguing from an (Anglo–) Irish perspective, have been looking into various facets of United activities. Nancy J. Curtin and Jim Smyth, among others, have sharpened our understanding of the United Irishmen by focusing on the movement's internal organisation as well as the development of popular politics. Without belittling the achievements of those working on the home movement, however, some studies have to be singled out as invaluable. Since it is beyond the scope of the national dimension of the United Irish movement, Marianne Elliott's pioneering *Partners in Revolution* set a new standard. In including Irish, British, and most importantly, French sources, Elliott considerably broadened our horizons with regard to the Franco–Irish alliance. However, one should also do justice to earlier efforts to examine the international implications of Irish radicalism. Nineteenth-century writers, in particular W.E.H. Lecky (*A History of Ireland in the Eighteenth Century*), W.J. Fitzpatrick (*Secret Service under Pitt*), Edouard Guillon (*La France et l'Irlande pendant la Révolution*), or R.R. Madden (*The United Irishmen. Their Lives and Times*), paved the way for modern historical investigations into the United Irishmen. Moreover, twentieth-century British historians, such as E.P. Thompson, A. Goodwin, or Roger Wells, have helped to elucidate the Anglo–Irish dimension of Irish radicalism. All of these cast light on the United Irishmen as an international phenomenon.[4] In the historiography

4   In order of appearance in the text: McDowell, R.B., *Ireland in the Age of Imperialism and Revolution 1760–1801*, 2nd edn (Oxford, 1991); Whelan, Kevin, *The Tree of Liberty: Radicalism, Catholicism and the Construction of the Irish Identity 1760–1830* (Cork, 1996); Bartlett, Thomas, *The Fall and Rise of the Irish Nation: the Catholic Question, 1690–1830* (Savage, Md., 1992); Curtin, Nancy J., *The United Irishmen. Popular Politics in Ulster and Dublin 1791–8* (Oxford, 1994); Smyth, Jim, *The Men of No Property. Irish Radicals and*

on the United Irishmen, there are countless references to Hamburg. Though
the role of the north German city is far from unknown, its importance for
the Irish republican movement has never been singled out for special attention.

In the years between 1796 and 1803, Hamburg functioned as a communications centre between the revolutionary movement in Ireland and the various
governments in France. The city reflected the different aspects of political
emigration from the British Isles to the Continent in the transitional years of
the French Revolution. Hamburg became the preferred point of entrance on
the Continent for the United Irishmen, since its legal status as a free city and
its commercial relations offered a wide scope for the Irishmen's activities. At
the same time, it provided the British and French governments with the opportunity of establishing a network of agents to keep a watch on subversive
activities. Hamburg, although supposedly neutral, represented one of the main
scenes in the conflict between the great powers in the years of the coalition
wars.

A study of events in Hamburg at the turn of the eighteenth century sup-
plements the historiography on the United Irishmen and adds an important
piece to the United jigsaw. Accordingly, the development of United affairs
in Hamburg in the years between 1796 and 1803 forms the principal topic of
this study. Emphasis will be laid on the question of radical migration to and
from Hamburg, and its emerging routes and patterns. What were the effects
of the 'Hamburg connection' on the radical movement as a whole? Since
United moves were subject to British scrutiny, it will be important to look
into the machinery of British espionage in Hamburg, its development as well
as the repercussions it had on the United movement. Apart from making use
of Irish and British sources, German material is consulted in order to examine
United Irish activities against their Hamburg background. Notwithstanding
that this book is, first and foremost, a survey of Irish history, the destinies
of the Irish radicals were closely connected with the north German city.
Thus, it will be vital to paint a picture of the United Irishmen in Hamburg
and to entice them out from the depths of the footnotes.

Popular Politics in the Late Eighteenth Century (Dublin, 1992); Elliott, Marianne, *Partners
in Revolution. The United Irishmen and France* (New Haven, London, 1982); Lecky,
W.E.H., *A History of Ireland in the Eighteenth Century*, vols: III–IV, New Impression
(London, 1913); Fitzpatrick, W.J., *Secret Service under Pitt* (London, 1892); Guillon,
Edouard, *La France et l'Irlande pendant la Révolution* (Paris, 1888); Madden, R.R., *The
United Irishmen. Their Lives and Times*, 3 ser., 7 vols (London, 1842–46), and revised edn,
4 vols (London, 1857–60); Thompson, E.P., *The Making of the English Working Class*, 3rd
edn (London, 1980); Goodwin, Albert, *The Friends of Liberty: The English Democratic
Movement in the Age of the French Revolution* (London, 1979); Wells, Roger, *Insurrection.
The British Experience 1795–1803*, 2nd edn (Gloucester, 1986).

CHAPTER I

Hamburg: the Historical Basis of a 'Special Case'

PRE-REVOLUTIONARY HAMBURG[1]

Many historians, in following Schramm's theory of its being a 'special case' in German history, have emphasised Hamburg's special position. Schramm, one of the outstanding German historians of the post-war period, argued that this position was due to a combination of geographical, political, social and economic factors which made Hamburg stand out against the eighteenth-century German background.[2] A critical observation of the city's history shows that this applies at an international as well as a national level. Hamburg's special position within the German *Reich*, or the Holy Roman Empire, is closely connected with its position in Europe.[3] As will be shown later on, the city's great importance as a crossroads on the Continent created the conditions for an interface of Irish and German history at the time of the French Revolution.

Despite belonging formally to the German *Reich* from the ninth century, Hamburg had an unclear relationship with the *Reich* and the neighbouring countries alike. Since early modern times, the city fathers had always attached great importance to neutrality. The absolute endeavour to preserve this neutrality often led to political instability and confusion about its position as well as to pressure from the great powers on the city to submit to their demands. From a quite early stage, the assembly of the representatives of the German

---

1 This chapter includes a short description of the peculiarities of Altona's history. In the rest of the book, distinctions between Hamburg and Altona will not be made and the name Hamburg will stand in for the two cities inasmuch as Altona does not differ from Hamburg. The two cities became one municipality as recently as 1937 although just being one mile away from each other.

2 See Schramm, Percy Ernst, *Hamburg. Ein Sonderfall in der Geschichte Deutschlands* (Hamburg, 1964).

3 Henceforth historical technical terms will often be used in German (italics), together with an English translation on their first appearance. In this way, long-winded and sometimes misleading English paraphrases will be avoided.

Reich (*Reichstag*) tried to tie Hamburg to the Empire. This seemed more than advisable since, in the fifteenth century, Schleswig-Holstein, the country immediately surrounding the city, came into the hands of the house of Oldenburg, the Danish reigning family, and was thus connected with the kingdom of Denmark. Hence, the *Reichstag* of 1510 asserted Hamburg's place in the *Reich*.[4] Furthermore, from the beginning of the sixteenth century, the imperial court at Vienna began legal proceedings to secure Hamburg's submission to the German Empire (*Reichsunmittelbarkeit*) in order to definitely settle the dispute over the city's status. When the court finally declared Hamburg an imperial city (*Reichsstadt*) in 1618, Denmark lodged an appeal against the decision, and Hamburg, accepting its subordinate position to Holstein and Denmark, agreed in 1621, in the Treaty of Steinburg, to pay homage to the Danish king. In the following years, Hamburg faced a constant threat of a Danish military intervention. Denmark, always opposed to the city's independence, undertook several attempts to annex the city and to exclude the *Reich*.[5] Thus, from quite early in modern times, Hamburg stood uneasily between the German *Reich* and Denmark, subject to the emperor, but at the same time paying contributions to both Danish king and German emperor.

In the first half of the eighteenth century, a third power, Prussia, itself an electorate of Brandenburg which had become a kingdom in 1701, became increasingly interested in the destinies of Hamburg. The elector of Brandenburg, as the count of Magdeburg, had traditionally been the leading prince of the circle of Lower Saxony, an administrative district of the north German states, the *Reichsstädte* and the cities of the Hanse. Now the kings of Prussia, especially Frederic William I and Frederic II, the Great, in reinforcing their position in northern Germany, offered their protection to the city of Hamburg. Despite several approaches to Hamburg, the relationship remained vague, and the kings of Prussia were not able to change the magistrates' mind about the city's policy of neutrality.[6]

Eventually, determined intervention by the new German emperor, Joseph II, smoothed the path for a satisfactory settlement of the situation. In 1766, he asked the Danish king to withdraw his appeal of 1618. Subsequent negotiations between Denmark and the *Reich* over the question of Hamburg's status were

---

4 Hamburg was no imperial city (*Reichsstadt*) and was still not officially invited to the *Reichstag* but was present at the assemblies since the beginning of the fifteenth century and had to pay contributions to the *Reich*'s charges (*Reichslasten*).

5 Thus, during the Great Northern War, Danish troops moved into Hamburg in 1712 and only left after the city had paid a huge sum of money to the Danish king.

6 See Wohlwill, Adolf, *Neuere Geschichte der Freien und Hansestadt Hamburg, insbesondere von 1789 bis 1815* (Gotha, 1914), 62–3 and 74 on Prussia's Hamburg policies in the eighteenth century.

finally completed in 1768 with the Treaty of Gottorp. Denmark dropped its demands, waived its financial claims and accepted the city's independence (which did not itself mean that Hamburg's disputes with Denmark came to an end). Hamburg's neutrality within the German *Reich* was legally fixed and agreed upon by the emperor. The city officially became a *Reichsstadt* and received a seat and the right to vote at the *Immerwährender Reichstag* at Regensburg. Thus, Hamburg was the youngest, but also the biggest German *Reichsstadt*, with 130,000 inhabitants in 1794.[7]

Apart from a determined policy of neutrality, Hamburg's sophisticated administration was a further essential feature of its special position. The democratic character of the city's politics as well as the extraordinary and comprehensive self-government of the burghers distinguished Hamburg from the rest of the *Reich* where feudal structures still prevailed. The government of the 'most enlightened German city' exclusively rested on its burghers.[8] Thus, noblemen could not obtain civil rights in Hamburg, purchase property or participate in the city's politics. Politics was restricted to a relatively small circle of Lutheran, propertied burghers (*Erbgessene Bürgerschaft*): some 3000 to 4000 participated in politics at the end of the eighteenth century.[9]

Hamburg's body politic rested on the constitution of 1712 (*Hauptrezeß*). The *Hauptrezeß* brought to an end a struggle about power and influence between the burghers and the magistrates which had been going on for centuries. Furthermore, it secured the city's democratic basis and created the *Erbgessene Bürgerschaft*. As laid down by the constitution, Hamburg's government and administration was in the hands of the Senate and the burgherly colleges (*Bürgerliche Kollegien*), both composed of men of great merit from the *Erbgesessene Bürgerschaft* but self-perpetuating in the absence of any process of election. The extraordinarily close cooperation within the administrative machinery, that is, between Senate and Colleges, was the basis of the city's body politic. Nevertheless, it was characteristic of the democratic nature of the

7 Hamburg's demographic development in the modern times: 1550: 20,000; 1600: 36–40,000; 1680: 48–58,000; 1710: 75,000; 1750: 90,000; 1787: 100,000; 1794: 130,000; Kopitzsch, Franklin, 'Hamburg zwischen Hauptrezeß und Franzosenseit-Bemerkungen zur Verfassung, Verwaltung und Sozialstruktur', in Rausch, Wilhelm, ed., *Die Städte Mitteleuropas im 17. und 18. Jahrhundert* (Linz/Donau, 1981), 182.

8 Kopitzsch, Franklin, *Grundzüge einer Sozialgeschichte der Aufklärung in Hamburg und Altona* (Hamburg, 1982), 137.

9 The *Erbgessene Bürgerschaft* and political participation was restricted to burghers, at least thirty years old, with a house in the city, land inside the city zone plus a sum of money of at least 1000 *Reichstaler* or land outside the city zone plus at least 2000 *Reichstaler*. Kopitzsch, op. cit., 187.

constitution that important decisions taken by the Senate and the burgherly colleges were submitted for the approval of the *Erbgessenene Bürgerschaft*.

The Senate, as the central representative assembly of Hamburg, was composed of an equal number of lawyers and merchants. It consisted of four Burgomasters (three had to have a doctorate in law and one had to be a merchant), 24 Senators (11 lawyers/13 merchants), 4 *Syndici* and 4 Secretaries all of whom had to have doctorates in law. The cabinet-like Senate managed all departments. Thus, Burgomasters and Senators, among other things, functioned as secretaries of state, diplomats, chief justices or chief constables (*Prätor*). On the other hand, *Syndici* and Secretaries, as the continuous element of Senate politics, had clearly defined areas of responsibility. In the course of the eighteenth century, they became influential ministers rather than mere advisers, as they were originally intended to be.

The burgherly colleges acted as a means of supervision and a counterbalance to the Senate. Furthermore, they provided the bureaucratic apparatus for the city's administration. Their responsibilities included all spheres of administrative work: special cases which were carried out by deputations (*Deputationen*), the supervision of the poor-houses, orphanages, prisons and other public institutions which were under the control of the colleges (*Kollegien*), as well as the administration of the city's finances through the *Kämmerei* and the *Kommerzdeputation* which were independent of the Senate's control. The burgherly colleges were organized on a hierarchic basis, including effectively overlapping 'colleges' of 15, 60, 120 and 180 members respectively. The College of the One hundred and eighty (*Gremium der Hundertachtziger*), as a representative body of all burgherly colleges, was composed of 4 colleges: 15 Elders (*Oberalte*), mostly experienced, senior officials who represented a strong conservative element in the city's government, constituted the highest authority within the hierarchy. Together with 45 Deacons (*Diakone*), they formed the College of the Sixty (*Gremium der Sechziger*) which cooperated with the Senate in matters of the church. The College of the Sixty plus 120 Subdeacons (*Subdiakone*) eventually made up the College of the One hundred and eighty.[10]

Although the city's administration rested on a hierarchy along property lines, it was based on democratic principles. Unlike many German and European states where hereditary nepotism and cliquish regimes were still the order of the day at the end of the eighteenth century, Hamburg's government represented a 'democracy of the wealthy'. Accordingly, the protection and promotion of the city's wealth through a policy of neutrality had traditionally been imperative for the Hamburg authorities in order to preserve the political

10 See Kopitzsch, *Grundzüge einer Sozialgeschichte der Aufklärung*, 146–78 on the foundations of Hamburg's administration.

and economic basis of its livelihood. The city's politics was strongly influenced by its prominent position in international politics, as seen above, but most of all by the ramifications of its commercial relations. Favoured by its geographic position Hamburg 'served as a commercial nerve center for half the continent'.[11] By means of the river Elbe, Hamburg was connected with the North Sea and the east German Oder towns (the *Friedrich-Wilhelm-Kanal* connecting the rivers Oder and Spree, and thus the Elbe with the Oder, was opened in 1668). Moreover, it lay on the eighteenth-century commercial routes between the east and the west, and the north and the south of Europe. The strength of its position in the world market was the fundamental basis of Hamburg's prosperity, which rested on a combination of commerce and manufacturing. Accordingly, commercial and political relations with foreign countries were of great importance to Hamburg whose diplomatic representatives and mercantile fleet were to be found in most parts of maritime Europe. Furthermore, the city served as a residence for foreign merchants since early modern times. The admission of the first merchant adventurers in 1567 reflects the city's openness towards foreigners, which was to become one of the essential features of the city's commercial development. It prompted a constant influx of merchants from the Netherlands, England, eastern Europe, Jews from Portugal, and from other economic powers of the time, trading with or alongside their German counterparts.[12]

In the sixteenth and seventeenth century, England and Holland were the city's preferred trade partners. According to the trade agreement of 1567, their merchants had full freedom of trade in Hamburg as long as the goods were not restricted by any privileges (*Privilegium*).[13] In the eighteenth century, commercial relations with England worsened because of Hamburg reinforcing its trade with France. England felt neglected in the face of several trade agreements between its rival on the Continent and Hamburg. The trade agreements with France in 1655, 1716, 1769 and 1789 obtained favourable conditions and lower taxes for the city's mercantile fleet berthing at French ports. Furthermore, the agreements included separate clauses saying that in cases of war between France and the German *Reich* Hamburg's citizens would be regarded as neutral if the German emperor granted the same rights to French

---

11 Lindemann, Mary, *Patriots and Paupers. Hamburg, 1712–1830* (New York, Oxford, 1990), 3.
12 Schramm, *Hamburg. Ein Sonderfall*, 21.
13 Hamburg's trade in England was not as unlimited until 1661 when a decree of Charles II granted full freedom of trade to Hamburg merchants (*Caroli II Magnae Britanniae Regis Privilegium civitati Hamburgensi concessum de libertate Commercii 1661*). See Laufenberg, H., *Hamburg und die Französische Revolution* (Hamburg, 1913), 29–32 on Hamburg's commercial relations with England.

citizens in Hamburg. Thus, in the course of the eighteenth century, France took the place of England as Hamburg's preferred trade partner.[14] Many of the city's merchant houses opened offices in Le Havre, Bordeaux, Nantes, Marseille, and other French cities, operating with their parent companies in Hamburg and establishing close economic as well as political links between the two economic powers. In the years of the First French Republic, the close relations with France and the French presence in Hamburg were to play an important part in attracting foreign radicals who were seeking to get in contact with French representatives.[15]

The revolutionary events on the Continent and the coalition wars changed the conditions of Hamburg's economy and its politics alike. The establishment of the Batavian Republic in 1795 and the English naval blockade brought about the elimination of Holland from the economic field. Hamburg then became the outstanding continental centre of trade and of the financial world as well as the only market for English transactions on the European mainland. Thus, according to Franklin Kopitzsch, the years between 1792 and 1798 were 'one of the most successful periods of trade in the history of Hamburg'.[16] In the face of a major European war, the city succeeded in benefitting from its central position until it eventually became involved in the power struggles between France and England at the end of the century.[17] The city's authorities, traditionally eager to stick to their principles of neutrality, were no longer able to stay out of the conflict involving Hamburg's most important trade partners.

ALTONA AND ITS HISTORICAL BACKGROUND

In the eighteenth century, the city of Altona was situated on the River Elbe, one mile north of Hamburg.[18] The short distance between two cities could nevertheless mean a great difference in a German *Reich* split into numerous little states, principalities and city states with different political, social and

---

14 In volume of imports to Hamburg in the years between 1789 and 1791 France led England, Holland, Spain, Portugal and the United States in order of importance (the United States took the place of Portugal after 1791). Kopitzsch, *Grundzüge einer Sozialgeschichte der Aufklärung*, 182.

15 See Laufenberg, *Hamburg und die Französische Revolution*, 33–41 on Hamburg's commercial relations with France in the seventeenth and eighteenth century.

16 Kopitzsch, *Grundzüge einer Sozialgeschichte der Aufklärung*, 183.

17 See chapter 5 of this study on Hamburg and the European conflict.

18 Today there are hardly any visible boundaries or transitions in the urban features of Altona and Hamburg, which became one municipality in 1937.

economic backgrounds. Altona, like Hamburg, had until the extinction of the Pinneberg family and county in 1640 acknowledged its place in the *Reich*. Its effective German status, however, ended in 1640 when it became a Danish possession, and hence, by virtue of royal inheritance, acknowledged the Danish king as its sovereign.[19]

In the 1640s, Denmark started to lay emphasis on the promotion of Altona, until the sixteenth century a mere village of fishermen and craftsmen. It received legal recognition as a city in 1664 and soon became the biggest Danish city after Copenhagen, with approximately 20,000 inhabitants in 1790.[20] Successive governments sought to establish Altona as an economic outpost in the Danish border area. In making use of the city's favourable geographic position and its waterways, Copenhagen tried hard to extend the pillars of Altona's economy – shipping companies, shipping and trade. It became the base of Danish herring shipping and of many other royal institutions. By the end of the eighteenth century, Altona's merchant fleet had developed into a competitor with its prosperous neighbour, Hamburg. Like Hamburg, Altona benefitted from the English naval blockade of the French and the Dutch coast, its economic boom peaking in the 1790s and in the 1800s.[21] With its liberal laws on religion and commerce Altona, like Hamburg, was a melting pot for foreigners of many different nationalities. Jews, for instance, had more rights in Altona than in other cities on the Continent. Due to an enlightened Danish absolutism, the city became a cultural centre of Schleswig-Holstein and a tolerant paradise for foreign merchants and emigrants alike. After 1792, it proved to be a centre for French royalists outside France as well as for republicans from all parts of Europe.[22] The competition with Altona thus became an important impulse for Hamburg and a catalyst for its economy in the eighteenth century. The reciprocal influence between Hamburg and Altona related to many levels of public life. It had become an essential feature of the development of the two cities whose destinies were always to remain closely connected.

19 The county of Pinneberg was part of the county of Holstein, which already belonged to Denmark since 1459 when the main line of the house of Schaumburg had come to an end. However, the count of Pinneberg had still continued to accept his subordinate position to the German emperor until 1640.

20 Grab, Walter, *Demokratische Strömungen in Hamburg und Schleswig-Holstein zur Zeit der Ersten Französischen Republik* (Hamburg, 1966), 23. Altona's demographic development in the modern times: 1570: 50; 1600: 250; 1664: 3000; 1710: 12,000; 1769: 18,050; 1780: 24,400; 1803: 23,099. Kopitzsch, *Grundzüge einer Sozialgeschichte der Aufklärung*, 217, 220 and 224.

21 In terms of numbers of ships it even surpassed Hamburg's fleet at the end of the eighteenth century, possessing 296 ships in 1803. Ibid., 225.

22 See ibid., 712–86 on Altona and the Enlightenment and Piper, P., *Altona und die Fremden, insbesondere die Emigranten, vor hundert Jahren* (Altona, 1914), 3.

HAMBURG AND THE FRENCH REVOLUTION, 1789–95

The changes in France in the year 1789 were generally welcomed in Hamburg. The takeover of power by the citizens met with great interest in a city of politically-minded burghers. Accounts of the Revolution were soon spread by Hamburg merchants doing business in France, such as J.C. Matthiessen and J.W. Archenholz,[23] who had witnessed the events in the streets of Paris in 1789. Due to their long-standing commercial relations the city's merchants had come into close contact with the situation in France and regarded the Revolution as a radical but necessary change to a repressive apparatus of state. Thus, educated and propertied liberals, like Klopstock, the well-known poet residing in Hamburg, or the merchant houses of Albert Reimarus, Georg Heinrich Sieveking, Caspar Voght, August Hennings and Chapeaurouge, were sympathetic to the revolutionary cause. The house of Georg Heinrich Sieveking that had already been a place for intellectual interchange in the years before 1789 soon became 'a meeting point of European standing', including many French liberals and admirers of the Revolution from all over Europe.[24] In talks and debates they expressed great enthusiasm for the ideas coming from France. In 1790, the Reimarus-Sieveking-Voght circle celebrated the anniversary of Bastille Day, incurring variously approval and indignation from the burghers of Hamburg.

In the first years after 1789, the Hamburg press was sympathetic to the new revolutionary principles. Hamburg, as well as Altona, accommodated a multitude of daily papers including, among others, the *Hamburgische Correspondent* as the top-selling newspaper in the whole of Germany, with 36,000 copies a day at the beginning of the 1790s. The mild censorship in Hamburg facilitated a wide coverage of the Revolution, but also eventually attracted the attention of the imperial government at Vienna. Annoyed about a press flirting with democratic ideas, Emperor Leopold III ordered the confiscation of all papers creating indignation and turmoil in December 1791. However, despite the Senate's subsequent efforts to suppress the democratic press, the city remained a centre for publications on the Revolution throughout the decade.[25]

At the beginning of the 1790s, revolutionary ideas fell on fertile ground in a plutocratic society with a highly unequal distribution of wealth. Hamburg's poor did not benefit proportionally from the city's flourishing economy, a

---

23 See chapters 3 and 5 of this study on their involvement in the activities of the United Irishmen in Hamburg.
24 Kopitzsch, *Grundzüge einer Sozialgeschichte der Aufklärung*, 206.
25 See Grab, *Demokratische Strömungen in Hamburg und Schleswig-Holstein*, 25–9 and Droz, Jacques, *L'Allemagne et la Révolution Francaise* (Paris, 1949), 135–9 on the immediate response to the revolutionary events in France.

fact which led to increasing social friction between the prosperous and the poor towards the end of the century.[26] Thus, the Big Strike of the Guilds was an expression of social discontent rather than a direct outcome of the French Revolution. It also highlighted the rivalry between the old crafts and their guilds and the rising manufactories and new methods of production in the textile, sugar, tobacco and clothing industries. In August 1791, in the first strike ever in the history of Germany, 7000 journeymen stopped working and demonstrated on the streets of Hamburg. Although diffuse allusions to a French-inspired ideology were heard among some of the journeymen, their actual claims were for better working conditions, higher wages and a reduction in working hours. Nevertheless, to the city's wealthy the turmoil was a reminder of the radical events in France. Within a week, the authorities had restored order, with little bloodshed, but with a determination hitherto unusual in Hamburg.[27]

The wealthy burghers, initially enthusiastic about the Revolution, quickly turned away after social discontent at home had begun to grow. Furthermore, from 1792, the emerging radicalisation of the Revolution in France through the Jacobins gave cause for concern. Radical politics spread to Germany and also found its way to Hamburg and Altona. In Altona, a Jacobin club was formed in 1792. Although it was apparently relatively small, with not more than 22 members (whose names and activities are not known) and of little importance, it caused great uneasiness among the city's authorities. French Jacobins also appeared in Hamburg making contact with liberal groups. Despite their interest in democratic ideas, Hamburg's friends of the Revolution, like the Reimarus–Sieveking–Voght circle, were moderate liberals and Enlightenment thinkers rather than radical revolutionaries. Thus, Jacobinism could never really establish itself as an authoritative force and actually remained isolated within the city. However, Hamburg gained the reputation of being a seat of rabble-rousers among German conservatives who, not without reason, feared

26 In the years between 1792 and 1799 the death rate largely exceeded the birth rate due to catastrophic conditions in the city's public health service. The increase in population in these years only resulted from a sharp rise in immigration. Efforts to relieve the state of affairs for Hamburg's poor had already started in 1788 with the establishment of the Poor House by Caspar Voght but failed to produce a satisfying improvement of social conditions. Grab, *Demokratische Strömungen in Hamburg und Schleswig-Holstein*, 30–1. See Lindemann, Mary, *Patriots and Paupers. Hamburg, 1712–1830* (New York, Oxford, 1990) for further information on social policies and the situation of the poor in Hamburg in the eighteenth century.

27 The series of strikes of various guilds that were to follow until 1795 only confirmed the Senate in its fear of the masses. See Wohlwill, *Neuere Geschichte der Freien und Hansestadt Hamburg*, 105–14 on the strikes of the 1790s.

that the city with its liberal laws would develop into a meeting point for radicals from all over Europe.[28]

The Altona authorities and the Hamburg Senate, which felt joined together in tradition and social position with the French *noblesse de robe*, were strongly opposed to the Revolution. Out-of-doors agitation and notorious political activities of foreign radicals had to be regarded as a threat to their own position. Accordingly, in view of the *terreur* in France, the activities of French republicans on Hamburg territory strained the relations between France and Hamburg. Furthermore, since 1792, Austria and Prussia, the two most powerful states of the German *Reich*, were at war with France, Hamburg's leading trade partner. Consequently, the Senate found itself in the difficult situation of balancing the city's economic interests and the political necessities of its position as a *Reichsstadt*.

In the face of full-scale war with France the imperial government at Vienna was deeply annoyed about Hamburg's persistent efforts to protect its neutral status. Although the German emperor had agreed on a financial contribution as a substitute for military assistance in May 1793, Hamburg's lack of willingness to participate directly in the war caused offence in Vienna. Accordingly, the court in Vienna, as well as Berlin, accused the city of neglecting its duties as a *Reichsstadt*. Moreover, it complained with emphasis about the city's continual commercial relations with France. In February 1793, the German emperor issued a decree proscribing the trade in livestock, grain, a number of important foodstuffs, and raw materials for military uses. The decree was intended to restrict Hamburg's trade with the *Reich's* enemy and to aim a decisive blow at France, which was burdened with food shortages and mercantile difficulties due to its isolation within Europe. Knowing that French economic distress was surely not to the city's detriment, the Senate strongly protested against the imperial instructions and attempted to bring about the discontinuation of the decree. These efforts failed, however, since Prussia and the circle of Lower Saxony insisted on Hamburg loyalty to the German war effort. In the following years, although the Senate tried hard to adhere to the imperial directives, it nevertheless strove to maintain the city's long-standing relations with France.

In a time of a major European war, Hamburg's links with France remained controversial. Shortly after the court at Vienna had placed restrictions on the city's freedom of trade in February 1793, the question of Hamburg's neutrality became a serious point at issue again. In February, the authorities of the circle of Lower Saxony pressed for Lehoc, the French representative at

28 See Grab, *Demokratische Strömungen in Hamburg und Schleswig-Holstein*, 101–12 and 140 on republican activities in Hamburg and Altona in the first half of the 1790s.

Hamburg, to be expelled.[29] His presence in the city had long been a thorn in the flesh of north German conservatives, since all other representatives from France residing in the *Reich* had already been expelled by an imperial decree in November of the previous year. Thus, the Senate finally had to comply with the demands and reluctantly told Lehoc to leave the city. Lehoc himself complained loudly about the Senate's procedure, calling it a violation of international law and an insult to the French nation. Soon after news of Lehoc's departure had reached Paris, the French government, taking vigorous action, ordered the confiscation of all Hamburg ships in France. Vexed about the uncertain nature of Hamburg–French relations, it wanted to show up Hamburg's city fathers as mere tools in the hands of France's enemies. But Paris knew full well that commercial relations with Hamburg were of vital importance for France's national economy and sought only a short, but sharp trial of strength. In March, the French government abolished the embargo, which nevertheless had caused heavy financial losses for Hamburg's trade.[30]

Arising from the difficulties of its special position, Hamburg had once more found itself in the midst of a conflict of the great powers at the beginning of 1793. In February, also Great Britain joined the coalition of conservative countries fighting France. The British declaration of war thus changed the balance of power in favour of the conservative forces. This, moreover, put additional pressure on Hamburg which was endeavouring to get along both with revolutionary France and the reactionary powers. It became increasingly difficult for the city to keep up a neutral line, since all warring parties were suspicious about discriminations against them in their commercial and political rivalry with their enemies. The city, faced with a multitude of conflicting interests and claims of the great powers, developed into a diplomatic theatre of war.

Hamburg hoped for an end to the war, which was disturbing its economy and its international relations, when a peace conference between France and Prussia finally seemed to offer a glimmer of hope. With the Peace of Basel in April 1795, Prussia and France suspended hostilities. Berlin pledged itself to be neutral and also officially consented to north German neutrality, thus meeting Hamburg's key demands. But although Prussian supremacy over

---

29 Lehoc was the official French representative at the circle of Lower Saxony with his residence in Hamburg. Originally appointed by Louis XVI, his credentials had not been renewed after the establishment of the French Republic in 1792.

30 The abolition had been preceded by the mediation of Hamburg's French born envoy in Paris, LaFlotte, who had presented a memorandum on behalf of Hamburg to the French government. See Wohlwill, *Neuere Geschichte der Freien und Hansestadt Hamburg*, 116–27 on the events of the beginning of 1793.

north Germany seemed to ensure the city's independence, the imperial court at Vienna did not agree to Berlin's high-handed approach. Hamburg was subordinate to Prussia, as the leading state in the circle of Lower Saxony, but first and foremost, it was a *Reichsstadt* and subject to imperial directives. Hence, Vienna rejected several requests of the Senate for imperial recognition of the city's neutrality and refused to put an end to Hamburg's war contributions. The city's magistrate had to realise that there was 'hardly any room for an independent political development of smaller powers', especially since France continued to assert itself as an authoritative force in the city, too.[31] Paris was annoyed about Hamburg's weak-willed attempts to preserve its independence after the Peace of Basel. Moreover, it was indignant about French royalists gathering in the city in great numbers. In the spring of 1795, the French government's disappointment took the form of bitter warnings to the Senate to restore the old friendship between France and Hamburg.[32]

France was absolutely determined to re-establish regular diplomatic relations with Hamburg. In June 1795, the Committee of Public Safety decided to send another envoy to north Germany. It appointed Charles Reinhard as French representative at Hamburg and Georg Kerner as his secretary. Reinhard's (and Kerner's) German descent seemed advantageous for his demanding mission. Born as Karl Reinhardt in German Schorndorf/Württemberg, fifteen miles east of Stuttgart, the delegate had been in the French diplomatic service and various government posts since 1792. Known to be a revolutionary idealist as well as an ardent admirer of the idea of the Hanse, he was concerned about French as well as Hamburg interests. Later on, his close relations with the Reimarus–Sieveking–Voght circle also culminated in a strong personal commitment to the city.[33] Officially, however, the delegate was forced to pursue French interests with unbending determination. When Reinhard arrived at Hamburg at the end of September 1795, he initially did not present his credentials as diplomatic custom required. In an explanation to *Syndicus* Doormann, on 8 October, he stated that this was an expression of the Republic's displeasure and that the old friendship would not be restored until the city had satisfied France's demands. Soon, the Senate got into further difficulties,

---

31 Kopitzsch, *Grundzüge einer Sozialgeschichte der Aufklärung*, 177.
32 See Wohlwill, *Neuere Geschichte der Freien und Hansestadt Hamburg*, 136–41 on the Peace of Basel and its immediate aftermath.
33 Furthermore, Reinhard soon fell in love with Christine Reimarus, daughter of J.A.H. Reimarus and sister-in-law Georg Heinrich Sieveking. They finally married in October 1796. See Laufenberg, *Hamburg und die Französische Revolution*, 64–71 and Wohlwill, *Reinhard als Französischer Gesandter in Hamburg und die Neutralitätsbestrebungen der Hansestädte in den Jahren 1795–1797* (Hamburg, 1875), 19–54 on Reinhard's position in Hamburg.

since the imperial court also put pressure on Hamburg. Vienna viewed with great suspicion France's efforts to bring about Hamburg's neutrality. It warned the Senate to be loyal to the *Reich* and not to recognise the French delegate, who had received letters of introduction from the recently established Directory on 26 December. In the covering letter, Delacroix, the new French foreign secretary, had instructed Reinhard to leave Hamburg in the event of his credentials not being accepted with due respect. The question of Reinhard's official recognition as the French representative soon developed into a bone of contention, but was never fully settled in the following years.[34]

The dispute over Reinhard's recognition clearly showed France's interest in Hamburg. The Directory attached great importance to the city's position as the outstanding commercial and political centre on the Continent. Accordingly, France laid stress upon its diplomatic presence in the city and started taking a more aggressive line from 1795. In the centre of this policy of confrontation was Charles Reinhard, the new representative at Hamburg. In the years to come, he proved to be decisive for French efforts to create a diplomatic network and highly important for European radicals trying to come into contact with the various revolutionary governments in France.

---

34 See Wohlwill, *Neuere Geschichte der Freien und Hansestadt Hamburg*, 144–61 on the dispute over Reinhard's recognition.

CHAPTER 2

Flirting with French Ideas:
the United Irishmen, 1791–5

The importance of the French Revolution for the development of modern nationalism at the end of the eighteenth century has never been in doubt.[1] Most twentieth-century historians describe the Revolution as a catalyst for the course of events in Ireland, thus hinting at the dramatic changes following the year 1789. Accordingly, the French Revolution added a further radical element to an already increasing politicisation in Ireland, which had started long before the sweeping changes on the Continent. The desire for a reform of the political system and for more representative standards had existed before 1789, but events in France showed that the reorganisation of a society based on the principles of self-determination and the sovereign power of the people was more than the wishful thinking of some philosophers. The Irish response to the Revolution was enormous. The wide coverage of French news in the press, books and theatre plays on the Revolution, as well as parades of the Volunteers, celebrating the anniversaries of the Storming of the Bastille in the early 1790s, showed the interest of all classes of Irish society – whether sympathetic or opposed – in the dramatic events on the Continent. The themes of republicanism and revolution were to prevail among progressives and conservatives alike for the greater part of the following decade.[2]

While Irish political debate in the first half of the 1790s was dominated by catholic demands for 'emancipation', a radical political association called the United Irishmen was founded in Belfast and Dublin in the autumn of 1791. The 'Society of United Irishmen' was meant to be the organ of Irish reform agitation striving for an improved and more representative parliament.

1 For the importance of the French Revolution for modern European nationalism see Dann, Otto and Dinwiddy, John, eds, *Nationalism in the Age of the French Revolution* (London, Ronceverte, 1988).
2 See McDowell, *Ireland in the Age of Imperialism*, 351–62 on 'Ireland and the French Revolution'.

Declarations of the Society illustrate that Irish reformers for the first time sought to create a nation based on protestants and catholics alike. The Revolution in catholic France had shown that catholics were capable of liberty. To Irish reformers, the overthrow of a catholic king as well as of the church structure proved that catholics could be free and overcome their priests. According to a policy document, issued by the Dublin Society on 5 December 1791, the object of the reformers was 'to make an United Society of the Irish nation; to make all Irishmen Citizens – all Citizens Irishmen'.[3] Another resolution said that 'This society is constituted for the purpose of forwarding a brotherhood of affection, a communion of rights, and a Union of power among Irishmen of every religious persuasion; and thereby to obtain a complete reform in the legislature founded on the principles of civil, political, and religious liberty.'[4] Stimulated by the French Revolution and French writings, the United Irishmen set their sights on a new nation. Nevertheless, the demands of these advanced patriots were still within the confines of the existing constitution, though on its outer limits. They did not plan to destroy the connection with Britain and the Crown, but wanted parliamentary reform as well as equal political representation.[5] Even committed conservatives, like Edmund Burke, could not but observe that 'the papers of the Society of united Irishmen are rational manly, and proper'.[6] In the following years, however, the United Irishmen gradually abandoned their ideas of constitutional reform.

After 1792, political disturbances in Ireland as well as the international situation placed Irish reformers in an awkward position. Since they were openly flirting with French ideas, the outbreak of war between Britain and France in February 1793 put the United Irishmen in an unfavourable light. The United target of sweeping constitutional reform was regarded as subversive at a time when war made it expedient to cooperate on behalf of national unity (although this had never really existed anyway). London and Dublin were not willing to tolerate any suspicious liberals disturbing British war efforts. Following the dissolution of the Volunteers at the beginning of 1793, the government started to harass the United Irishmen at law. After several legal

3 Reproduced in Madden, *The United Irishmen*, 1st ser., 2nd vol., 315–177.
4 The Declarations, Resolutions and Constitution of The Societies of United Irishmen, reproduced in Cronin, Sean, *Irish Nationalism. A History of its Roots and Ideology* (Dublin, 1980), 23.
5 See Elliott, *Partners in Revolution*, 27 on the ideological background of late eighteenth century Irish radicalism.
6 Edmund Burke to Richard Burke, Jr, 2 November 1792, in Copeland, Thomas W., *The Correspondence of Edmund Burke*, vol. VII (Chicago, 1968), 283. Burke's correspondence is an interesting and accurate reflection of the development of conservative attitudes towards the increasing radicalization in Ireland in the years leading up to his death in 1797.

cases against United leaders in 1792, Dublin Castle increased its tactic of court proceedings against prominent United leaders, like Simon Butler, Oliver Bond, veteran radical James Napper Tandy, as well as Archibald Hamilton Rowan and William Drennan. More timid United men, such as William Drennan, eventually withdrew from active politics, leaving behind a leadership that was prepared to continue its activities at all costs. Harsh government measures as well as the Society's involvement with the French were finally to set off the radicalization of the United Irishmen in the course of 1794–5.

Soon after the outbreak of war, French policy-makers had begun to put out feelers towards Ireland. The government in Paris had revived the traditional French interest in Ireland in the face of a bloody counter-revolutionary war in the west of France that was supported by Britain.[7] The initial missionary approach of revolutionary France, as laid down by the decree of 19 November 1792, offering French aid to all peoples striving to recover their liberty, had soon given way to more practical policies responding to the necessities of a European war. Accordingly, Ireland was seen as the vulnerable backdoor to the arch-enemy in the north rather than another step on the way to inter-national revolution. However, the overall picture of France's policies regard-ing Ireland in the early years of the war is somewhat blurred. Due to confused processes of decision-making and uncertain conceptions of French foreign policy-makers, French overtures were lacking a clear sense of direction. Some of the missions in the initial stages of the war are certainly indicative of the half-heartedness of French efforts. In the first half of 1793, five inexperi-enced Irish exiles, namely William Duckett, Sidderson, Edward Ferris and Nicholas Madgett, were sent on a propaganda mission to Ireland. They had been instructed to spread news of the French Revolution, but were arrested on arrival in London. Discharged shortly afterwards, the Irishmen remained in the British Isles, where 'they were left entirely free to work out their own campaign on the spot'.[8] Colonel Eleazer Oswald's journey to Ireland in the late spring of 1793 further illustrates French *laissez-faire* with regard to Irish policies. The American exile was commissioned to sound out the Irish dis-affected without holding out the prospect of help for the Irish independence movement. When Oswald finally did make promises of French military aid, he found most United leaders reluctant to engage in subversive activities.

---

7 See Guillon, *La France et L'Irlande Pendant la Revolution*, 48–83 on French invasionary
   policies concerning Britain in the seventeenth and eighteenth century and Sutherland,
   D.M.G., *France 1789–1815. Revolution and Counterrevolution*, 2nd edn (London, 1988),
   166–72 on the French civil war in the west in 1793.
8 See Elliott, *Partners in Revolution*, 59. See ibid., 56–9 on the mission of Duckett and his
   friends as well as French policies regarding Ireland in 1792–3.

While the United Irishmen still held to their target of an unarmed and constitutional reform, half-hearted French overtures did not attract a great deal
of serious interest among the Society's leaders; and it was not before 1794–5
that the idea of a Franco–Irish alliance firmly gained ground.[9]

Embittered about their war-time enemy, French policy-makers increasingly
turned towards the British Isles in the second half of 1793. Since Ireland was
viewed as an integral part of France's British campaign, the French authorities grew to develop a more serious interest in England's disaffected colony.[10]
In the winter of 1793–4, an Irish exile in France, the Revd William Jackson,
was sent on a mission to his native country in order to make contact with the
United Irishmen. He managed to meet some of the most influential United
leaders. Accompanied by his old friend Cockayne, who reported Jackson's
movements to the British government from the time the French agent arrived
in London in January 1794, Jackson made contact with Leonard McNally,
Simon Butler and Edward Lewins. The latter soon arranged for them to
meet Archibald Hamilton Rowan. At the beginning of the year, Rowan had
been brought to trial for distributing a seditious libel, found guilty and finally
given a two-year sentence. It was in Newgate prison, where he eventually met
Jackson in April. Frustrated by his own and the Society's hopeless situation,
Rowan was attracted by Jackson's offer of a possible French invasion. He
asked Theobald Wolfe Tone, one of the United founders of 1791, to be present at the talks and to 'draw up a statement of the situation of Ireland'.[11]
Although Tone deeply mistrusted Jackson, his survey 'indicated that a French
invasion in sufficient force would be supported'.[12] The French agent received
copies of the statement from Rowan and tried to send them to France through
the open post. Warned by Cockayne, the government intercepted Jackson's
letters and arrested him at the end of April. He was finally brought to trial
in 1795 and found guilty, but committed suicide before being executed. The
Jackson affair finally provided the government with the chance to aim a decisive blow at the United Irishmen. In May 1794, the Society's books and papers
were seized. The Jackson affair opened the way to a more radical and militant
form of United agitation.[13]

The Belfast societies, less divided than the single large Dublin society which
itself continued to meet during the winter of 1794–5, began to form new units
of United Irishmen as secret, oath-bound bodies with a new structure and a

9   Ibid., 60–1 on Oswald's mission.
10 Ibid., 61–3 on France's foreign policy regarding Great Britain.
11 *Autobiography of Archibald Hamilton Rowan*, ed. W.H. Drummond (Dublin, 1840), 212.
12 McDowell, *Ireland in the Age of Imperialism*, 442 and Elliott, *Partners in Revolution*, 64–5.
13 See Elliott, *Partners in Revolution*, 63–6, McDowell, *Ireland in the Age of Imperialism*,
    441–3, Curtin, Nancy J., *The United Irishmen. Popular Politics in Ulster and Dublin*,

new kind of secrecy. The loose openness of the early societies no longer seemed reasonable in the face of vehement government attacks on Irish radicals. Repressions led the United Irishmen to reconsider their notion of political reform in Ireland. In looking back some prominent United leaders later illustrated the gradual character of this phase of structural and ideological transformation.

> While the formation of these Societies was in agitation, the friends of liberty were gradually, but with a timid step, advancing towards Republicanism. They began to be convinced that it would be as easy to obtain a Revolution as a Reform, so obstinately was the latter resisted; and, as this conviction impressed itself on their minds, they were inclined not to give up the struggle, but to extend their views. It was for this reason that, in their text, the words are, 'an equal representation of all the people of Ireland,' without inserting the words 'in Parliament'. This test embraced both the Republican and the Reformer, and left it to future circumstances to decide to which point the common strength should be directed.[14]

Gradually the idea of a republican nationalism spread to all ranks of the society. In order to pursue their goal, the United Irishmen had to build up an effective national movement. Thus, the northern radicals began reconstituting a nation-wide organization with a new and tighter structure. In the course of 1795, they approached the emerging United clubs in Dublin, which had survived political confusion and government suppression, to bring about a union of the two movements.[15] The radical organization spread rapidly from the middle of 1795, being especially strong in Ulster, where the numbers rose to 121,000 by June 1797. By the same time there are said to be 56,000 United Irishmen in Dublin, Kildare, Meath and Westmeath.[16] Although no obvious pattern of organization existed outside Ulster and Leinster, the United Irishmen had successfully attracted new members from many classes of Irish society. When the Leinster provincial committee was formed at the beginning of 1797,

1791–1798 (Oxford, 1994), 61 and *Autobiography of Archibald Hamilton Rowan*, 210–14 on the Jackson affair.

14   Memoir of the State Prisoners, 1798, in *Memoirs and Correspondence of Viscount Castlereagh, Second Marquess of Londonderry*, ed. Charles Vane, 3rd marquess of Londonderry, vol. I (1848), 355.

15   See Elliott, *Partners in Revolution*, 67–74 on this phase of transformation in 1794–5 and see McCracken, J.L., 'The United Irishmen', in Williams, T. Desmond, *Secret Societies in Ireland* (Dublin, New York, 1973), 63 on the new structure of the United Irishmen.

16   McDowell, *Ireland in the Age of Imperialism*, 473 and 476.

the Leinster and Ulster executives constituted the national leadership.[17] Furthermore, the political organization served as a model for the formation of a military organization in 1796.[18] The reconstruction of a new underground society and its growing radicalization indicated the United Irishmen's determination to bring about political change. Further events in the course of 1795 eventually 'led the minds of reflecting United Irishmen to look towards a Republic and separation from England.'[19]

The dissatisfaction of Irish radicals had come to a climax in 1795. Years of peaceful political activities were apparently in vain. Catholic political participation had finally been rejected by the Irish parliament in May 1795. After years of flirting with a revolutionary, French-inspired ideology, Irish radicals were now prepared to translate these principles into action. French overtures in the first half of the 1790s seemed to show that *the* democratic power in Europe was willing to assist the Irish radicals at establishing an Irish republic independent of British influencing control. The involvement with the French was eventually to catapult the United Irishmen from a national into an international context.

17 Ibid., 477 and 479–82.
18 See McCracken, J.L., 'The United Irishmen', in Williams, *Secret Societies in Ireland*, 64 on the military structure of the United Irishmen.
19 Memoir of the State Prisoners, 1798, in *Memoirs and Correspondence of Viscount Castlereagh*, I, 355.

CHAPTER 3

Converging on Hamburg: from the American Exiles to the Dispatch of Jan Anders Jägerhorn, 1795–7

By 1795, the United Irishmen's hope of bringing about change by peaceful means had been shattered once and for all. French assistance to an Irish independence movement seemed to be the only way out of the Irish stalemate resulting from a spiral of pressure and counterpressure; or in other words, the vicious circle between growing government pressure and popular radicalization in the first half of the 1790s ended in a United policy of rapprochement with revolutionary France. France had already developed into a Mecca of republicanism since the early days of the Revolution. It had a magnetic attraction for radical movements, which had sprung into existence in Poland, Italy, Germany, as well as other countries, and which strove to translate French principles into action. Would-be republicans from all over Europe courted successive French governments, trying hard to get France's attention for their respective mother countries. Accordingly, the French Revolution triggered off a political migration, planned and prepared as well as forced and unintentional, since migration could mean both an overhasty flight and a purposive political mission. It often centred around France, as the model for a modern democracy, but was not necessarily restricted to it. The great war of the conservative powers against France and complicated political alliances in and outside Europe had created quite ramified patterns of migratory routes. The French Revolution also led to a confusing picture of political activities: the high politics of war and coalitions and, at the same time, revolutionary movements, missions, undercover diplomacy, emigration and espionage were all part and parcel of the age of Revolution and reactionary retaliation.[1]

---

1 See Dann, Otto and Dinwiddy, John, eds, *Nationalism in the Age of the French Revolution* (London, Ronceverte, 1988) and Gough, Hugh, 'The French Revolution and Europe 1789–99', in Gough, Hugh and Dickson, David, eds, *Ireland and the French Revolution* (Dublin, 1990), 1–13 on the European dimension of the French Revolution.

I

In the case of the United Irishmen political emigration started as early as 1793. After several legal cases against United Irishmen in 1792, Dublin Castle had begun to increase its efforts to prosecute prominent United leaders. When Napper Tandy, a veteran radical and popular street politician since the early Volunteer days of the late 1770s, faced a charge of felony for taking the unlawful Defenders' oath, he preferred to flee the country in order to escape legal punishment. At the end of March 1793, he first left for England, supposedly using a wherry to Holyhead, and stayed there for the following two years. Tandy finally turned up in America, where he, according to Theobald Wolfe Tone, arrived from Hamburg in 1795.[2] In the American capital of Philadelphia, Tandy met with a little group of United Irish exiles, namely Archibald Hamilton Rowan, Theobald Wolfe Tone and Dr Reynolds, who sooner or later fled Ireland in the wake of the Jackson affair which lasted from arrest in April 1794 to sentencing in May 1795. Soon after being informed about Jackson's arrest in April 1794, Rowan escaped from his prison with the intention of leaving the country as quickly as possible. He set sail from Sutton on board a fishing wherry, accompanied by three hired helpers. In crossing 'the British channel' the crew found itself 'enveloped by a British fleet coming up the channel; but the ships which served as a convoy kept between them and the French coast', so that they passed unobserved and landed at Roscoff Bay in Brittany.[3] It was not before the beginning of June 1795 that Rowan left France, disgusted by ill treatment and the confusion of French politics. He embarked on board the vessel *Columbus*, reaching America on 15 July 1795.[4] Shortly after his arrival in Philadelphia, Rowan was joined by Theobald Wolfe Tone. After his name had been publicly mentioned in Jackson's trial, Tone lost little time in leaving Ireland for fear of prosecution. The Tones had set sail from Belfast on board the *Cincinnatus* on 12 June 1795 and eventually landed at Wilmington on 1 August. Within a week, they moved to Philadelphia, where they met up with Rowan and Tandy; the latter had arrived at the city around the middle of July.[5] Little is known about Dr James

2   *Life of Theobald Wolfe Tone*, ed. his son William T.W. Tone, 1st vol. (Washington, 1826), 136 and Coughlan, Rupert J., *Napper Tandy* (Dublin, 1976), 97–109. See Elliott, *Partners in Revolution*, 44–50 on the spring assizes of 1793 and subsequent government repression. Little is known about Tandy's stay in England and also about the date and circumstances of his departure for America.

3   *Autobiography of Archibald Hamilton Rowan*, ed. W.H. Drummond (Dublin, 1840), 218 and ibid., 210–19 on Rowan and the Jackson episode.

4   Ibid., 219–79 on Rowan's residence in France and his passage to America.

5   Elliott, Marianne, *Wolfe Tone. Prophet of Irish Independence* (New Haven, London, 1989),

Reynolds, another victim of the Jackson episode, and his passage to America. At the beginning of August 1795, he turns up in Tone's diary and, one month later, in Rowan's letters to his wife. He seems to have been well settled by the time his fellow United exiles reached the New World. Thus, with Reynolds already established at Philadelphia, and Rowan, Tandy and Tone arriving in July and August, within a fortnight of each other in 1795, the first community of United *émigrés* emerged in America.[6]

Soon enough, reports on the four 'acting somehow suspiciously' were trickling in to the governments in Dublin and London.[7] In fact, Tone and Tandy continued actively fighting for the Irish cause. Although Reynolds 'is a great politician', according to Rowan, his efforts were mostly limited to local American politics rather than to returning to his native country in order to resume his former endeavours with the United Irishmen.[8] Rowan himself was acquainted with Adet, the French minister, and General Thomas Mifflin, Governor of Philadelphia, but was extremely anxious not to cause his family too much worry. Writing to his wife on 20 April 1796, he affirmed that after

> some malignant or ill-informed traveller has said to G.M. that I agitate politics here, which I know must not only make you think meanly of my sense, but also lightly of my love. I assure you, however, that, except on general topics, I scarcely open my lips.

In fact, in the years to come, Rowan's republicanism cooled down substantially.[9]

Napper Tandy, already absent from Ireland since 1793, had not yet abandoned his hopes of actively taking part in Ireland's fight for freedom. After years of carefully manoeuvring around in England, and probably encouraged by the tireless Tone, Tandy got in contact with the minister plenipotentiary of France at Philadelphia.[10] As a few years later in Paris, Tandy and Tone wooed France's favour in order to seek assistance for the republican movement in Ireland. It was Wolfe Tone, however, who was eventually chosen as

---

240–61 on Tone's involvement in the Jackson affair, its aftermath and his departure for America. See *Autobiography of Archibald Hamilton Rowan*, 282 on the date of Tandy's arrival.

6 Ibid., 283–4, Rowan mentioning Reynolds, 7 and 21 September 1795 and *Life of Theobald Wolfe Tone*, I, 131.

7 Nat. Arch. 620/28/24, John Lyster, London, to E. Cooke, 21 January 1797. See also various reports of Leonard McNally on the United exiles in America: Nat. Arch. 620/24/165, 620/36/277, 620/10/121/29, 32 and 49; PRO H.O. 100/62/149.

8 *Autobiography of Archibald Hamilton Rowan*, 284. See also Nat. Arch. 620/36/227 on Reynolds' political activities.

9 Ibid., 293.

10 Coughlan, *Napper Tandy*, 109–13.

the Irish agent to the French government in December 1795. Tone's untiring persistence and his bold and visionary argumentation in favour of Ireland breaking away from England was crucial for Adet's decision. Moreover, there was still a score to settle with the British after their support of the bloody counter-revolutionary war in western France in the previous years; and Ireland seemed to be the appropriate target for France's search for revenge.

On 10 December, Tone's brother Arthur was sent to Ireland to communicate the news to the leading radicals in Belfast and Dublin. He reached Belfast on board the *Susannah* in January to find the underground Society of United Irishmen growing rapidly. Tone himself took ship from New York on 1 January and, after a speedy crossing, landed at Le Havre de Grace on 1 February, as the United Irishmen's first ambassador to France.[11]

II

Tone's mission to France was to determine the society's destiny in the years to come. The leadership in the Society that had emerged in 1794–5 was prepared to enlist French military assistance for an Irish independence movement. The mission characterized a decisive step in the Society's radicalization, as well as a further step in Tone's personal maturation process as a republican, as superbly described by Marianne Elliott.[12] Although Rowan had had contacts with the French authorities during his short stay on the Continent, it was Tone, who conscientiously established official United–French contacts in France. It was this mission that laid the basis for later overtures and further United visitors. In the light of Tone's experience, later United *émigrés* did not shy away from difficulties in language and from the problems of adaptation to an unusual environment. Before Tone, it had been the safety of distant America that attracted the first United exiles. The British naval blockade of the French and the Batavian coast proved to be an almost insuperable obstacle in the direct route to France; and regarding this, Rowan's adventurous passage to Roscoff on board a fishing wherry did not really set a realistic example. In the following years, the arduous detour via America to France was replaced by a more direct continental route, and the New World was headed for only as a last place of refuge. Nevertheless, with the American exiles of the mid-1790s, 'the migratory phase' of the United Irishmen had got under way.

11 See *Life of Theobald Wolfe Tone*, I, 130–6 and Elliott, *Wolfe Tone*, 260–78 on Tone's stay in America.
12 Ibid.

Soon after his arrival at Le Havre, Theobald Wolfe Tone transferred to Paris. He lost no time in getting down to the heart of his mission, despite little knowledge of French and no familiarity with fast-moving French politics. Since October 1795, the Directory of Five had been at the head of the government of France. It had replaced the Committee of Public Safety without necessarily escaping some of the weaknesses the Committee had suffered from. The work of the Directory, too, was affected by personal animosities and disputes over areas of responsibility, at the highest level as well as within the respective government departments. Tone, unfamiliar with questions of competence and personal relationships, lost no time in making an approach to the French authorities. Within a week of arriving in Paris, he called on Delacroix, the French foreign minister, and Nicholas Madgett, head of the Bureau de Traduction, who was subordinate to Delacroix and responsible for Irish missions in the years before. To them, he presented his ideas of sending a French invasionary fleet of 15,000 to 20,000 men to Ireland. The French landing was supposed to mark the beginning of a rebellion in Ireland, which was ready to rise, according to Tone. But the Irishman soon became dissatisfied with the foreign ministry's handling of the matter. As early as 24 February 1796, he turned to Carnot, the Director charged with the conduct of war policy. In March, Carnot introduced Tone to General Clarke, a man of Irish descent in the war ministry, who was now entrusted with looking after Tone and Irish affairs.[13] Thus, within a month, Tone had taken matters to some of the leading men of the French government and, most importantly, he had found a ready hearing. Britain's involvement in the bloody counter-revolutionary war in the west of France had caused great bitterness and fury among French policy-makers in the foreign and the war ministry alike. The French government was keen on retaliation and Tone's plans of a French invasion of Ireland seemed to offer an opportunity to aim a decisive blow at the arch-enemy in the north. The French were thus able to take revenge for England's support of the *chouannerie* in western France by promoting a *chouannerie* in Britain. Wolfe Tone had filled the French with enthusiasm about an invasion of Ireland. In the spring of 1796, he eventually convinced French foreign policy-makers of the necessity of sending an agent to Ireland to communicate with the United leadership.[14]

The search for a suitable agent turned out to be a difficult undertaking, since Delacroix in the foreign ministry and Carnot in the war ministry pur-

13 *Life of Theobald Wolfe Tone*, II, 12–54 on Tone's account of his early negotiations in February and March 1796.

14 See Elliott, *Partners in Revolution*, 85–90 on the background to French plans of a *chouannerie* in Britain and the search for an agent to Ireland.

sued their own foreign policies. Conflicts within the French government thus made a collective way of proceeding impossible. It also contributed much to the misunderstandings, confusion and problems of coordination that characterized the United–French alliance in the following years. Furthermore, Wolfe Tone himself made the search more difficult, since he rigorously brushed aside some of the suggested agents on ludicrous pretexts. The mission proposed by Tone, however, turned out to be an almost total failure, since the leading French foreign policy-makers, Carnot and Delacroix, did not put aside their animosities in favour of a consistent Irish policy. Thus, the two camps did not take concerted action and even hindered one another in producing promising results. The efforts of rival missions that were sent off in the spring of 1796, were wrecked before they actually arrived in the British Isles. Passing through Hamburg, the agents' covers were blown and further moves were doomed to fail.[15]

One of the candidates, who had been turned down by Tone, was the young Kerryman, William Duckett, who had already taken part in the 1793 propaganda mission. Tone was misled by the slightly mysterious appearance of his 'brother Ambassador', as he called Duckett, half-amused, half-jealous. The paths of the two Irishmen were to cross several times after their first encounter in Delacroix's ante-chamber on the 26 February 1796, but Tone never shed his almost childish envy and initial antipathy towards his fellow Irishman, who was held in such high esteem by Clarke and other members of the French government. Despite Duckett's apparent contribution to the Irish republican cause and his intimacy with leading figures in the foreign as well as the war ministry, Tone dismissed him as a 'great blackguard', a 'rascal' and a 'scoundrel'.[16] Although Duckett was described as 'elusive' and 'enigmatic' by historians and even suspected of being one of Pitt's agents, he was one of the most straight-forward and devoted Irish republicans in the 1790s.[17] Apart from Tone, he proved to be the most important Irish-born adviser of the French government and a determined advocate of a French-assisted rebellion in 1796. A just evaluation of Duckett is all the more desirable, as he was one of the key figures in France's ramified spy network. Importantly, his activities as a French agent were closely connected with the city of Hamburg, through

15 PRO F.O. 33/12/190–1; F.O. 33/13/48 and 187; Elliott, *Partners in Revolution*, 87–95 on conflicting French foreign policies and on the missions passing through Hamburg.
16 *Life of Theobald Wolfe Tone*, I, 247–8 and II, 45, 141, 151, 171, 207–9, 219–20 for remarks on Duckett.
17 Wells, Roger, *Insurrection. The British Experience 1795–1803*, 2nd edn (Gloucester, 1986), 36 and 53; Madden, R.R., *The United Irishmen, their Lives and Times*, 2nd ser., vol. II (London, 1843), 66–72 on Duckett.

which he passed or where he resided on numerous occasions in the second half of the 1790s.

Born in Killarney in 1768, Duckett early emigrated to France in order to attend the College des Irlandais of Paris. The novice completed his studies in the stormy month of July 1789. Most certainly impressed by the sweeping events of the early years of the Revolution, the young cleric developed into an ardent republican. Increasingly, he got involved in French politics, his name turning up on a number of occasions. In the autumn of 1792, Duckett and a group of politically-minded seminarians started a coup d'état within the Irish College, aiming at its control and its revenues. They succeeded in replacing the superior, and on 29 October, Duckett was elected Provisor; his fellow seminarian, Nicholas Madgett, was nominated Administrator of the College des Irlandais.[18] A few weeks later, on 18 November, Duckett attended a banquet given by the English-speaking residents of Paris in White's Hotel. At the banquet, liberals like Lord Edward Fitzgerald, John and Henry Sheares, Thomas Paine and also Duckett drew up an address, celebrating French military victories over the Austrians and the Prussians.[19]

In 1793, after winning his first political spurs, Duckett and three other ex-students from the Irish College, including Nicholas Madgett, were recruited by the French government in order to spread revolutionary ideas in Ireland and England. After being initially arrested in London, Duckett got down to his propaganda mission. As Junius Redivius, he published several letters in the London *Morning Post* and the Belfast *Northern Star*, in which he heavily criticised the British government. Moreover, he established contacts with radicals on both sides of the Irish Sea, which proved extremely useful for his later missions to the British Isles.[20] Duckett returned to France, presumably in 1794, but was sent to Ireland again in the spring of 1795. Furnished with 14,000 livres from the Committee of Public Safety, he was instructed 'to assist Jackson for his trial'. He went back to Paris after Jackson's death 'and returned from thence in September with several letters directed among others to Mrs Jackson & Mrs Hamilton Rowan.' According to a letter of 9 September 1796

18 Cousin of the above mentioned head of the Bureau de Traduction of the foreign ministry.
19 The banquet in White's Hotel was followed by a propaganda decree on 19 November 1792, offering French aid to all peoples striving to recover their liberty.
20 See Swords, Liam, *The Green Cockade. The Irish in the French Revolution. 1789–1815* (Dublin, 1989), 61–7; Elliott, *Partners in Revolution*, 58–60; Kennedy, W. Benjamin, *Duckett, William (1768–1841)*, in Baylen, Joseph and Gossman, Norbert J., eds, *Biographical Dictionary of Modern British Radicals, Vol. I: 1770–1830* (Sussex, New Jersey, 1979), 134–5 and NLI pos. 210, MS. Life of William Duckett, by Raoul Duckett (Bordeaux, 1946), 4–15 on Duckett's early years in France and his first missions to the British Isles.

from Nicholas Madgett, his former fellow student and member of the mission of 1793, who knew Duckett very well,

> it was no secret in my relation's House that the object of his mission to Ireland was to prepare the minds of the people for insurrection, acquire friends by persuasion & money and transmit intelligence to my relation ... The mischief he may have done as an individual tho highly deserving the notice and animadversion of Gov' is nothing, when Compared to the facility he may have procured to persons of more Consequence and note, of Corresponding with France, and thus opening the way to general disaffection and the Love of French Liberty.

Madgett, who meanwhile had become a bitter opponent of the Revolution, also informed the English government about Duckett's contact and the mode he passed on information: Duckett's correspondence was generally addressed to Richard Ferris, Delacroix's secret agent, who was residing in London under a false name. Using various covers, Ferris then passed on the letters to Madgett's cousin in the French foreign ministry.[21]

Thus, by the time Tone arrived in France, Duckett had already developed into a key figure in a French spy network aiming at the infiltration of radical circles in Ireland and England. Like his 'brother Ambassador', he was dedicated to the idea of a French invasion of Ireland, as the necessary prerequisite for an Irish rebellion. After he had returned from England at the end of 1795, he vehemently argued for speedy action in several letters to the French government. On 30 May 1796, he wrote to the Directory:

> The independence of Ireland necessarily means the destruction of the British government. This event is bound up with the approval of French liberty ... Today there are no people more disposed towards a revolution than the Irish people ... Her [Ireland's] independence has to come from outside. Ireland well contains the necessary force for that great operation, but it is imperative, that the lever to set this force in motion finds help from within the country. In saving Ireland, the French people have to use her independence as a principal base for her proper liberty ... And now one should ask about the reasons for that unpolitical negligence, not to say criminal negligence, of the French government, not to derive benefit from this open hatred against the British. Where are the people to support the Defenders? Where are the newspapers about Ireland? One could think, that the English government is not dealing

21 Nat. Arch. 620/25/39, Secret letter of Nicholas Madgett, 9 September 1796.

with France just as well. One can also assure, that if the French government had launched into the same actions as the cabinet of Saint James
has unfolded amongst us, Ireland would already be free and independent
and England could not recruit its armies on land and sea; it could not
develop sufficient resources, deprived of a population of four million
people. It is hard to believe, but it is not less true, and this is a copy of
a table presented to the parliament of Ireland by the secretary of war,
since the commencement of the present hostilities this country has supplied 200,000 men, just as many land as naval forces. Half of the English
navy is composed of Irishmen ... [22]

In using his experience of several missions to Ireland, Duckett confirmed
that an alliance of catholics and presbyterians, joined together in mutual hatred for British rule, was ready to rise. Only a French 'lever' was required
to put things in motion. The French could thus support the Irish in bringing
about their independence; and at the same time, France could place a decisive
blow at its enemy in depriving England of Irish resources and manpower.
Moreover, Duckett offered once again to go to Ireland to spread propaganda
and to prepare the minds of the Irish people for revolutionary changes. He
declared, 'I have no other ambition than the liberty of Ireland, and I will
know no peace until I see the Irish people enjoy their full rights.'[23]

Duckett's offer to go to Ireland was disregarded in the spring and summer of 1796, but his ideas of an invasion of Ireland did not fall on deaf ears.
Duckett's as well as Tone's efforts certainly had an effect on the French authorities whose support for an Irish expedition was unanimous by the summer,
according to Marianne Elliott. Louis Lazare Hoche, victor of the Vendée, had
been made commander of the Irish expedition on 20 June, and suitable
preparations were in full swing.[24]

In Ireland, the apparent tranquillity that had prevailed throughout the first
half of the year seemed to have come to an end by mid-1796. From the beginning of the summer, reports issued from Dublin Castle show rising concern
about the growth of lawlessness and radicalism in Ireland.[25] Defenderism had
spread into the counties of Armagh, Down, Cavan, Monaghan, Dublin, Meath

---

22 Arch. Nat. AF, III. 186 b D 859, Duckett to the Directory, 11 prairial an IV (30 May 1796),
    reproduced in Guillon, E., *La France et l'Irlande Pendant la Révolution* (Paris, 1888),
    159–62; See ibid., 159–65 on Duckett's letters to the Directory.
23 Ibid. (4 June 1796), 163.
24 Elliott, *Partners in Revolution*, 92–3.
25 See TCD MS. 1762–3 (Pratt Papers, Copy of MS. U.840, Original in Kent County
    Office) on Camden's reports to Portland in 1796.

and Kildare. Especially in the North, numerous clashes with the protestant Orangemen had led to a rapid increase of Defenderism. For the Irish government, the apparently unstructured movement presented a confusing picture, because it reflected a strange hotchpotch of traditional agrarian grievances, religious ardour and revolutionary French influences. However, it was the Defenders' revolutionary radicalism and their numbers that attracted the United Irishmen and that made the Society woo the Defenders when forced underground in 1794-5. Despite the hesitancy and the uneasiness of many United leaders to be associated with the radical Defenders, they 'recognised the numerical strength which an alliance with the Defenders would bring to a truly national independence movement.'[26]

Accounts of secret meetings of Defenders and United Irishmen caused great concern among the Irish authorities by mid-1796, when some form of cooperation between the two movements seemed to have got under way. The Irish government became alarmed by accounts of increased activities of the United Irishmen. The remnants of the old Society had been re-organized in the course of the previous year, with some experienced United Irishmen forming new units as oath-bound bodies with a new structure and a new kind of secrecy. By the summer of 1796, the United Irishmen's membership had increased substantially, with strongholds in the north-east of the country and Dublin, from where it was spreading west.[27] Worried about the infectious force of popular discontent, Dublin Castle was anxious to nip disaffection in the bud. Early in the year, an Indemnity Act was introduced as a safeguard against prosecution. It referred to persons, who had committed unlawful acts in suppressing rebellion, retrospectively since 1 January 1795. Accompanied by the Insurrection Act, which gave increased legal power to the justices of the peace of the respective counties, it provided the government with a *carte blanche* to stamp out popular discontent. With the suspension of the Habeas Corpus Act in October, it also curtailed individual rights, and thus had established an almost unlimited state of emergency by the end of the year.

Apart from internal consolidation, Ireland's state of defence became another important issue for Irish policy-makers in the second half of 1796. In the summer, the withdrawal of British troops to the European theatres of war was met with the establishment of yeomanry corps, which were to act as an auxiliary military force as well as to take part in domestic police operations.

26 Elliott, *Partners in Revolution*, 95-6.
27 See McCracken, J.L., 'The United Irishmen', in Williams, *Secret Societies in Ireland*, 63 on the new structure of the United Irishmen and McDowell, *Ireland in the Age of Imperialism and Revolution*, 474-6 on the society's development in 1796.

In the course of the summer and autumn of the year, rumours of plans for a French invasion had begun to trickle in to Dublin Castle, which now feared to become directly involved in the European war. Alarmed by internal troubles and intelligence of a projected French invasion, Camden was at pains to convince the English government that Ireland's defence alert was to be greatly strengthened. Although he insistently endeavoured to draw the Home Office's attention to the threat of a French–Irish connection, London's response was merely half-hearted.[28]

III

With regard to United links with France, the English as well as the Irish government were groping about in the dark in 1796. Although Dublin Castle had helping hands on the fringes of the Society, such as Leonard McNally who, like Drennan, did not become a member of the reactivated Society, but unlike Drennan, became an informer in the wake of the fear the Jackson arrest and trial had engendered among radicals, it did not succeed in infiltrating the decision-making bodies of the movement. Thus, McNally still thought Tone to be in America by 26 July 1796, keeping 'quite retired' and 'preparing a work for the Press'.[29] Government records of the year 1796 show how little was known about actions within the top level of the United Irishmen. Most importantly, they illustrate almost total British ignorance of United moves outside Ireland; understandably enough, since the government had not been forced into looking out for United continental missions before 1796.[30]

Thus, it is hardly surprising that Lord Edward Fitzgerald and Arthur O'Connor's journey to the Continent was not mentioned in the papers of the responsible British government offices in 1796. While the two energetic noblemen had been members of the Irish parliament, they had been ardent admirers of revolutionary principles and sympathetic to the Society's cause long before they joined the United Irishmen in 1796. Arthur O'Connor, as well as Lord Edward, had visited France in 1792; and subsequently, the revolutionary French experience was to be of great importance in their political thinking. After the failure of the various reform efforts in Ireland in the first half of the 1790s, it was this French-inspired republicanism that induced the

28 TCD MS 1762/239–44, 441–2 and MS 1763/1, 16, 75–9 on rumours of a projected French invasion and reports on Ireland's defence in the second half of 1796.
29 PRO H.O. 100/62/149. See also Nat. Arch. 620/10/121 for examples of McNally's intelligence.
30 See PRO 100 and F.O. 33 for 1796.

two to turn their backs on parliamentary politics and to approach the radical movement in 1796.

His standing and his well known liberal views contributed much to Lord Edward's popularity among Dublin and Ulster United leaders, who welcomed his suggestion of reinforcing United–French contacts in the spring of 1796. To them, Lord Edward had proposed to get in touch with the French, in making use of his acquaintance with the French representative in Hamburg, Charles Reinhard, whom he had got to know in 1792, when Reinhard was residing in London, as a secretary to the French envoy, F.-B. Chauvelin. In April, Fitzgerald travelled to London, where he met his personal friend, Arthur O'Connor. Accompanied only by his wife Pamela, he then continued his journey, arriving in Hamburg about 10 May 1796.[31]

Lord Edward had married the foster-daughter of Phillipe Duc d'Orléans and the Comtesse de Genlis while in France in 1792. Pamela's family connections were to offer a suitable cover for Edward's mission. Her cousin, Henriette de Sercy, was about to marry Johann Conrad Matthiessen, one of the wealthiest Hamburg merchants who was 19 years her senior, on 19 May. Among the expected guests were Madame de Genlis, Pamela's beloved foster-mother who had been residing in Hamburg since 1794, and her son-in-law, General de Valence, who had arrived in the city after the establishment of the Batavian Republic in 1795. Edward and Pamela were put up at Madame de Genlis' abode, an estate in Silk, just outside Hamburg, which was also the home of General de Valence, his wife Madame de Sillery and, up to the day of her wedding, Henriette de Sercy. In 1795–6, the estate at Silk was one of the major meeting places for leading figures of the *Ancien Régime*, such as Talleyrand, Lafayette, Dumouriez or Abbé Louis. Thus, since Hamburg had offered shelter to thousands of French *émigrés* with quite complex connections in and outside the city, Fitzgerald's trip to the Continent had nothing of the secrecy of later missions and appeared more like pleasant holidays of a typical nobleman.[32]

31 See Wohlwill, Adolf, *Reinhard als Französischer Gesandter in Hamburg und die Neutralitäts-bestrebungen der Hansestädte in den Jahren 1795–1797* (Hamburg, 1875) on Reinhard. See Elliott, *Partners in Revolution*, 98–103, Lecky, W.E.H., *A History of Ireland in the Eighteenth Century*, IV, new impression (London, 1913), 501–4, 520–2 and MacDermot, Frank, 'Arthur O'Connor', *I.H.S.*, XV (1966), 52–4 for accounts of Lord Edward and Arthur O'Connor's mission.

32 Ham. Staats. Wedde I, Nr. 29, Bd. 77, Hochzeitenprotokoll de Anno 1796. See Harkensee, Heinrich, *Beiträge zur Geschichte der Emigranten in Hamburg*, II *Madame de Genlis* (Hamburg, 1900) for information on Pamela's family connections and on French *émigrés* in Hamburg. See Sillem, W., 'Conrad Johann Matthiessen', *Mitteilungen des Vereins für Hamburgische Geschichte*, 11 & 12 (November & December 1891), 303–12 & 319–25.

However, Lord Edward did not remain idle. Soon after his arrival in Hamburg, he called on Charles Reinhard, who was staying in Altona for a short time. On account of the dispute between France and the Senate over Reinhard's recognition, the French representative had left Hamburg in March and was residing in Bremen until September. Only occasionally, he returned to Altona to look after his diplomatic tasks.[33] It was there that Lord Edward met Charles Reinhard and advocated a French invasion prior to an insurrection. He stated that 150,000 Irishmen were ready to rise, among them 10,000 armed Defenders, and that weapons and munitions were needed. Fitzgerald emphasized that a French invasion was necessary to explode Irish discontent. He also expressed his readiness to proceed to Paris to present his plans to the Directory. Reinhard's account of the meeting, dated 18 May, shows that Lord Edward's visit did not fail to have an effect on the French representative. Despite the Irishman's 'royalist' connections, Reinhard was convinced of his integrity and republicanism. He was clearly taken with the idea of an Irish insurrection and its importance for France.[34]

A few weeks later, Lord Edward went to see Reinhard again, this time accompanied by Arthur O'Connor, who had arrived in Hamburg in the meantime. O'Connor confirmed Fitzgerald's account of the state of affairs in Ireland and suggested Cork, Waterford and also Dublin as suitable targets for a French attack. The invasion would spark off an insurrection in Ireland, bind the bulk of British forces to Ireland and thus place a decisive blow at France's enemy. Self-confidently, O'Connor told Reinhard, 'We only want your help in the first moment; in two months we should have 100,000 men under arms; we ask your assistance only because we know it is your own clear interest to give it, and only on condition that you leave us absolute masters to frame our government as we please.'[35] Enthusiastic about O'Connor's self-assured appearance and his clear-cut ideas, Reinhard advocated French support for the Irish independence movement. The French government, however, decided not to give way to the two Irishmen's requests to be admitted to Paris. The Directory was obviously interested in their plans, but did not want to put the mission at risk by blowing the Irishmen's covers. O'Connor and Fitzgerald should proceed to Switzerland to communicate with the French minister at Basle, Francois Barthélemy. As normal travellers, they would not invite any suspicion.

33 Wohlwill, *Neuere Geschichte der Freien und Hansestadt Hamburg*, 152–61 on the dispute between France and the Senate in 1796.
34 Reinhard to Delacroix, 29 floréal an 4 (18 May 1796), after Lecky, *A History of Ireland*, IV, 501–3.
35 Reinhard to Delacroix, 18 prairial an 4 (6 June 1796), reproduced in Lecky, *A History of Ireland*, IV, 503–4.

The two Irishmen seemed to have left Hamburg shortly after the meeting with Reinhard of the beginning of June. Arriving in Basle, they soon had conversations with Bartélemy. Impressed by the eloquent O'Connor, he attempted to comply with his request for personal negotiations with the Directory. Details of the Irishmen's meetings with Barthélemy and the latter's correspondence with the French authorities in Paris can be found in the works of W.E.H. Lecky and Marianne Elliott, who document French eagerness to use Irish discontent for the war with England.[36] The highly ambitious Hoche, the newly appointed commander of the Irish expedition, regarded the Irish plans as an opportunity to make his mark militarily. Hoche as well as the French government had welcomed the reports of Fitzgerald and O'Connor with keen anticipation. In France, little was known about the state of disaffection in Ireland, since Tone had been the last direct contact for some time. Therefore, Hoche took a personal interest in O'Connor passing on information, as he seemed to be the more able of the two negotiators. In the middle of August, Hoche eventually arranged to meet O'Connor at Angers, in the west of France, to clarify the particulars of the forthcoming expedition to Ireland.[37]

As early as July, Lord Edward had returned to Hamburg to see Pamela, whom he had left with her family more than a month earlier. In the meantime, two Irishmen had called on Reinhard. In the middle of June, Carnot's agent, Richard O'Shee, had arrived in Hamburg and, giving credence to Lecky's assumption, received instructions from Reinhard. The object of his mission was to keep a close eye on the Defenders, their numbers, leaders, strength and, importantly, their connections with the Ulster presbyterians. He was authorised to promise 10,000 French soldiers and arms for 20,000 rebels, which would soon be sent to the north or the north-west of Ireland. O'Shee was then to conclude his mission by setting up communication routes with France through Copenhagen, Cadiz, Stockholm, Amsterdam and Hamburg. However, nothing is known about the further course of the mission after O'Shee had left Hamburg. It is unclear whether he even succeeded in getting to Ireland. He eventually returned to Paris on 27 October; considerations about O'Shee's steps from June until October remain speculative to this day.[38]

---

36 Lecky, *A History of Ireland*, IV, 520–2 and Elliott, *Partners in Revolution*, 101–2.
37 See MacDermot, Frank, 'Arthur O'Connor', *I.H.S.*, XV (1966), 53 and Elliott, *Partners in Revolution*, 102 for accounts of the meeting at Angers.
38 Lecky, *A History of Ireland*, IV, 519–20 and Elliott, *Partners in Revolution*, 88–90 and 104–5 on O'Shee's mission.

The second Irishmen, who went to see Reinhard in the time of Lord Edward's absence, was William Duckett's brother. In a letter to Delacroix, dated Bremen, 5 July 1796, the French minister mentioned that Duckett called on him in Altona, with letters, which he wanted to be transmitted to Paris, to his brother, it must be assumed. In the latter half of 1796, William Duckett had temporarily fallen out of favour with Hoche. Because of the Irishman's constant moaning about poverty, the general had ordered him to proceed to Paris and to be available on call. But in the long term, French foreign policy-makers were not able to do without Duckett and fell back upon his valuable services soon after Hoche's ill-feeling about the Irishman in the summer and autumn of 1796. Little is known about William's younger brother, Sidney. He as well appears to have been in the service of the French, 'employed in finding out agents', according to later sources. At any rate, he turned up again in 1798, when he supported William on another mission.[39]

Events in Hamburg reveal that French efforts concerning the Irish expedition were in full swing in the summer of 1796. Investigations about the state of affairs in Ireland were necessary to make progress with preparations for the forthcoming enterprise. Communications with the Irish radicals had to be improved, appropriate routes to be established. Neutral Hamburg, half-way between France and Ireland, now proved to be a suitable starting point for French as well as Irish missions. The English naval blockade of the French and the Dutch coast acted as a deterrent, since taking the direct route would have threatened life and mission of any foolhardy agent. Hamburg offered the most suitable opportunity to directly get in contact with the French as well as to transmit information to them. It accommodated one of the most important political outposts for France, with Reinhard as an able diplomat and creator of French foreign policy.

Using Hamburg as a crossroads appeared inconspicuous and less dangerous to Lord Edward and Arthur O'Connor, too. They had avoided casting suspicion on their journey, keeping even close relatives in ignorance of their plans.[40] However, the British and the Irish government did not suspect the two Irishmen's mission and did not take action against them. Unmolestedly, O'Connor and the Fitzgeralds left Hamburg for England in September 1796 and finally returned to Ireland in October.

39 NLI pos. 210 MS. Life of William Duckett, by Raoul Duckett (Bordeaux, 1946), 48–53 and Kennedy, *William Duckett*, in Baylen/Gossman, *Biographical Dictionary*, 137. See *Memoirs and Correspondence of Viscount Castlereagh, Second Marquess of Londonderry*, ed. Charles Vane, 3rd marquess of Londonderry, vol. 1 (1848), 326, Lord Castlereagh's notes, August 1798, and chapters 4–5 of this study on William Duckett and his brother.
40 See Campbell, Gerald, *Edward and Pamela Fitzgerald* (London, 1904), 107–9 for Lord Edward's letters from Hamburg, 29 July and 29 August 1796.

IV

In many respects, this famous journey of 1796 represented a turning point. It smoothed the way for Irish radicals using the continental route via Hamburg in later years. The experience gained served as a model for future agents and proved to be especially helpful for travellers immediately following Arthur O'Connor and Lord Edward. Secondly, the mission of 1796 had an influence on the development of the United movement in Ireland. The news of the forthcoming French expedition, delivered by the two travellers, favoured the widening and militarization of radicalism. Thus, the formation of a United military organization at the end of 1796 most certainly was connected with O'Connor's negotiations with Hoche. Probably encouraged by Hoche, the United Irishmen also put a greater emphasis on thoroughly organizing a nationwide movement in order to create the necessary conditions for an Irish rising and the projected French landing. Moreover, the mission was a decisive step in the personal development of O'Connor and Fitzgerald. Both had only been flirting with radical ideas before they went to the Continent, but henceforward became active members of the United Irishmen. At the end of 1796, they were in the newly established national executive committee, together with Robert Simms, Richard McCormick, and shortly afterwards, William James MacNeven, Thomas Addis Emmet, Joseph Orr, Bartholomew Teeling and Alexander Lowry.[41]

Once again, it was Arthur O'Connor, who courageously set to work in the immediate aftermath of his return in October. While Lord Edward returned to his Kildare cottage, O'Connor moved house to Belfast. There, he published an address to the electors of Antrim, announcing his intention to take part in the county's parliamentary elections, as a 'pretext and a platform for subversive propaganda', according to Frank MacDermot.[42] In November, he started off for Cork, where his brother Roger had established contacts with some of the leading Munster United Irishmen, above all with Edmund O'Finn, a frequent traveller to the Continent in the revolutionary years. In the meeting with the United Irish representatives, arranged by Roger, Arthur O'Connor stated that 'an Invasion of this Country would to a certainty be attempted, and that it ought to be a primary object to have the whole country in a state of the most perfect organization.' Accordingly, he recommended the formation of an executive directory in Cork, which should closely cooperate with the respective committees in Dublin and Belfast. The Munster

---

41 Memoir of the State Prisoners, 1798, in *Memoirs and Correspondence of Viscount Castlereagh*, I, 359–61 and Elliott, *Partners in Revolution*, 108–9.
42 MacDermot, 'Arthur O'Connor', *I.H.S.*, 54.

United Irishmen seem to have followed O'Connor's instructions in the years to come. An executive committee was established as well as communications with the United brethren in Dublin and Belfast, namely Oliver Bond, James Putnam McCabe, Henry Sheares and one of the Binns brothers. At any rate, Arthur O'Connor was trying hard to make his contribution to United efforts to improve the Society's national organization. He returned to Belfast in the latter half of November, the invasion he had agreed with Hoche immediately lying ahead.[43]

In France, Hoche's headquarters at Brest were feverishly preparing for the Irish expedition. At the beginning of November, Hoche and Tone had agreed to send the latter's adjoint, Bernard MacSheehy, to Ireland to gather detailed information on the current state of affairs. Leaving Brest on board the American vessel *Washington* on 7 November, he made his way to Ireland, via the Isle of Wight, Portsmouth, London and Holyhead, and finally arrived in Dublin on 26 of the same month. After meeting Bond, McCormick, MacNeven and Lewins, he lost no time in setting out for France in order to communicate the news to Hoche as soon as possible. MacSheehy reached Brest on 18 December, three days after the French fleet had left for Ireland.[44]

In the months before, busy activity had prevailed in France. In the run-up to the expedition, the French had also started sending arms to the disaffected in Ireland. Yet, not all ships reached their goals. Around 10 December, the American *Olive Branch*, under captain Allen, 'loaden with 20,000 stand of arms and a very complete Field Artillery Train, destined for Ireland North about' was seized by the English navy. Despite the failure of the *Olive Branch* to carry through its mission, the incident shows that the French were willing to stand by the promises, which had, in all likelihood, been made to O'Connor. As already demanded by O'Connor in his first conversation with Reinhard in the beginning of June, and most likely he repeated this claim in the meeting with Hoche, the Irish rebellion had to be equipped with French arms. Accordingly, Hoche tried hard to optimise preparations for the Irish expedition, although his efforts met with great difficulties, due to the desperate state of the French navy.[45]

43 PRO P.C. I./44/A.155, Communication of Thomas Conway, 13 April 1799.
44 NLI pos. 198 (Archives Nationales AF III 186b doss. 859 & 860), MacSheehy's account of the mission, 19 December 1796; TCD MS 873/526. For detailed descriptions of the mission see Swords, *The Green Cockade*, 125–8; Elliott, *Partners in Revolution*, 104–6 and VanBrock, F.W., 'Captain MacSheehy's mission', *Irish Sword*, X (1972), 215–28.
45 PRO H.O. 100/62/364. See also H.O. 100/62/340–1, 346, 348, 366, 405–6; Nat. Arch. 620/26/96, 620/34/2; TCD MS 1763/94–5, 103 for information on the *Olive Branch*, arms shippings and gunrunning in the autumn of 1796. See Elliott, *Partners in Revolution*, 109–11 on French preparations.

In Ireland, tensions heightened in the last few months of 1796. Dublin Castle had increased pressure on the disaffected. Especially in the North, the radical movement was hit hard by waves of arrests and harsh legislative measures that had been introduced by the government to crush discontent once and for all. In turn, the United Irishmen responded to government reprisals with untiring efforts to build up an effective countermovement underground. Encouraged by the prospect of the forthcoming French invasion, the Society's numbers grew steadily. The military organization, even though still in its infancy, was supposed to be the nucleus of a longed-for national rising. The United Irishmen were at pains to prepare the ground for the arrival of the French comrade in arms.[46]

Much has been written on the fate of the French expedition at the end of December 1796. Therefore, descriptions of military details are to be avoided. However, unfavourable winds and lack of coordination within the fleet's command had made Hoche's efforts fail and soon led the generals to break off the expedition altogether. The fleet finally returned to France without putting one soldier ashore.[47]

In the months before, English and Irish authorities had been warned about French plans to invade Ireland, but had subsequently failed to take steps against a possible invasion. Despite Camden's anxious reminders to Portland to arrange for security measures to be taken, the British government did not substantially reinforce Ireland's defences. It was soon to become clear that the Irish coast was insufficiently protected against enemy attacks. At Christmas, Dublin and London were shocked at learning about a French fleet off Bantry Bay.[48]

The news was a surprise for the United Irishmen, too, since they had not been informed about the time and place of the landing. Even in the event of a successful invasion, it would have been rather difficult for the Irish radicals to suit their actions to a possible French campaign. Without being initiated into French plans, United efforts to proceed in conjunction with a French military expedition most certainly would have been doomed to fail. At any rate, the United Irishmen did not raise their hands in rebellion at the close of 1796. In the eyes of most radicals, however, France had offered evidence of its willingness to assist the Irish fight for freedom. The Bantry Bay expedition reinforced the belief in a Franco–Irish alliance and nurtured hopes of soon bringing about Ireland's independence. United numbers grew rapidly

46 Elliott, *Partners in Revolution*, 106–8.
47 See Guillon, *La France et L'Irlande*, 246–83 and Elliott, *Partners in Revolution*, 109–16 on the Bantry Bay expedition.
48 See PRO H.O. 100/62/156–8, 314, 381; TCD MS. 1762/239–44, 255, 441–2; TCD MS. 1763/16, 89, 94 for government accounts of French invasionary plans before December.

after Bantry Bay, amounting to 121,000 in Ulster and 56,000 in Dublin, Kildare, Meath and Westmeath by June 1797.[49] Despite the expedition's failure, the infectious force of Irish radicalism continued undiminished.

The enthusiasm of the French authorities for another Irish invasion cooled down substantially after December 1796. Seeing that the enemy had not even been engaged in battle, French losses were considerable. The remnants of the returning fleet were in a wretched condition. France had lost 5000 men and eleven ships. In the face of the Irish fiasco, dejection and dissatisfaction prevailed among French foreign policy-makers and led them to turn their attention increasingly towards the continental war against Austria. The United Irishmen's radical attitude was questioned, since they had not even made an attempt at rising in those crucial days at the end of December. Had O'Connor and Lord Edward exaggerated their accounts of the strength of Irish radicalism? In the light of the Bantry Bay experience, future overtures of Irish agents were to meet with a more cautious reception from respective French governments.[50]

V

Likewise frustrated by the outcome of the Irish expedition, Theobald Wolfe Tone returned to Paris on 12 January 1797. All his efforts in favour of the Irish cause seemed to have been in vain, and yet, his frustration did not last for long. The very same day, he received a letter from his wife, in which she reported on the Tones' journey from America to the Continent. Shortly before Christmas, his wife Matilda, his children and sister Margaret had reached Hamburg, where they heard of the failure of the expedition. This piece of news had caused Matilda a lot of worry, as she was not informed about her husband's fate until late January. The pressing uncertainty weakened her, all the more considering her bad health at the time of arrival in Hamburg. Anxious about his wife's state of health, Tone wrote back to her on 13 January. In view of Matilda's illness, he gave her detailed pieces of advice. He also urged her to remain in Hamburg, since a journey to France would be too perilous in the winter. Furthermore, Tone encouraged Matilda to take up residence in a village outside Hamburg in order to avoid the damaging conditions of a big city.

In the course of his correspondence with his family, which occupied Tone in the first months of 1797, he also learned about his sister's relationship

49 McDowell, *Ireland in the Age of Imperialism*, 473 and 476.
50 Elliott, *Tone*, 330–2 and *Partners in Revolution*, 118–19.

with Frederic Giauque. Born in Neuchâtel, Switzerland, the young merchant
had been residing in Philadelphia for the last three years. He had met Margaret
Tone on board the American vessel bound for Europe, and after a courtship
of only a few weeks, the two married in Hamburg on 29 January. The young
couple soon settled down into a well-ordered life. The same month, Giauque
went about his business and started paying aliens tax as early as 23 January.
Moreover, the Giauques then moved into the house of the Hamburg merchant, Johann Hinrich Schrader, at Rödingsmarkt 61, before they finally purchased their own home at Speenshörn 1 later in the year.[51]

Tone's frustration about the Bantry Bay failure soon wore off in the beginning of 1797, and he again began to look into the future. He realized that
his Hamburg connections might be of great benefit to the Irish cause. In his
letters to Matilda, dated 13 and 17 January, he openly thought about using
Giauque as a medium of communicating with Ireland. Some time later,
Tone got down to expounding his plans to Matilda: Messieurs Holtermann,
residing at Neven-Wall 123, and Wilson were to be the bearers of the
Hamburg letters; one Monsieur Benard was named as Giauque's correspondent in Paris.[52]

It is unclear whether Tone's plans actually took shape, but his diary reveals
that he lost little time in presenting matters to Hoche, who had returned to
his old headquarters on the Rhine in the meantime. While in Paris, Tone informed the general about his intention to absent himself and travel to Hamburg
in order to take his family to France on 31 January. Hoche, who was still
flirting with the idea of attacking the British Isles, welcomed Tone's proposal. He suggested the Irishman should meet a contact in Hamburg, without
informing him about the person's identity and without giving any further details of his ideas. Tone was puzzled about Hoche's intentions. 'Who is my
lover that I am to see at Hamburg, in God's name?', he wrote down at the
end of the day.[53] It is still uncertain whom Hoche had in mind. It is hard to
believe, because of the animosities between the two Irishmen, but quite possible that he was thinking of William Duckett. On 14 January, the French agent
had been seen in London and there is no reason to cast doubt on Nicholas
Madgett's report, since he was well acquainted with Duckett from his student days at the College des Irlandais.[54] Duckett had never stopped trying to

51 *Life of Theobald Wolfe Tone*, II, 337–40 and 381–99 on Tone and his family concerns. See
     Ham. Staats. Kämmerei I, Nr. 225, Fremdenschoßbücher, Bd. 2, 1793–1811, p. 150; Wedde
     I, Nr. 29, Bd. 78, Hochzeitenprotokoll de Anno 1797; Neues Hamburger und Altonaer
     Address-Buch, 1797 & 1798 (Hamburg, 1797 & 1798) on the Giauques in Hamburg.
52 *Life of Theobald Wolfe Tone*, II, 381–99.
53 Ibid, 342.
54 Nat. Arch. 620/25/39, N. Madgett to ?, London, 14 January 1797.

re-establish his good relations with the Directory after falling out of favour with Hoche in the second half of 1796. He had been re-engaged by the French government by the end of the year, when he appears to have translated Hoche's proclamation to the Irish nation in the run-up to the Bantry Bay expedition.[55] Little is known about Duckett's moves and the circumstances of his journey to England, but it must be assumed that he took in Hamburg on the way to Britain. Being familiar with travelling via Hamburg and being the only United traveller in that part of Europe at that particular time, he, in all probability, would have stopped there on the way back from England. Thus, there is a possibility that Duckett was the person Tone was supposed to meet in order to pass on information to Paris. Whoever Hoche had in mind, his plan of a mission to Hamburg did not materialize in the first months of 1797. But Tone did not let up. In February, he suggested that 'in consequence of my sister's marriage, to open a communication with Ireland through Hamburg; at which General Hoche caught directly.'[56] Hoche, who had shifted the main emphasis of his efforts to the fight against Austria, had not lost touch with the idea of an invasion of Ireland, an enterprise, which could still mean an enormous gain in prestige to the ambitious general. Therefore, Tone found a ready hearing for his Irish plans. In the course of the year, the system of communication, with its centre in Hamburg, was expanded. In connection with this, an important part fell upon Frederic Giauque, as well as Henriette Matthiessen, née de Sercy, as conveyors of information.[57]

At the end of March 1797, the unending months of passivity in Paris seemed to be over for Tone. On the 29 of the month, he set out for Cologne in order to join Hoche's headquarters on the Rhine, but also to search for means to meet his family.[58] At the same time, the United agent, Edward Lewins, arrived at Hamburg. In February, Lewins, himself a member of the Dublin executive, had been appointed by a secret committee to take up again negotiations with France. In writing to Henriette Matthiessen, the committee had made provisions for giving the French advance notice of Lewins' mission. He had passed through London on 20 March to get himself the necessary travel documents for the journey to Hamburg.[59]

55 NLI pos. 210, MS. Life of William Duckett, 25–55.

56 *Life of Theobald Wolfe Tone*, II, 344. See also pages 346 and 355 on his Hamburg plans.

57 See PRO H.O. 100/70/347, 348 and H.O. 100/75/7, Samuel Turner's account of the Hamburg communication; See also *Memoirs and Correspondence of Viscount Castlereagh*, vol. I, 289–90 as another example of Giauque's activities.

58 *Life of Theobald Wolfe Tone*, II, 350–60 on Tone's journey to Cologne.

59 Nat. Arch. 620/29/5. Elliott assumes, that Lewins could have obtained the passport from Duckett, which might well be the case, since the latter was seen in London some time before. Nat. Arch. 620/28/96. See Elliott, *Partners in Revolution*, 130.

After arriving on the Continent, he soon set about calling on Reinhard, who was still residing at Altona on account of the continuing dispute over his official recognition. On 31 March, Lewins was received by the French representative. Reinhard had also invited de Nava, the Spanish minister, to be present at the meeting, as the latter was sympathetically inclined towards his fellow ambassador as well as towards the Irish cause. De Nava, acquainted with the country owing to a journey to Ireland, started to examine Lewins minutely for the veracity of his mission. He inquired about the state of discontent in Ireland and about the numbers of disaffected sworn in associations. Lewins, who had been well prepared for his task, assured him that 100,000 men would be standing by to assist the French in the event of a landing. He explained that especially the North would be in a state of perfect organization, ready to rise at short notice. In accordance with his instructions, Lewins then requested 20,000 to 25,000 troops and 80,000 stand of arms from the French, as well as a loan of 500,000 livres from Spain.

Although Lewins apparently represented his request to the best of his ability, de Nava and Reinhard were somehow muddled about the Irishman's unemotional manner. In his letter to Delacroix, dated 5 April 1797, Reinhard recommended detaining Lewins, who had asked the French minister to be allowed to proceed to France via Lübeck. It should be found out first whether the Irishman was an 'Agent de Pitt', before placing confidence in his mission. He advised making inquiries as soon as possible, since the rising temperature in Ireland would brook no delay. Moreover, Reinhard emphasized the importance of proceeding in conjunction with the Spanish, because he considered them to be useful and loyal to France. Hamburg could thus develop into a 'point de contact avec l'Irlande' and be of great use to French war politics. Reinhard called Lewins' mission into question, despite the Irishman having a letter of introduction from Lord Edward. In the letter, he had assured Reinhard of Lewins' loyalty and honesty. Lord Edward had also conceded that, although he believed his friend to be firmly attached to the French cause, he would suggest dispatching an agent to Dublin. In this way, Lewins' integrity could be clarified, and more importantly, the French could gain an insight into the present state of affairs in Ireland. Finally, Fitzgerald proposed a man named Jägerhorn, as being most suitable for such a mission, since his Swedish passport would prevent him from arousing supicion.[60]

Lord Edward had met Jägerhorn in Hamburg in the previous year. The Swedish officer had taken refuge there after being forced to flee his native country. In the 1780s, he had been one of the leading conspirators in a

---

60 NLI pos. 198 (Archives Nationales AF III 59 doss. 231), Reinhard to Delacroix, 16 germinal an 5 (5 April 1797), including Lord Edward's letter of introduction.

movement striving to establish an independent Finland. After staying in
Russia and Paris, he settled down in Reinbeck, two leagues from Hamburg,
in the territory of Holstein, in 1793. By 1796, he had become a well-known
figure in the colourful *émigré* world of Hamburg. Among others, he was on
intimate terms with Madame de Genlis, the Matthiessens and General de
Valence, through whom he had got to know Lord Edward at their estate in
Silk in 1796.[61]

Reinhard strongly approved of sending Jägerhorn to Ireland as quickly as
possible in order to sort out the uncertainties about Lewins' mission. He
once again emphasized that the communication with the radical movement
was essential for Franco–Irish plans. With regard to Jägerhorn, Reinhard did
not think much of making him familiar with too many secrets. The Swede's
knowledge of details of his mission was to be clearly defined. His friend,
General de Valence, who was eager to prove his loyalty to the French
Revolution, was chosen to brief Jägerhorn on how to proceed.[62]

Jägerhorn eventually set sail for England in April 1797. Accompanied by
his fellow Swedish exile, Daniel Vilhelm Padenheim, he arrived at Yarmouth
and immediately started out for London. Padenheim, acquainted with England
from earlier visits, arranged for Jägerhorn to take up residence in London,
since only himself had acquired the necessary passport for continuing the
journey to Ireland. Furnished with a letter from Jägerhorn, Padenheim travelled further to Dublin, where he called on Lord Edward, who 'was on the
point of setting out for London, to escort one of my sisters.'[63] Jägerhorn
eventually met the Irishman in London at the beginning of May. Fitzgerald
showed himself visibly relieved in the face of French efforts to re-open communications with the Irish republican movement. He immediately got down
to the heart of matters. Self-confidently, he stated,

> that the number of the defenders of the Confederation of the Irish is
> daily increasing, and that their energy had re-doubled in proportion as
> the English government is become persecuting and vexatious. The con-
> federation formed under the name of the United Irishmen, established
> in a society of 36 persons, has fully organized its form and political ex-
> istence. The numbers of the men who have devoted themselves to the
> defence of the rights of their country amounts to nearly 100,000; and,

61 Lesch, Bruno, *Jan Anders Jägerhorn. Patriot Och Världsborgare Separatist Och Emigrant*
    (Helsingfors, 1941). I am greatly indebted to Petri Mirala for making this book available
    to me and for translating it in extracts.
62 NLI pos. 198 (Archives Nationales AF III 59 doss. 231), Reinhard to Delacroix, 5 April 1797.
63 Letter from Lord Edward Fitzgerald to Mr Jägerhorn, in *Memoirs and Correspondence of
    Viscount Castlereagh*, vol. II, 261.

reduced to those who are capable of bearing arms, it comprehends at least 40,000 combatants. The whole Irish nation, with the exception of persons pre-corrupted by the English Government, is animated by the same spirit ...

Lord Edward then went into details of a possible French expedition. He outlined the mode of forwarding arms and ammunition, which should best be sent to the ports of Carrickfergus, Loughfoyle or Loughswilly. He also referred to the necessity of dispatching qualified French officers to assist the untrained radical force of Ireland.[64] Lord Edward evidently indicated the United Irishmen's clear-cut ideas of how to proceed and also their determination not to waste time in idleness. Jägerhorn's mission eventually removed lingering French doubts about Lewins. As Reinhard put it in matter-of-fact fashion

> the authenticity of the mission of Mr Lewins was verified; important details respecting the state of Ireland were given; it was ascertained that there was no derangement in the plan, and in the resources of the united patriots.[65]

Once again, Hamburg had been the starting point of France's Irish policies. Although steps were taken in prior consultation with Paris, Reinhard did not confine himself to merely implementing government instructions. He himself developed into a creator of French foreign policy and considerably contributed to the actual shaping of French actions. He brought an influence to bear on the choice of respective agents, the briefings and instructions they received. Reinhard also quite independently negotiated with Irish agents calling at Hamburg, as seen in the instance of the missions of Lord Edward, Arthur O'Connor and Edward Lewins. The French representative displayed a personal interest in Irish affairs, striving to turn Hamburg into a 'point de contact avec l'Irlande', as he put it himself. This interest is also reflected in the efforts of Hoche and Tone, who tried hard to reconstruct contacts with

---

64 Ibid., vol. I, 288–9, Reinhard to Delacroix, Report of Mr Jägerhorn, 13 July 1797.
65 Ibid., vol. I, 282, Reinhard to Delacroix, 25 messidor an 5 (12 July 1797). See ibid., vol. I, 270–89 and vol. II, 248–65 for British accounts of the Jägerhorn mission, including the communication between Reinhard and the French government, the correspondence between Jägerhorn and General de Valence/Lord Edward, and the examination of Mr Jägerhorn in 1799.

the Irish republican movement in the aftermath of the Bantry Bay failure. The French expedition had shown clearly that the Franco–Irish alliance substantially suffered from communication difficulties. It was also thanks to the city's geographical and political situation, that Hamburg's position as co-ordinating point for communication with Ireland was strengthened. Encouraged by the favourable reception respective missions could expect on the part of the French, Irish agents preferred using the Hamburg route. In connection with this, Arthur O'Connor and Lord Edward's trip to Hamburg formed a prelude to future United missions. From an Irish as well as from a French angle, the two Irishmen set an example, which was to come in useful in the following years. Thus, for instance Edward Lewins gained a great deal from his connection with Lord Edward and from the latter's testimonial, but he was received with scepticism, since he lacked the enthusiasm of his two pre-decessors. However, French caution was also due to the failure of the United Irishmen to rise at the time the French lay off the Irish coast. After Bantry Bay, France had come to doubt the genuineness of Irish overtures, which they had seen demonstrated by Lord Edward and Arthur O'Connor in pre-senting matters to Reinhard. Moreover, the rising temperature in Ireland in the first half of 1797 made it more difficult for the French to reach a better understanding of the state of affairs. In many respects, the heightening ten-sions in Ireland were to have an effect on the situation in Hamburg, too. The relative tranquillity that had surrounded the missions of Lord Edward, O'Connor and Lewins was to be a thing of the past. On the part of the British government, too, the Irish crisis produced a change in political outlook. London had become aware of the international dimension of Irish radicalism and of the importance of Hamburg.

CHAPTER 4

Turner and the Race for Information, 1797–8

Shocked by a French fleet off Bantry Bay some months previously and by re-curring rumours of continued French invasion efforts, the Irish and English authorities were roused to action in the first half of 1797. Starting in the spring, Dublin Castle substantially increased pressure on the Irish republican movement, which was at the height of its strength at the beginning of the year. The governments at Dublin and London also became more aware of United moves outside Ireland. Accordingly, both governments began to put greater emphasis on extending a network of intelligence in order to meet the inter-national dimension of Irish radicalism. Due to heightening tensions in Ireland and to a change of scope of radical activities, United migration started to mount rapidly after the dispatch of Edward Lewins in the spring of 1797. The German city of Hamburg not only grew into a hotbed for devoted Irish re-publicans, but became the focus of British and French government attention. Increasingly, the great powers became aware of the city's importance as a point of convergence between the front lines, each of them trying not to fall behind in a race for information.

I

In the middle of 1797, events were moving fast for the United Irishmen on the Continent. After nearly two years in America, Napper Tandy returned to Europe in May. According to Rupert Coughlan, the French ambassador 'in the name of his government, had invited him to repair to France to as-sist in the formation of an expedition to Ireland.'[1] He finally set sail from New York on 20 March and reached Cuxhaven, at the mouth of the Elbe, at the beginning of May. Although Tandy tried to disguise himself under the

---

1 Coughlan, *Napper Tandy*, 113.

alias of Jones, he attracted the attention of Harward, an English representa-
tive residing at Cuxhaven. After berthing at Cuxhaven, Jones had 'ripped the
Bolster of his Bed + took from thence an immense quantity of Letters for
Ireland, which were put into the Post Office here by the Captain of the Vessel',
Harward also commented on the conspicuous and boorish behaviour of Tandy.
Three or four days later, 'two Irishmen from the North of Ireland', later identified as Bill and Angula, arrived at Cuxhaven. They hurriedly enquired about
an American vessel, certain letters and an 'elderly Man', answering Tandy's
description. But Tandy had already left Cuxhaven. The two Irishmen immediately proceeded to Hamburg, where they finally met up with Tandy
around mid-May. The veteran radical had already got in contact with Reinhard.
The French representative had received him with great respect and took care
of arrangements for the Irishmen's passage to Paris. Tandy and his companions
left Hamburg and reached France towards the end of May 1797. Frazer, the
English minister in Hamburg, did not learn who had actually slipped through
his fingers until the middle of June.[2]

Tandy's stay in Hamburg was short, but significant. The Irishman's mission to Europe had obviously been well prepared and only superficially seems
the rash action of a choleric, 'elderly Man'. Although his appearance in
Hamburg and Cuxhaven certainly had much of the eccentricity that Tandy
was reputed to show, it was above all his absolute radicalism that made him
stand out. His persuasiveness also seems to have impressed Reinhard, who once
again proved favourable to the United cause. It was the Irishman's determination that was to affect the balance of power among the United Irishmen
on the Continent in the course of the following year. His constant craving
for admiration soon led him to demand a leading position among United
men in France. Tandy's arrival coincided with the beginning of a new phase
of United presence on the European mainland. The relative cohesion among
earlier missions to France came to an end. Discord began to make itself felt
among United Irishmen, both on the Continent and in Ireland. Moreover,
Tandy's stay in Hamburg also coincided with Edward Lewins' residence in
the city, since the latter departed only as late as 20 May. It is surprising that
no mention is made of a meeting of the two radicals, who were acquainted
since the early days of the Dublin United Irishmen. To avoid each other
must have been more difficult than to meet, because both were in close touch
with Reinhard. Explanations must necessarily remain speculative, but one is

2   PRO F.O. 33/13/89, Frazer to Grenville, 23 May 1797; PRO F.O. 33/13/97, Harward
    to Frazer, 2 June 1797; Nat. Arch. 620/31/61, Grenville to Pelham, 9 June 1797; PRO
    F.O. 33/13/119, Frazer to Grenville, 20 June 1797; Coughlan, *Napper Tandy*, 114 on
    Tandy's arrival on the Continent.

led to believe that personal animosities between the two Irishmen already became apparent in Hamburg. Some time later in Paris, Tandy fell out with Lewins as well as with Tone, who now had to dispense with his special position as the United Irishmen's only ambassador to France.

On 20 May, Edward Lewins had left Hamburg. Although he had received a letter of introduction from Reinhard, the latter continued to put little confidence in the Irishman. Jägerhorn had not yet returned from his mission, so that the issue of Lewins' integrity still remained to be clarified. Furthermore, Reinhard had been made suspicious in the face of confusing newspaper reports on the situation in Ireland. Why had Lewins not made mention of the United Irishmen's internal troubles and why should Reinhard give his 'confidence to any other than him alone?'[3] After charging Johann Conrad Matthiessen to forward his correspondence, Lewins set out for the south of Germany in order to meet Hoche. On 29 May, he was received by the French general in the north Hessian city of Kassel. There, Hoche was condemned to passivity after the preliminary peace with Austria, which had been accepted by Bonaparte on 18 April. Accordingly, an expedition to Ireland still appeared very attractive to the ambitious general. Immediately, Hoche got down to enquiring from the Directory about its Irish plans, but he soon had to realise that the French government showed little commitment in favour of another Irish invasion attempt. Public interest in an expedition to Ireland had decreased after the Bantry Bay failure and the government in Paris did not want to risk any troops without a prior attempt at rising on the part of the Irish. For the moment, Irish affairs had been assigned to the Batavian Republic. General Daendals and Admiral DeWinter, as commanders of a projected expedition to the British Isles, had been given the task of preparing the enterprise. Accordingly, Lewins set out for the Hague at the end of June, accompanied by Wolfe Tone, who had met his family in Holland in early May after a separation of seventeen months. Hoche, who was to have the overall command of the Irish expedition, had instructed the two Irishmen to be at the disposal of the Dutch and to furnish those responsible for the preparations with information on Ireland.[4]

II

In Ireland, events came thick and fast in the first half of 1797. Tensions had heightened after the French Bantry Bay failure, which had nevertheless nur-

3 *Memoirs and Correspondence of Viscount Castlereagh*, I, 272–7, Reinhard to Delacroix, 13 prairial an 5 (31 May 1797).
4 PRONI D.3030/210, Secret note, undated [received from Cuxhaven, 16 August 1798 and

tured radical hopes of change. Dublin Castle was faced with increasing political unrest, both from the radical and the loyalist side. Especially in Ulster,
the major radical stronghold, the situation seemed to escalate. There, United
numbers had grown enormously, amounting to 121,000 by June.[5] In the spring
of 1797, the Irish government started to take large-scale countermeasures
against the radical threat. Ulster was struck by waves of arrests, and by the
summer, large numbers of United leaders were in detention. At the beginning
of March, Dublin Castle initiated the disarming of the military bulwark of Irish
radicalism. On 13 March, the entire province was put under martial law, followed by excessive acts of violence on the part of the military. Government
measures did not fail to hit their target, all the more as the northern radicals
were completely taken by surprise. Soon, the Ulster movement was in disarray,
struggling to withstand government reprisals.

Against this background, the story of one of the most enigmatic double-lives
commenced in the spring of 1797. Although often alluded to in modern historiography, Samuel Turner's career as a secret agent has never been singled
out for special attention. Therefore, it is a matter of necessity to remove remaining inaccuracies and inconsistencies in order to do justice to Turner's
importance for Hamburg and the British Continental spy network. Samuel
Turner of Newry, born in 1765, was the son of a gentleman of good fortune.
He was educated at Trinity College Dublin and completed the study of juris-
prudence in 1787. Turner was called to the Irish Bar in 1788, and he appears
to have served as a justice of the peace for Armagh and Down afterwards.
Nevertheless, very little is actually known about his professional career in the
years between 1788 and 1797. It was not until 1797, however, that Turner
joined the Society of United Irishmen, sworn in by Abraham Walker, who
afterwards fled to America. It speaks well for his persuasive power that he
was admitted into the national executive committee within the next months.
At that time, the committee was at pains to prevent the execution of a number
of United Irishmen standing trial at the spring assizes in the counties of Antrim
and Down. Turner's legal advice came in useful. Together with Alexander
Lowry, Bartholomew Teeling and Anthony McCann, all of whom were to
penetrate through to France within the next six months, he was busy 'col-
lecting money to fee Council and to bribe or buy off witnesses etc. etc' in
order to preserve his United brethren from conviction.[6]

enclosed in a letter from Wickham to Castlereagh, see *Memoirs and Correspondence of
   Viscount Castlereagh*, I, 270–2]; Elliott, *Partners in Revolution*, 154–8 on Lewins and France's
   Irish policy in the spring and summer of 1797; see *Life of Theobald Wolfe* Tone, II, 355–80
   and 405–41 on Tone's family reunion and the mission to Holland.
5 McDowell, *Ireland in the Age of Imperialism*, 473.
6 PRO H.O. 100/70/340–1, Camden to Portland, 9 December 1797, including Downshire's

Despite increasing government pressure, the Ulster movement was at the height of its numerical and organizational strength in the early spring of 1797. With great enthusiasm, the Ulstermen endeavoured to strengthen the Society's cohesion, to improve its military power and to prepare the ground for a speedy Irish rising, if necessary independent of French help. United activity prevailed throughout the whole province. Apart from Belfast, Newry was one of the principal centres of disaffection and a major 'republican stronghold', as recently described by Tony Canavan. Numerous reports show clearly the precarious state of affairs in the Newry region in early 1797.[7] The Irish authorities could not avoid reacting to the radical menace, which seemed to shake the very foundations of government control. Joseph Pollock, often used as a man for special tasks by the government, was a loyal magistrate for the county of Down who devoted his energies to the troubled town. His reports served as an important source of information for the government, but also for the second marquess of Downshire, who showed a special interest in crushing the radical threat. 'Through his electoral influence' and extensive estates 'in his power base of Co. Down and elsewhere, he was the most powerful political magnate in late-eighteenth-century-Ireland.' Downshire spared no effort to 'effectively prevent the Mischief intended by those cunning Vipers', as he put it himself some months earlier.[8] In a letter to Downshire on 21 March 1797, Joseph Pollock named John Gordon, Robert Maitland and Sam Turner as the 'chief and violent persons as agitators of late'. With the help of Pollock's information, the Irish government started to substantially increase pressure on the Newry radicals in the following weeks. By 12 April, Turner was reported to have 'been through the Mountains, lying in dirty Cabins'.[9] Although there was still no warrant out for his arrest, Turner found himself in an awkward situation. Since he was obviously associated with the United Irishmen, the authorities only waited for him to act rashly.

account of his meeting with Turner of 8 October 1797. See *The Dictionary of National Biography* (London, since 1917), vol. XIX, 1282–3 on Turner's early life.

7 Canavan, Tony, *Frontier Town. An Illustrated History of Newry* (Belfast, 1989), 112. See PRONI D.607/E/41, 42, 45, 51, 67, 86, 145, 147, 185, 210 and 'Report of the Committee of Secrecy, 30 August 1798', in *Journals of the House of Lords of Ireland, vol. VIII: 1798–1800* (Dublin, 1800), 139 as well as McDowell, *Ireland in the Age of Imperialism*, 576 on the state of affairs in the Newry region.

8 See PRONI D.607/E on Pollock; Malcomson, A.P.W., 'The Gentle Leviathan: Arthur Hill, Second Marquess of Downshire, 1753–1801', in Roebuck, Peter, *Plantation to Partition. Essays in Ulster History in Honour of J.L. McCracken* (Belfast, 1981), 102–18 on Lord Downshire; Nat. Arch. 620/25/150, Downshire to Cooke, 6 October 1796.

9 PRONI D.607/E/214, Pollock to Downshire, 21 March 1797; Nat. Arch. 620/29/247, J. Carleton, Newry, to Col. Ross, 12 April 1797.

A famous incident on 16 April finally made sure that Turner did not fall into oblivion. In the meantime, the Irish government had reinforced troops in Ulster. Ranking officers were staying in Newry, among others Lieutenant-General Lake, Brigadier-General Knox and General Lord Carhampton, the latter of whom met Turner in an inn on Easter Sunday, 16 April. There, Carhampton told Turner to take off the green handkerchief around his neck, because it obviously represented a 'symbol of rebellion'. The United Irishman refused to do so and after some arguing, Carhampton tore off the handkerchief. Although the incident did no harm to Turner, since the general later apologized to him, it contributed much to his reputation as a brave and unbending radical. In the days following, the incident was on everyone's lips. On the evening of 16 April, J. Carleton, himself a magistrate in Newry, addressed Col. Ross, still very close to it all. 'Sunday is come', he wrote, 'and I am alive and well, but remember what I say, that unless Sam Turner and other busy agitators are taken up without waiting for forms, the U.I.'s will pour in on us like a torrent, and sweep us all away.' Three days later, Brigade-General Knox criticised Carhampton's faux-pas, but also stressed the importance of taking more vigorous action:

> Lord Carhampton at Newry took a green handkerchief from the neck of one of the principal Enragés. To what does that tend? Certainly not to subdue. Lord Carhampton says it is necessary to turn the tide. It is so, but it must be so effectually turned, that it will not flow again.

The Turner episode shows that the radical spirit in Ulster remained unbroken, despite measures that had been taken in the previous months to root out radicalism in the North. The incident made it clear to the Irish government that a tighter rein had to be kept on the undaunted Ulster troublemakers.[10]

After the incident with Lord Carhampton, events came thick and fast for Turner. For the following month, it is rather difficult to trace his whereabouts. He was obviously occupied in doing his share to hurry along northern preparations for the intended rising. Together with Ulster's main militants, Teeling, Lowry, John Orr and John Tennent, he worked ceaselessly, attending meetings, instructing followers and extending the Society's military organization. However, Turner's apparent tirelessness in favour of the United cause should not blind one to the fact that he was already looking for a way out of his diffi-

---

10 Madden, R.R., *The United Irishmen, Their Lives and Times*, 2nd edn, 1st ser., (Dublin, 1857), 548, Newell's narrative of the Turner episode; Nat. Arch. 620/29/270, Carleton to Ross, 16 April 1797; PRONI T.755/IV/2/290, Knox to Pelham, 19 April 1797, T.755/IV/2/264-9 and McDowell, *Ireland in the Age of Imperialism*, 570 on the army in Newry on Easter Sunday.

culties as a victim of persecution. His activities as a United Irishman jeopardised his life, and Turner did not shut his eyes to his precarious situation. Records in the National Archives suggest that a person answering Turner's description spent a few days in Dublin at the end of April. Very carefully, the United Irishman from the North approached Francis Higgins, trying to establish 'a confidential communication' with the government through Higgins, its long-standing agent. A letter to the government, written by Higgins on 13 June 1801, verifies the assumption that the informer was acquainted with Turner and that 'he paid a Debt of 35 Pounds [for the latter] when he got off to Hambro'. Thus, it can be presumed that Turner was flirting with the idea of offering his services to the government as early as April 1797, long before October, which is the date generally acknowledged by historians.[11] However cautiously Turner first approached the idea of defecting from the United cause, he translated it into action within the next month. In May, the Irish government once again tightened its policy on Ulster. On 17 May Camden issued a second proclamation, thus extending

> His Majesty's Pardon to all such as are sensible of their Errors, and willing to return to their Allegiance, do hereby promise His Majesty's gracious Pardon, to all such Persons, so seduced or intimidated, as have taken an Engagement to the said Societies, or any of them, who shall, on or before the 24th day of June next, surrender themselves to any of His Majesty's Justices of the Peace, being of the Quorum of the Counties in which they shall respectively reside, and take the Oath of Allegiance, and enter into sufficient Recognizance with two sufficient Sureties ... [12]

Some three or four days later 'the celebrated Knight of the Green Handkerchief Mr (or if you will) General Turner' is reported to have fled from Newry. Just in time, he escaped arrest, since 'on 22 May 1797, a detachment of the 22nd Light Dragoons arrested a number of Newry townsmen suspected of treasonable activities, among them John Gordon. In a further series of arrests four days later, ten men were taken.'[13] Turner spent the following week in

---

11 Nat. Arch. 620/18/14, Francis Higgins' information, three letters, written between 30 April and 6 May 1797; Nat. Arch. 620/18/14, Higgins' letters, 30 May 1797 and 13 June 1801. See Froude, James Anthony, *The English in Ireland in the Eighteenth Century*, vol. III (London, 1881), 319–22, McDowell, *Ireland in the Age of Imperialism*, 533–4 and Elliott, Wolfe Tone, 368–9 as some examples on Turner's defection.

12 PRONI T.739/1&2, Proclamations by the Lord Lieutenant & Council of Ireland, 17 May 1797; see Elliott, *Partners in Revolution*, 126–30 and Curtin, *The United Irishmen*, 78–87 on the Irish government's Ulster campaign in 1797.

13 Nat. Arch. 620/30/195, Major John Giffard to Cooke, Newry, 26 May 1797; Canavan, *Frontier Town*, 114 on the military in Newry; see also PRO P.C. I/38/A.122 on Turner fleeing Newry around 20 May 1797.

Dublin, having daily conversations with leading United Irishmen, such as Sampson, Bond, Jackson and Dixon. Around 25 May, he left Dublin on his way back to the North. By that time, he had made up his mind. In a 'time of arrests and atrocity, murder and execution', his life was hanging by a thread.[14] In dire straits, Turner decided to take advantage of the late proclamation. Around 26 May, he approached Joseph Pollock in Newry, who some time later summarised their meeting.

> ... The Chancellor has superseded in the Commission of our two
> Counties Mr Turner of this Town, who thought it necessary to sur-
> render under the Proclamation, and entered into Recognizance (by mis-
> take only 100 Pounds. But perhaps that may be corrected. I wrote to the
> Chancellor on it.) as common Culprits do. He on purging himself began
> to white-wash, as some call it, as many others and I have reason to
> think that, if we have Access to his List of Recognizances, which by the
> Proclamation may be returned either to the next Sessions of the Peace
> (now about sitting in Armagh) or next Assizes, we shall receive Names
> that will discover much of the political Situation of the Country, the
> rank & numbers of Conspirators, etc. etc. ... The Chancellor says that
> Turner is not of the Quorum in either County, and that such acts as
> Surrenders to him are therefore void. The proclamation certainly runs
> so. This will help the Terror, if thought necessary, and if Government
> chuse to consider or appear for the moment to consider, such Surrenders
> as not entitling to pardon. The fact must be, I should think, and as I
> explained at large to the Chancellor, that Turner did not examine prop-
> erly his friends, perhaps any who surrendered, for all may have been
> his friends and they went to him in great bodies. Government might
> perhaps find it prudent to take up some who surrendered to him, on
> the ground of insufficiency of surrender, and to give the rest fair notice
> afterwards to make a proper Surrender to some proper Magistrates. If
> you adopt my idea even in part, I should suppose that the less time that
> is lost the better. A Session for County Down is to held here on Monday
> next but it would be better to have sooner the list I speak of, even if T.
> would return it to us then, which I am confident he won't, as he must
> wish to conceal it while he lawfully can. You will please to recollect he
> was Justice for Armagh & Down.[15]

14 Canavan, *Frontier Town*, 114; Nat. Arch. 620/10/121/61, MacNally on Turner's stay in
    Dublin, 27 May 1797.
15 Nat. Arch. 620/31/50, Pollock to Pelham, 7 June 1797; see also Nat. Arch. 620/30/200,
    Pollock to Pelham, 26 May 1797, for the date of Turner's defection.

Today, Turner's attempt to 'white-wash' his involvement with the United Irishmen and to excuse his radical activities as being a result of 'not examining properly his friends' seems more than doubtful. Also Goodwin's assumption that he had 'been alienated from the cause of Irish independence largely by his conviction that the southern Catholics had determined to use it to put through large-scale confiscations of landed property' is a possible reason and is consonant with the anti-catholic sentiment expressed in some of his letters. However, it was not the primary motive behind Turner's decision to change sides.[16] Most likely, it was sheer fear for his life that induced him to defect from the Society's cause rather than a sudden and fundamental change of his political views. The hectic rush and the shady circumstances that surrounded his defection suggest as much. Moreover, the reference to the chancellor as having 'superseded' Turner as a magistrate and as a consequence some recent magisterial actions of Turner been deemed invalid is in itself significant. If he had within some comparatively short time previously been struck off as a magistrate, his position as a marked man would be all the clearer to him. Nevertheless, Pollock's letter reveals that Turner's treachery was not merely an act committed under the influence of emotion. The United Irishman did not only want to save his own skin but had made provisions for selling his services as dearly as possible. He had apparently received submissions by a great number of United Irishmen up to and even beyond the last hours of office, concealing from them the fact that 'such acts as Surrenders to him' were legally invalid. It is unclear whether he had planned to betray his United brethren when accepting their submissions. At any rate, at the end of May 1797, he did not scruple to use 'his List of Recognizances' as a means of gaining advantage for his negotiations with Pollock. Thus, even though he appears to have been driven to despair because of increasing government repression, one can not help wondering whether Turner had been a wolf in sheep's clothing some time before he gave himself up at the end of May. By accepting United submissions, he had possibly ingratiated himself with the United Irishmen he was about to betray as a form of cover for his present or future hostile action against them. Throwing a glance at the future conduct

Pollock's letter to Pelham (7 June 1797) does not reveal the date of Turner's surrender. After examining all possible dates, Turner's meeting with Pollock in Newry seems to have been around 26 May. The meeting and the following correspondence between Pollock and the Chancellor (mentioned in Pollock's letter) hardly could have taken place in the short period between 5 and 7 June, the day Pollock wrote the above letter. Since Turner stayed in Dublin from around 27 May until around 5 June, the meeting in all likelihood took place during Turner's last stay in Newry between 25 and 26 May.

16 Goodwin, Albert, *The Friends of Liberty. The English Democratic Movement in the Age of the French Revolution* (London, 1979), 435.

of the highly calculating government spy, one would certainly assume that he had prepared his meeting with Pollock carefully. However, since Turner was at pains to conceal his treachery, he could not allow himself much leisure for extensive conversations with Pollock, who in turn had little time to confer with the Irish government. Thus, for Turner, the terms of his surrender obviously left a great deal to be desired. Nothing is known about the instructions he received and the safety precautions on his behalf. Moreover, the question of payment for his future services does not seem to have been clarified to Turner's satisfaction. However, some five months later, he was to pursue the matter again.

Outwardly, Turner remained loyal to the United Irishmen. At the end of May, he went to Dublin 'for the purpose of conveying intelligence, from the leaders [t]here, to those in the North.' On 28 May, he left the city again and set out for Ulster.[17] There, preparations were in train for the forthcoming national meeting in Dublin, which was to take place in the first week of June. It was destined to serve as a decisive military stock-taking and intended to set the pattern for a United policy on the questions of an Irish rising and the French alliance. Around 5 June, Turner, Bartholomew Teeling, Alexander Lowry, Joseph Orr and John Tennent proceeded to Dublin and presented Ulster plans to the national meeting. Accordingly, Teeling was supposed to 'raise the lads in the county of Louth', Turner himself was 'to raise them in and about Newry' and Alexander Stewart was to stir them in Armagh. The Ulster leaders reckoned the northern movement would easily bring together 20,000 men, just as many as Arthur O'Connor would bring together in the South. The country north of Newry was designed to 'employ the attention of General Lake's army', while the major part of the rebel forces would attack Dublin. However, the Ulster proposal met with disapproval. 'The Leinster directory refused to co-operate, on the grounds that the southern organization was incomplete.'[18] Moreover, according to Turner's own account, 'the Dublin part of the Executive Committee did not like this plan', since it was vehemently opposed to the idea of a rising independent of French help. 'After much altercation and dispute [they] refused to act in concert with the Northerns ... '. The Ulster leaders thereupon made their ways home, angry and willing 'to begin the business by themselves.'[19]

Shortly after the split in the national executive committee, Ulster's main militants, Turner, Lowry, Orr, Tennent, John Byrne and Teeling met again in the latter's house in Dundalk. There, they decided to send emissaries to

17 Nat. Arch. 620/10/121/62, McNally's information, 29 May 1797.
18 Curtin, *The United Irishmen*, 87.
19 PRO H.O. 100/70/341-2, Turner's account of the national meeting.

each of the northern counties to consult United colonels about their readiness to come forward in an immediate rising. The Ulster militants were determined to bring their full weight to bear and to launch an attack without the support of the divided Dublin leadership. However, the meeting in Dundalk had to be cut short. A man named Corcoran had got wind of government troops approaching Dundalk. He had also learned that warrants were out for the arrest of the Ulster United leaders and that the army was on their trail. 'He arrived in Dundalk in time to disperse the meeting'. In great haste,

> Barclay Teeling, Sam Turner, John Byrne and Alex. Lowry retreated with Corcoran to one Kelly a Farmer about two small miles from Dundalk where they hid themselves that night in a Barn, in the morning Corcoran was ordered by them to go to Dundalk to know if there was any danger of the Military. Finding none they went to Dundalk. Turner, Lowry and Teeling went to Newry.'[20]

After hiding himself for a short while, Turner fled, according to his own account, 'to the mountains of Morne, from thence took a boat & went to Skerries, thence nearer to Dublin where he stayed two days and afterwards went off by Waterford to London where he stayed ten days. He then went to Hamburgh. The others fled different ways, but all met again upon the Continent by the way of Hamburgh.'[21]

Turner's last days in Ireland are characteristic of the circumstances that surrounded his defection from the radical movement. However precipitately he left the country around mid-June, he left it as a traitor to the United cause. After worming himself into the confidence of his United brethren, his escape to the Continent now proved to be an ideal cover for his employment as a government spy. In the eyes of the United Irishmen, Turner was a rebel fleeing his native Ireland because of his political convictions. In reality, his flight was part and parcel of his efforts to hide the truth from his United companions and enter upon his new role as an informer on the Continent. The Irish government, however, lost no time in making provisions to conceal his conversion. As early as June 1797, his name was included in a list of fugitives from Newry. Moreover, Turner was one of the persons listed in the Fugitive Act (Act. 38th Geo. III, ch. 80) in the following year. Government circles took a lot of care over this new source of information, although responsibility for dealing with Turner had not been clearly assigned for the time being.[22]

20 TCD MSS. 869/8/36, Conlan's information, 1798, respecting the meeting in Dundalk and the subsequent flight of the Ulster militants.
21 PRO H.O. 100/70/342–3, Turner's account of his flight from Ireland.
22 Nat. Arch. 620/31/185, list of fugitives from Newry, June 1797; Madden, *The United*

Frantically, Turner's militant companions had scattered to various parts of the country, before they met again at Randalstown in the North some time after 14 June. There, a gathering had been called together in order to receive a general return of the United leaders and their readiness to participate in an immediate rebellion independent of French assistance. At the meeting, the Antrim colonels objected to acting without the French and thus foiled plans for a speedy rising. Since they lacked unanimous support within their own ranks, the Ulster militants were now in difficulties. Frustrated by the situation within the movement and persecuted by government troops, they decided to go to France, 'as it would not be safe for them to remain longer in the country.'[23] By 26 June, Teeling, Tennent, Lowry and Orr had left Ireland, furnished with letters from Arthur O'Connor. When they arrived at Hamburg around mid-July, travelling via London, Teeling, Tennent and Lowry called on Giauque, who then brought them into contact with the French minister. The Ulster delegates told Reinhard that the 'principal motive of their voyage was the necessity of calming the anxiety of the mass of United Irishmen' concerning communications with France, since the Irish radicals had already 'started to grumble about the indifference, which was demonstrated on the part of the French.' Sympathetic towards the Irishmen, Reinhard tried to allay their worries and to convince them that the United Irishmen could rely on France. Moreover, Giauque informed the Ulstermen that Wolfe Tone, his brother-in-law, was on board a Dutch fleet preparing for Ireland. Thus, with sufficient news to 'spur on the spirits' of the Irish radicals, Teeling started out for Ireland around 20 July. Lowry and Tennent also left Hamburg, and on 5 August, joined Tone on board the *Vreyheid*. By the end of September, the two reached Paris, where they eventually reunited with their Ulster companions, Teeling, Orr, Patrick and John Byrne as well as Anthony McCann and Thomas Burgess, from Co. Louth, later in the year.[24]

In the aftermath of the June crisis, further Ulster militants sought their salvation in fleeing the country. The Revd James Quigley, a catholic priest from Armagh, left Ireland on learning that a warrant for his arrest had been

Irishmen, 2nd ser., 2nd vol., 521 and 3rd ser., 1st vol., 326 on the Fugitive Act; PRO H.O. 100/70/113–7 and 335 on the authorities' handling of Turner's information.

23 *Report of the Committee of Secrecy, 21 August 1798* ... Commons [Ireland], append. XV, DCCCLXVII, information from John Hughes.

24 PRO H.O. 100/70/343–4, Turner's account of the flight of the Ulster leaders; Reinhard to Talleyrand, the newly appointed Minister of Foreign Affairs, 13 thermidor an 5 (30 July 1797) and also Reinhard to Delacroix, 6 thermidor an 5 (23 July 1797), in *Memoirs and Correspondence of Viscount Castlereagh*, I, 289–92 on Reinhard's meeting with the Ulster radicals; *Life of Theobald Wolfe Tone*, II, 428–43 on Tone, Tennent and Lowry; Madden, *The United Irishmen*, 3rd ser., 2nd vol. (Dublin, 1846), 51–63 on Tennent.

issued soon after the Dublin meeting. He first travelled to Liverpool, from where he proceeded to Manchester. There, he got in touch with local radical circles and informed them about his mission to France. He also presented an address from the 'national committee of Ireland', which confirmed French willingness to invade the British Isles. The Manchester brethren must have been taken with Quigley's exposition, since they were busy trying to make it possible for him to continue his journey. A subscription was held, and after a stay of three days, Quigley set out for London. In the capital, he joined the Revd Magaulay and the Revd MacMahon, a presbyterian minister from Down. The latter had also taken part in the Randalstown meeting around mid-June, after which he was informed that there was a warrant out for his arrest. He fled via Bangor and Scotland and arrived in London some time later. There, the three Ulstermen tried to establish contacts with their British counterparts. According to Albert Goodwin, Quigley especially was successful in 'cementing his relations with English and Irish republicans', which were to come in useful on later journeys. With the help of their English brethren, the Irish radicals eventually took ship for Cuxhaven. From there, they proceeded to Paris in order to join the United Irish community, which by now had substantially increased due to the Ulster crisis.[25]

In many respects, events in Ulster in the spring and summer of 1797 began to bring an influence to bear on the entire United movement. Firstly, they greatly affected the dynamism of Irish radicalism. Owing to increased government activity, the northern leaders were concerned about the continued existence of the Ulster movement. Therefore, they did not want to waste time in waiting for another French fleet, but bring into action the still considerable radical force of Ireland as soon as possible. Henceforth, their argumentation in favour of a rising without delay was marked by a note of urgency, which again led to a division within the national executive committee on the issue of French assistance in general. The Ulster crisis of June shows clearly that the United Irishmen were far from united in the summer of 1797, a fact which some time later also became noticeable among the Irish exiles in

---

25 Nat. Arch. 620/1/4/2–3, Nugent to Cooke, 7 August 1797 and Nugent to marquis of Hartford, 12 August 1797; PRO P.C.I/42/A.144, P.C.I/41/A.136, A.139, A.140, Robert Gray papers & examination of Mary Perrins, 1798; 'Report of the Committee of Secrecy, 30 August 1798', in *Journals of the House of Lords of Ireland*, vol. VIII, 1798–1800 (Dublin, 1800), 149; Goodwin, *The Friends of Liberty*, 432–5; Maguire, W.A., 'Arthur MacMahon, United Irishman and French Soldier', *Irish Sword*, IX (1969–70), 212–3; McEvoy, Brendan, 'Father James Quigley', *Seanchas Ardmhacha*, V (1970), 257–8 on MacMahon, Quigley and their flight to the Continent in 1797; see also Elliott, *Partners in Revolution*, 134–50 and Wells, *Insurrection*, 69–78 on further details concerning the connections between the Irish and the English radical scene in 1797–8.

France. The divides among the United Irish in Paris, and their exacerbation by the arrivals of 1797, themselves reflected the pattern of conflict within the leadership in Ireland.[26] Secondly, the increased migration outside Ireland for the most part took place in the form of hasty flights rather than purposive political missions, since fleeing the country often meant the only way out for a harassed United Irishman.[27] Without exception, the known Ulster militants travelled via England on their way to Hamburg (including Cuxhaven as one of the Hamburg harbours), from where they eventually set out for France. Thus, a definite pattern of United migration was strengthened by 1797. Thirdly, events in Ulster indicate a decisive change in government policies with regard to the United Irishmen. Dublin Castle started to keep a tighter rein on Irish radicalism, a fact which in turn substantially furthered United migration to the Continent. The Irish as well as the British government not only got the United Irishmen moving, but also began to gain a more detailed insight into the machinery of United moves. Starting in the spring and summer of 1797, growing numbers of accounts, which were trickling in to Dublin and London, illustrate that the authorities became aware of the importance of the international dimension of Irish radicalism. Accordingly, secret information was handled with utmost caution. The 'importance of secrecy' was one of the main priorities in dealing with arriving pieces of news, which were confined to relatively few government officials. An intelligence network was still not in operation in 1797; it was not before 1798 that the British government effectively reacted to United migration outside Ireland.[28]

III

With the United Irishmen in disarray and divided on the issue of French assistance, the radical potential could not be effectively exploited. In addition, the United Irishmen's difficulties were aggravated by the lack of communication with their French ally, whose Irish policy was anything but transparent in the summer of 1797. Whereas the Irish radicals moved to France in droves,

26 See Cullen, L.M., 'The Internal Politics of the United Irishmen' in Dickson, David, Keogh, Dáire & Whelan, Kevin, eds, *The United Irishmen: Republicanism, Radicalism and Rebellion* (Dublin, 1993), 192–6, Curtin, *The United Irishmen*, 87–9 and Elliott, *Partners in Revolution*, 189–213 for information on the conflict within the United leadership in Ireland.
27 See PRONI T.755/V/129–33, D.607/E/300, Nat. Arch. 620/31/96 as exemplary reports on increased migration and the flight of numerous unnamed Ulster radicals in the summer of 1797.
28 PRO H.O. 100/70/114, Portland to Camden, 25 August 1797. See PRO H.O. 100/69 and 70 as examples of government handling of intelligence in the spring and summer of 1797.

no French mission had reached Ireland since the end of 1796. Moreover, no news had been received from Lewins or any other radical wanderer, until May, when a letter written by Tone eventually put an end to United uncertainties. It also soothed Ulster's displeasure at the stalling tactics supported by the Dublin leaders. In the letter, Tone reaffirmed French intentions to send another expedition and emphasized the need to dispatch an agent to France in order to update the French government with regard to the state of affairs in Ireland. In July, the executive decided to entrust William James MacNeven with the task of travelling to France. Since MacNeven was a 'moderate', this decision certainly bears the mark of the moderate camp in the Dublin leadership who in mid-year were temporarily in the ascendant. Unlike Lewins who had been told to ask for 20,000 to 25,000 French troops, MacNeven was instructed to request 'rather a small number of men, with great quantity of arms, ammunition, artillery and Officers ... '. Five to ten thousand men would be enough to assist the steadily increasing radical movement. MacNeven was also required to make it clear to the French that Ireland would 'in no event ... come under the dominion of France, but [that] it was offered to pay the expenses of the expedition.'[29]

En route for England, MacNeven left Ireland on 27 June 1797. On 7 July, he set sail from Yarmouth and eventually arrived at Hamburg around the tenth. He saw Reinhard immediately, and, as on the twelfth, Reinhard reported his conversation with MacNeven, who used the alias of Williams to Delacroix. He judged the meeting with mixed emotions. Although he believed MacNeven 'to be a man thoroughly acquainted with the facts, in their entirety and their interconnections', the French minister described the Irishman's conduct as 'so circumspect, that there is nothing to oppose his return'. Reinhard took a critical view of the plan of the Dublin moderates to await a French landing before stirring up a rising. He saw it as preferable for French interests that 'the Irish should show themselves' without waiting for help from outside. Reinhard also strongly advised Delacroix against permitting the Irishman to travel to France. 'In consequence', he told MacNeven,

> that the presence of Lewins and Furnes [Turner] in France, the favourable reception of the former by General Hoche, the promises and proofs already given, ought to be sufficient to fix the uncertainty of the Irish; that it was of less importance to increase the number of agents in France, than to animate the minds and the courage of his countrymen; that it was essential to establish firmly a chain of correspondence, by which both parties might mutually obtain information with despatch;

29 MacNeven, William James, *Pieces of Irish History* (New York, 1807), 189–90; see Elliott, *Partners in Revolution*, 150–3 on the circumstances of MacNeven's dispatch.

that, in this manner, he would completely fulfil the end proposed by his mission.

Reinhard's account shows that he was ill disposed to the cautious conduct of the Dublin leadership. He was somewhat irritated by their policy of wait-and-see, which must have appeared like lukewarm radicalism to him. Reinhard's unenthusiastic appraisal of MacNeven seems to suggest that MacNeven's 'moderation' was patently obvious. Moreover, in view of the French representative's enthusiasm for the Irish cause, his cool reaction to MacNeven's report may by implication illustrate from a French perspective the caution to which in Dublin both Lord Edward and O'Connor were opposed. He decided to detain MacNeven in Hamburg and to wait for further instructions, although the latter had expressed the strongest desire to proceed to France.[30]

Soon after his arrival in Hamburg, MacNeven drew up a plan respecting a landing in Ireland, which was to be presented to the Directory. He pointed out Oyster Haven, Lough Swilly, Killybegs and Galway as some of the most favourable landing places. He, however, warned against putting into Carrickfergus and Lough Foyle, which had been recommended by Lord Edward in his London meeting with Jägerhorn at the beginning of May. MacNeven also added a detailed account of the state of affairs in Ireland, making the assurance that the whole country was favourably disposed to the radical movement. He stated that 'even in the places where the system of the United Irishmen is not entirely adopted, we can reckon upon the cooperation of the poor and middling classes. Their hatred of English despotism, and the vexations which they have to endure on the part of their lords, cause the most ignorant of them to act in the same spirit as the most enlightened Republicans ... '. In accordance with his instructions, he then asked for 5000 to 10,000 French troops, 'a numerous staff, engineers, and general officers', which should be commanded by General Hoche. Stressing that 'there is reason to fear that many patriots will be discouraged' by increasing government reprisals, he pointed out that 'it is necessary to accelerate the expedition as much as possible ... '. Finally, MacNeven once again confirmed the missions of Tone as well as Lewins, who was to be the new Irish plenipotentiary in France. Like his predecessors, Lord Edward, O'Connor and Lewins, he tended to overestimate the radical disposition of the Irish people, which can be put down to wishful thinking rather than an intention to pull the wool over French eyes. MacNeven was detained by Reinhard until August, when he finally turned up in Paris.[31]

30 Reinhard to Delacroix, 25 messidor an 5 (12 July 1798), in *Memoirs and Correspondence of Viscount Castlereagh*, I, 277–86; *Life of Theobald Wolfe Tone*, II, 428 on the date of MacNeven's departure from Yarmouth.
31 Ibid., 295–306, MacNeven's memorial relative to a landing in Ireland.

The French minister was better disposed towards Turner who had reached Hamburg some weeks earlier. Furnished with letters from Lady Pamela Fitzgerald, he approached her sister, Madame Matthiessen. He also got in touch with her brother-in-law, General de Valence, who was still eager to make 'his peace with the Directory'. In making use of his family connections, the Frenchman acted as a mediator between French government officials and arriving United men. Soon, Valence also introduced Turner to Reinhard. The minister was clearly taken with the Irishman's appearance. Turner's 'ardent character' and his argumentation in favour of a 'speedy explosion' lived up to Reinhard's idea of an Irish revolution. Accordingly, he issued Turner with an American passport in July and engaged him to proceed to France in order to meet Hoche.

Before he left Hamburg, Turner set about applying himself to his new task as a government spy. He had already kept an eye on MacNeven, whom he knew as one of his opponents at the Dublin meeting at the beginning of June. Both had been admitted to the French minister, but it was Turner, who enjoyed Reinhard's favour to a greater extent. Unsuspectingly, the French minister associated with Turner, confident that he was an ardent republican. Thus, Turner was familiar with MacNeven's moves right from the time the latter had arrived in the city. He was also acquainted with his efforts to establish contact with the French government. Accordingly, he reported back to London. With Turner's help, the British government was able to intercept parts of Reinhard's correspondence with France in the summer of 1797, including MacNeven's memorial. Thanks to its Hamburg spy, Whitehall had now access to first-hand information on radical moves on the Continent and it slowly began to realise that the United Irishmen had to be fought not only in Ireland but abroad.[32]

Apart from Turner, MacNeven and the Ulster militants, William Duckett also stayed in the free German city in July. Like his compatriots, he called on Reinhard, trying to win him over to assist his plans. His mission must have appeared unfathomable to the French minister, who eventually refused to give him money to continue his journey to the British Isles. While detained in Hamburg, Duckett wrote to Truguet, ex-Minister of the Marine and of the Colonies. In the letter, he regretted the changes that had taken place in the ministry of the marine (i.e., Truguet's removal). He also expressed his hope that the French government and the new minister would

32 PRO H.O. 100/70/343, Turner's account of his arrival at Hamburg; Reinhard to Delacroix, 25 messidor an 5 (12 July 1797), in *Memoirs and Correspondence of Viscount Castlereagh*, I, 277–86; PRO H.O. 100/113–7, 123–8, 139–41, 331–6 on the British government and Turner's information, August 1797; see *Memoirs and Correspondence of Viscount Castlereagh*, I, 272–306, intercepted letters, May–July 1797.

still 'prosecute the same plans and the same projects'. Since even 'the best-
informed persons' had begun to 'entertain their doubts and their fears' concerning the reliability of the French, Duckett pressed for Truguet to provide
the necessary means to fulfill his mission as soon as possible. However, although Duckett was insistent that Reinhard should support his efforts, he
was not permitted to leave for England in July 1797. Owing to the French
minister's unyielding attitude, he was forced to stay on in Hamburg until the
end of the year. The mission Duckett had in mind is unclear, but it certainly
was unpopular with Reinhard and also with MacNeven, who 'refused to recon-
cile himself with Mr Duckett' while in Hamburg. Being in the service of the
ministry of the marine, all the indications are that he was engaged to revive
the naval mutiny, which had shaken parts of the English navy in the months
before. Duckett's involvement in the Great Naval Mutiny at the Nore and
Spithead is unclear. After all, he does not appear to have actively fanned the
flames of discontent among Irish seamen in the spring and summer of 1797.
More likely, his proposed July mission seems to be a belated attempt on the
part of the French to reap the benefits of an English crisis, which had taken
France by surprise.[33]

Increasingly, in the summer of 1797 Hamburg had turned into a halting-
place for Irish republicans. While French eagerness to send another expedition to Ireland had cooled off substantially, the United Irishmen sought their
salvation in exerting all their strength to prevent United matters from falling
into oblivion. MacNeven, Turner, Duckett and their Ulster compatriots all
used Hamburg as a stepping stone for their respective missions; and yet, as
seen in the instances of MacNeven and Duckett, the free German city did
not merely serve as a Continental starting point for United travellers, but
represented a major obstacle which had to be negotiated. In connection with
this, Reinhard's position as the French representative was of utmost importance. Apart from Hoche, he had developed into one of the outstanding advocates of Irish affairs and had a say in the fate of most missions. Being the
first French authority encountered on the way to France by many United
Irishmen, he also had an influence on the image of France's Irish policy. In
reality, French policy-makers, however, showed themselves less committed
and enthusiastic about a far-reaching involvement in Ireland than Reinhard

33 Reinhard to Delacroix, 6 thermidor an 5 (23 July 1797) and Duckett to Truguet, no date,
   in *Memoirs and Correspondence of Viscount Castlereagh*, I, 290–5; NLI pos.210/70–3,
   Duckett's account of his stay in Hamburg; Kennedy, 'William Duckett', in Baylen/Gossman,
   Biographical Dictionary, 137 on Duckett in 1797; see Elliott, *Partners in Revolution*, 134–50,
   Wells, *Insurrection*, 79–109, Dugan, James, *The Great Mutiny* (London, 1966), Goodwin, *The
   Friends of Liberty*, 406–35 on the Great Mutiny and its Anglo–Irish dimension.

in his meetings with United radicals. Thus, the French minister presented a distorted picture of French intentions, which in turn led to inflated hopes on the part of the United Irishmen. Reinhard himself did not shut his eyes to the 'delicacy of [his] position', which he put down to 'having no assurance to give, no central authority to direct me'. Reproachfully, he commented on French attitudes towards the Irish republican cause in July and stated 'that to show coldness and uncertainty is the way to weaken the springs of a machine, the working of which, under every hypothesis, the Republic has an interest in humouring and directing.' However, the French government does not seem to have approved of Reinhard's conduct, since he was removed from office some time later. French foreign policy had already changed in emphasis to hurrying along peace negotiations with Austria, and since June, also with England. Henceforward, the preferential treatment of Irish radicals was to be a thing of the past.[34]

IV

Turner was still in Hamburg in the middle of July. He had been required to stay on for some time by Madame Matthiessen, who was awaiting intelligence from her sister, Lady Pamela Fitzgerald. Among the expected letters were to be instructions for his conduct and for his proposed mission to France. Furnished with letters of recommendation to Hoche and Delacroix, which he had received from Reinhard, Turner eventually left Hamburg and arrived at Paris around 26 July. In Paris, he met up with his Ulster companions. He lodged with Alexander Lowry and an Irishman named Black, and also associated with Joseph Orr, the Byrne brothers, Anthony McCann, Napper Tandy and Bartholomew Teeling, who had been sent back to France in order to lay stress on the militants' call for immediate French assistance.[35] In all probability,

---

34 Reinhard to Delacroix, 25 messidor an 5 (12 July 1797), in *Memoirs and Correspondence of Viscount Castlereagh*, I, 285; see Elliott, *Partners in Revolution*, 153–8 on French foreign policy in the summer of 1797.

35 PRO H.O. 100/70/343–6, Turner's account of his stay in Paris. Turner's mention of Teeling being in Paris appears somewhat baffling. However, although Elliott believes Teeling to have returned to Paris some time later, his presence in the French capital at an earlier date is very possible. After leaving Hamburg for England around 20 July, he probably transmitted information to John Chambers, member of the Dublin executive, who was staying in London from late July until the beginning of September. According to Leonard McNally, 'Chambers while in London has had frequent conferences with persons from France.' Nat. Arch. 620/10/121/75 and 71; see Elliott, *Partners in Revolution*, 161.

Turner, while in Paris, also ran into MacNeven. After Reinhard's agreement to the resumption of his journey, MacNeven had finally reached the French capital in August. There, he drew up a second memorial, in which he urged the Directory not to postpone the Irish expedition. Turner mixed with his compatriots without arousing suspicion; and also among French officials he was regarded as an upright radical. He called on Delacroix, who had been removed from office in July and who eventually referred him to his successor in the foreign ministry, Talleyrand. In September, Turner concluded his first fact-finding mission on behalf of the British government. He left Paris on the nineteenth. En route to Hamburg, he travelled via Lisle, Rotterdam and Amsterdam and eventually arrived at the free German city at the end of September. In Hamburg, Reinhard provided him with a 'passport which would enable him to return there when he chose.' Without knowing it, the French representative thus supported Turner's betrayal of the United Irishmen.[36]

Turner was still not quite clear about the particulars of his new career after his talks with Pollock in May/June. The Irish government, too, did not know how to handle this important source of intelligence. Responsibility for Turner had not been clearly assigned. After Pollock had informed Dublin Castle about his catch in June, Chief Secretary Thomas Pelham, Lord Lieutenant Camden and the Under-Secretary of State in the Civil Department, Edward Cooke, looked after Turner. Soon also the British Home Department was involved, in the persons of Home Secretary duke of Portland and the under-secretaries Charles Greville and John King. Thus, matters were confined to a few high-ranking government officials in Ireland as well as England. This illustrates Turner's importance as the British government's first 'international' United agent. Unlike McNally, Francis Higgins or Edward Newell, whose activities were restricted to Ireland, Turner attracted attention on both sides of the Irish Sea.[37]

In the beginning of October 1797, Turner himself put an end to government uncertainties about its Hamburg spy. On 8 October, late at night, he went to Lord Downshire's town house in Hanover Square, London. Downshire, who had been absent from Ireland since mid-April, had already in earlier instances offered evidence of his readiness to use the help of informers, a fact Turner most certainly knew about. Thus, it was surely no accident that he called at the door of Ireland's most powerful political magnate. Turner's face does not appear to have been completely unfamiliar to Downshire, which led

36 PRO H.O. 100/70/343–6, Turner's account of his stay in Paris; MacNeven, *Pieces of Irish History*, 190–1 on MacNeven in Paris.
37 PRO H.O. 100/70/93, 113–7, 123–8, 139–41, 331–6, 339–51 on the Irish/British government and Turner, including Downshire's account of his meeting with Turner.

the historian Fitzpatrick to assume that the October meeting was probably not the first communication between Downshire and his 'friend'. However, often alluded to as the all-important break with the United Irishmen, Turner's famous cloak-and-dagger visit to Downshire was certainly more of an attempt to fathom out the circumstances of his position as a government spy.[38] After unmasking, he entered into negotiations with Downshire, with the proviso 'that he should never be called upon to appear in a Court of Justice for the purpose of prosecuting any persons that might be taken up in consequence of his Discoveries or Information.' Turner emphasized that his intentions as a United Irishman had originally been 'perfectly pure' in aiming to bring about parliamentary reform, but that he was shocked about the measures and the violence now being employed by the Society. Therefore, he told Downshire, 'he had come to England to make every discovery in his power and to prevent such mischief befalling his Country ... '. Turner then put Downshire in the picture about United activities, starting with his admission to the Society up until his journey to France. In great detail, he commented on events, allowing Downshire to look at the decision-making bodies of the United Irishmen. For the first time, a United leader from the top level of the Society 'talked', and Downshire certainly deemed himself lucky about his catch. However, since the government did not immediately 'ratify the promise' Downshire had made to Turner, the informer disappeared from the lodgings, where he had been put up after their first meeting. He still feared for his life and apart from his continuing mistrust of government henchmen, he now lived in dread of being exposed and assassinated by his United companions.[39]

Turner succeeded in keeping his betrayal a secret. While in London, he conferred with Lord Edward who asked him to stay in Hamburg as the United Irishmen's mediator in the north German city. Lord Edward also had meetings with the newly returned MacNeven. Turner, like MacNeven, seems to have presented an optimistic picture of French attitudes towards another expedition to Ireland, since Lord Edward lost no time in hurrying off to Dublin, determined to initiate an Irish rising before the arrival of the French. He was convinced about France's willingness to send another fleet before the end of

38 PRONI D.607/E/250 and Malcomson, 'The Gentle Leviathan', in Roebuck, *Plantation to Partition* on Downshire; see PRONI D.714/5/1, D.607/F/473, 537, 569 & D.607/G/57, 66, 76, 82, 89, 92, 94, 100–1, 106, 143, 159, 170A, 174 , Nat. Arch. 620/10/121/60 and PRONI D.607/E/319 for examples of Downshire's connections with informers, such as Leonard McNally, Dutton ('the Newry informer') and Nicholas Magin ('the Saintfield informer'); see Froude, *The English in Ireland*, III, 319–22, McDowell, *Ireland in the Age of Imperialism*, 533–4 and Fitzpatrick, *Secret Service under Pitt* (London, 1892), 1–69 for some pieces of historical writing on Downshire's meeting with Turner.
39 PRO H.O. 100/70/339–51, Downshire's account of his meeting with Turner.

the month, probably not knowing that Hoche, the most important French advocate of Irish invasion plans, had died on 19 September. Up to his death, Hoche had encouraged Irish hopes of French assistance. As late as early September 1797, he had assured MacNeven that he would apply all his energies to get another expedition off the ground. Accordingly, United emissaries to France were blinded by the general's optimism, which was far from being in accordance with the scepticism displayed by the Directory. At any rate, although Hoche was unjustified in promising immediate help for the Irish radical movement, his death was a bitter set-back for the United Irishmen who lost their keenest supporter. Moreover, the defeat of the Dutch naval forces at Camperdown on 11 October shattered United hopes of an invasion of Ireland by the Texel fleet. Fitzgerald's optimism, however, may have been a key fact in the rising fortunes of the 'radicals', and in their success in the November quarterly elections to the executive which strengthened the hand of the 'radicals' and accelerated the effort to spread the military organisation of the Society in Leinster. If the Camperdown defeat excluded the prospect of imminent invasion (which would have united 'moderates' and 'radicals'), as a proof of French good intentions it strengthened the position of the 'radicals'.[40] At the end of 1797, the United Irishmen were awaiting the French with feverish excitement. But nothing seemed to happen, despite reports indicating French readiness to assist the Irish, which had been conveyed by Teeling in July, as well as by Turner and MacNeven in October. Only with great difficulties, United leaders succeeded in keeping under control the militant wing of the Society. Although the Ulster United men had been weakened earlier in the year, the movement as a whole was gaining ground towards the end of 1797. Due to insufficient information, however, the Society was in the dark regarding the Franco–Irish alliance. While United missions had increased substantially in 1797, communications with France had not improved correspondingly. The migration of Irish radicals to the Continent led to self-perpetuating confusion, since the Irish exiles in Paris, like their brethren at home, were divided amongst themselves. The divides among the United Irish in France closely mirrored the divides in Ireland about whether to rise immediately or to await the certain French help. Accordingly, the exchange of information between the home movement and the Continent reflected the fragmentation within the Society. Rather than clarifying the co-operation between France and Ireland, United missions accelerated misunderstandings within the organisation.[41]

---

40 PRO H.O. 100/75/7–10, Turner's intelligence, 19 November 1797; *Life of Theobald Wolfe Tone*, II, 443–7, Tone's account of Hoche's death.

41 See Elliott, *Partners in Revolution*, 158–62 on French attitudes towards Ireland in the second half of 1797.

On 17 November, Turner finally reached Hamburg after staying in England for some weeks. Immediately, he called on Giauque, who read to him a letter that Teeling had sent off from Paris towards the end of October. In the letter, Teeling showed himself well pleased with the course of his mission, indicating that French help was about to come. As to Lewins' position, which had become a subject of dispute among militant Irish leaders, Teeling confirmed that the former's 'conduct has been in every sense of the word worthy the confidence we reposed in him … '. On the evening of the same day, Turner set about reporting on Teeling's correspondence, which had been 'endorsed to Giauque under cover to Reinhard'. He wrote to Downshire that the letter was sent to one Bell in London, who would then forward it to a Mr Thompson, Kildare Street, Dublin, but that it was in fact addressed to Arthur O'Connor. On receiving news from his 'friend', Downshire immediately informed Dublin Castle, which in turn passed on information to Whitehall. Thus, with the help of Turner's accurate intelligence, Teeling's letter was intercepted at the Dublin post office on the 8 December.[42]

After uncovering Teeling's correspondence, Turner carried on performing his task as a government informer with almost meticulous care. In the following two weeks, he gave detailed accounts of events in a series of letters to Downshire. On 18 November, Turner received further news from Paris. In a letter, dated 11 October, his old friend Alexander Lowry informed him about the despondency among the United Irish at Paris on account of Hoche's death. With Lowry's letter, Turner went to Reinhard on the same day. The French minister showed himself 'extremely glad to see' him and asked him to stay in Hamburg, 'as the only mode in which [he] could serve [his] country and the Republic.' Obviously flattered by this warm reception, Turner reassured Reinhard that he already 'had arranged matters with Lord Edward for that purpose.' He then continued in telling the French minister about the London meeting. In his conversation with Turner, Lord Edward had expressed his intention of 'bringing matters to a crisis without the French.' Moreover, Fitzgerald had stated in the meeting that O'Connor was about to come to France 'in order to have Lewins removed'. This seems hardly surprising, because Teeling's account in favour of Lewins' conduct never reached its destination. It is unclear whether Turner intentionally tried to sow the seeds of discord among his United companions, but by making possible the interception of Teeling's letter to Dublin and backing the more extreme camp in Paris, the 'radical' Ulsterman certainly added to the depth of the divide among the United Irishmen themselves. However, Turner then put

42 PRO H.O. 100/70/331–52, including Turner to Downshire, 17 November 1797, Teeling's letter, Camden to Portland, 6 & 9 December 1797 and Downshire's letter to Camden.

Reinhard in the picture about the growing restlessness among United militants, who felt that 'the spirit of republicanism was losing ground in Ireland.'
Lord Edward and Arthur O'Connor's plans certainly did not incur Reinhard's
displeasure, since the latter had already shown his preference for militant
Irish hotheads in earlier instances. On parting, Reinhard requested the Irishman
to call on him twice or thrice a week and to keep him up-to-date on Irish affairs. Shortly after his meeting with the French minister, Turner also called
on DeNava, the Spanish representative residing in Hamburg. It was through
DeNava that he found out further details of MacNeven's mission. On the
night of 18 November, Turner supped with General de Valence, who told
him about Lord Edward and Arthur O'Connor's trip to the Continent in the
previous year. Thus, within a few days after his arrival on 17 November,
Turner had come to be a welcome visitor in Hamburg's French and francophile
circles. He gained ready access to confidential matters, which he promptly
conveyed to Downshire. On 19 November, he reported on his conduct. In his
letter, Turner also called special attention to the correspondence of Henriette
Matthiessen, whom he knew to be in contact with Lady Lucy Fitzgerald in
London and her sister Pamela in Ireland. Furthermore, he gave directions to
intercept letters to a Swiss residing in London, called Chabout. To his countryman, Turner wrote, 'Giauque often encloses letters for Ireland, tho' Chabout
is wholly ignorant of what's going on.' Thus, Turner revealed an essential
part of the United Irishmen's system of communication with France, which
was centred upon the Giauques and the Matthiessens as conveyors of information. Turner transferred his intelligence to Captain Gunter of the *Nautilus*,
a ship doing regular service between Hamburg and Yarmouth. Gunter then
posted the letters in Yarmouth, from where they eventually got to Downshire.[43]

Coincidentally, another Irishmen with the same name resided in Hamburg
at the same time. Samuel Turner of Cognac, an Irish-born merchant who had
emigrated to France some fourteen years before, had arrived in Hamburg in
1797. However, as L.M. Cullen rightly concluded, 'contemporaries, if not
the historian, were at least free from the dilemma posed by the presence of
two Samuel Turners in Hamburg. Samuel Turner of Cognac, except for his
employment of the alias of Johnson, in Hamburg itself used his real name
without interruption ... The remote possibility that the two Samuel Turners
were one and the same person, afloat on a sea of aliases, has to be excluded.'[44] Simultaneously, Samuel Turner of Newry lost no time in settling

43 PRO H.O. 100/75/7–10, Turner to Downshire, 19 November 1797.
44 I am grateful to my supervisor, Professor L.M. Cullen, for allowing me to have a look at
    his unpublished manuscript on the brandy trade.

down into his new double life in Hamburg. By the end of November, he had taken up residence at 120, bey-dem-Luchthause. While he was secretly forwarding intelligence to Downshire under the name of J. Richardson, he had assumed the alias of Roberts to ostensibly conceal his radical identity as Samuel Turner. He was still in dread of his treachery being found out, all the more considering his exposed position among United *émigrés*. Thus, he did not want to risk being associated with the English minister residing in Hamburg and soon informed Downshire that he could not 'continue any mode of seeing Mr Frazer ...'. Since Turner was afraid of jeopardizing his mission, he asked Downshire to take into account the difficult circumstances of his new task as an informer. On 1 December 1797, he wrote to him that 'it will be requisite for your Lordship to lay aside every emblem of nobless and adopt the stile of an Irish *Sansculotte*, for fear of accidents ...'. Bearing in mind Turner's contacts with Hamburg's liberal elite and French *émigrés* of high standing, he certainly did not answer the description of an impoverished rebel. However, he soon asked for more money. 'Mr Pitt may let me have a cool-five-hundred, which shall last me for six months to come', he wrote to Downshire on 1 December and he explained that 'to get the information here has cost me three times the sum; and to keep up the acquaintance and connections I have here, so as to get information, I cannot live on less.' Turner reassured Downshire that 'no pains on [his] part [would] be spared' to successfully carry out his mission.[45]

By the end of 1797, 'the celebrated Knight of the Green Handkerchief' had changed into Lord Downshire's 'most sincere and obliged Servant'. After ingratiating himself with the United Irishmen, Turner did not scruple to betray them to the authorities in Dublin and London, knowing full well that his information could mean their certain death. He had sold his services to the crown and fawned upon the French authorities and liberals of high standing in Hamburg and France in order to contribute to British efforts to infiltrate the United Irishmen. Judiciously, the radical chameleon had made a new life for himself in the north German city, where he had established himself as the official United mouthpiece. Turner did not only betray his United companions but tried hard to betray them painstakingly, and he does not appear to have suffered from a guilty conscience. On the contrary, with skill and ease, he endeavoured to 'play the old boy a trick', as he put it himself.[46] Although

---

45 PRO H.O. 100/75/7–10 & 11, Turner to Downshire, 19 and 28 November 1797; Nat. Arch. 620/33/107, Turner to Downshire, 1 December 1797.

46 PRONI D.607/F/432, Richardson to Richardson, 27 September 1798. This letter, the fact concealed by the author's irony or his Newry humour, is by Turner himself. There is no mistaking his handwriting.

Turner made a great effort to cultivate a certain sense of the comic in his information to the authorities, he was possessed of a heavy and laboured sense of humour at best. His efforts to gather information without arousing suspicion seem to have made him highly tense. Moreover, his letters reveal that Turner was preoccupied with making a profit out of his activities as an informer; and to all appearances, his avarice, coupled with a strong craving for admiration, had been an important reason for actually offering his services to the government. His defection from the radical cause, however, nobody had realized. Downshire had succeeded in smuggling a United leader into Europe's communication nerve centre, which had also turned into a centre for Irish affairs by the end of the year, since missions to France had almost exclusively gone via Hamburg. Turner, the first United spy on the Continent, helped the British to shed some light on the Franco–Irish alliance. It was thanks to him that the governments at London and Dublin gained an insight into the machinery of revolutionary Hamburg.

V

In 1797–8, also the French began to turn their attention towards Hamburg's importance for the exchange of information with the United Irishmen. Due to growing numbers of Irish radicals in France and to a waning commitment to another expedition to Ireland, the Directory now attached importance to cutting down on Irish entries into France. In connection with this, Hamburg was to be a checkpoint for United travellers arriving from the British Isles. Accordingly, Paris put special emphasis on French diplomatic presence in Hamburg in order to prevent France from becoming a hotbed for United refugees, whose numbers again increased in 1798.[47]

Although very little is actually known about Duckett's activities after July 1797, when Reinhard had prohibited him from travelling on to England, he appears to have remained in Hamburg in the following months. He had taken up lodgings with Prof. Unzer, one of Altona's outstanding Enlightenment reformers. From there, he started to correspond with the Directory in the autumn of 1797. While he was still waiting for new instructions towards the end of the year, he had devoted time to establishing contacts in Hamburg and Altona and to gathering information, which he then conveyed to the French government. Duckett's letters to the Directory reveal why he came to be regarded as an enigmatic and elusive figure even (or should one say especially) among his countrymen. Due to a strong feeling of distrust, Duckett mostly

47 Elliott, *Partners in Revolution*, 140–2 and 168–70 on France's Hamburg policy.

kept to himself and he does not appear to have mixed with the United Irishmen staying in Hamburg. He obviously did not think much of most Irish radicals, who simply did not have his experience. Duckett also dissociated himself from Reinhard. After the French minister had refused to support his efforts to proceed to the British Isles in July, Duckett's relationship with him was more than troubled. On several occasions, he cast suspicion on Reinhard, whom he assumed to violate French interests with dishonest wheeling and dealing. Although his accusations appear to be completely unfounded, Duckett's unwarranted assertions showed Reinhard in a bad light. In his letters to the Directory, however, he also called to mind the necessity of supporting the Irish republican cause. On 20 December 1797, he stated that 100,000 Irishmen would be ready to ally themselves with the French. He urged that the Directory should spare no effort to take vengeance for the 'outrageous inhumanities' that the English oppressors had perpetrated. Owing to his marked sense of mission, Duckett once again offered his services as an agent with insistence. 'I think, I might be of some use for my country', he wrote to the Directory, 'and I know that you will find few people, who love her partisans and hate her enemies more than I do.' However, the French government did not feel compelled to instruct Duckett to leave Germany in the autumn and winter of 1797–8. He remained in Hamburg, where a new task was waiting for him.[48]

In early 1798, Duckett was assigned to the post of secretary to Léonard Bourdon, one of the most dreaded and hot-blooded Jacobin orators in the days of the *terreur*. The Frenchman had been acquainted with Duckett since the turbulent events at the College des Irlandais in the autumn of 1792. Bourdon reached the city in the second half of January and soon gave rise to uncertainties about his mission, which had been the subject of much speculation before he had even set foot on Hamburg territory. Towards the end of January, he was introduced to the Senate by Reinhard, who had been removed from office in December, but who continued to function as French representative until his departure for Florence on 25 February. Although Reinhard presented him as a trade agent on behalf of the French government, it soon emerged that the famous ex-Montagnard did not confine himself to France's commercial interests. In a series of meetings at the residence of Langau, the French consul in Hamburg, Bourdon revealed the political nature of his mission in front of several hundred republican-minded French exiles. In his speeches, he pronounced himself in favour of French commercial links with Hamburg, but criticised the city's relations with Britain.

---

48 NLI pos.210/62–81, including Duckett's letters to the Directory, 29 October, 20 November and 20 December 1797.

Forcefully, Bourdon sought to fight this liaison with arguments and he directed warnings to the Hamburg authorities not to try France's patience. He also dropped hints about a French expedition against England, requiring the Senate to declare its position if this should arise. Furthermore, Bourdon addressed himself to his listeners and stated that no efforts should be spared to strengthen the cohesion and the spirits of the French community residing in the city. Thus, the legate argued a case for an aggressive French policy with regard to Hamburg. Bourdon spoke with a vehemence, which was reminiscent of his glowing speeches in the National Convention some five years earlier. Soon, he was known in the city under the name of 'Léopard' Bourdon. He also got in contact with well-known local republicans and democratic circles, trying to swear them to French principles. For instance, he joined the Philanthropic Society, which had been founded by Reinhard's secretary, Georg Kerner, in April 1797 and modelled on the French Theophilanthropic Society. Thus, Bourdon started to create a great deal of unrest not only among the French residents in Hamburg.

With the help of Duckett, his secretary and agent, Bourdon also got in touch with Irish and English radicals passing through the city. He looked after their concerns and subsequently conveyed information to Paris. Filled with enthusiasm about the commitment United travellers had shown, he advocated Irish efforts to achieve independence. Accordingly, he urged the Directory to affirm French intentions to assist Ireland's fight for freedom. Moreover, Bourdon realized the necessity of furthering missions between France and Ireland in order to improve insufficient communication with the radicals. With this aim in view, a pool should be provided to pay for an efficient network of professional agents, which was to be established in Hamburg. In order to counteract English efforts to set up a system of espionage, which Bourdon witnessed under way in the city, he strongly declared himself in favour of intensifying French endeavours regarding Hamburg.

Bourdon was hardly welcomed with open arms in Hamburg. He had offended the city's authorities, who were seriously disturbed about the French trouble-maker. Towards the end of February, the Senate decided to ask Talleyrand to withdraw Bourdon. Shortly afterwards, the courts of Berlin, Copenhagen and Petersburg also intervened, vehemently demanding Bourdon's recall. Since the French agent had also aroused the suspicion of Reinhard's successor, Roberjot, the Directory could not avoid summoning back Bourdon. Accompanied by Duckett, he eventually left Hamburg on 20 April 1798.[49]

---

49 Swords, *The Green Cockade*, 67 on Duckett, Bourdon and the disturbances at the College
    des Irlandais in 1792; PRO F.O. 33/14/30–1, 36, 43–4, 66, 92–3, 111–2, 122–5, F.O.

Although Bourdon's mission had come to an end relatively soon, it illustrates French efforts to make use of Hamburg, as *the* outstanding Continental nerve centre of information. It had become plainly recognizable that England had already started to be active in concentrating on Hamburg, and Bourdon was quite right in calling for French countermeasures. Bourdon's demands did not fall on deaf ears. Soon after his departure, a number of French agents arrived in Hamburg, such as Francois Lamarque or Parandier, who had already gained experience in undercover activities on various occasions. The French tried hard to infiltrate Hamburg's democratic circles and to intervene in the city's underworld of spies. However, a certain amount of discontinuity had necessitated a change of French attitudes towards Hamburg. The Directory had become increasingly dissatisfied with its Hamburg diplomatic representatives. Reinhard had to leave the city, because his marriage with a respected Hamburg lady and his unauthorized negotiations with foreign radicals had made him seem highly biassed. Roberjot, his successor, only stayed in the city for a mere four months. After arriving on 14 March, he already packed his bags in June, before being replaced with Marragon on 1 October 1798. Although French efforts regarding Hamburg appear somewhat confusing, they show clearly the Directory's determination to do justice to the city's importance for the exchange of information. After the peace agreement with Austria, signed at Campoformio on 17 October 1797, the French government had momentarily put the main stress on the war with England and also took up again the idea of an expedition to Ireland and/or England. French activities in Hamburg reflect this change in emphasis and illustrate that the main focus of the European war had shifted towards the north. This change in the free German city did certainly not make things easier for the United Irishmen, who were now deprived of Reinhard's active support. The tranquillity and the anonymity that had surrounded Irish missions in the previous years were a thing of the past by 1798. Hamburg had become increasingly transparent, since too many agents kept an eye on the travellers passing through.[50]

33/15/20 on the English representative and speculations on Bourdon's mission; Ham. Staats. Senat Cl. 1, Lit.Pb, Vol. 8c, Fasc. 2, Nr.21, Lelarge's reports on Bourdon, 2 February and 23 March 1798; Laufenberg, *Hamburg und die Französische Revolution*, 70–1, Grab, *Demokratische Strömungen in Hamburg und Schleswig-Holstein*, 206–18, Wohlwill, *Neuere Geschichte der Freien und Hansestadt Hamburg*, 48–63 on Bourdon's mission and its Hamburg background; NLI pos.198 (Archives Nationales AF III 57 doss. 225), Bourdon's correspondence with Paris; see Wohlwill, Adolf, *Georg Kerner. Ein deutsches Lebensbild aus dem Zeitalter der Französischen Revolution* (Hamburg, Leipzig, 1886) on Kerner and the Philanthropic Society.

50 Grab, *Demokratische Strömungen in Hamburg und Schleswig-Holstein*, 219–30, Wohlwill,

VII

Very little news had reached Ireland in the second half of 1797, at a time when growing fragmentation within the United Irishmen would have necessitated frequent consultations with France. Although United militants had come to a brittle agreement with the Society's moderates to hold back a rising until the arrival of French assistance, they had no wish to delay that event. Many radicals had begun to blame the Society's emissaries in France for protracting negotiations with the Directory. In France, too, the United Irishmen were far from forming an integrated whole at the end of 1797. Friction had arisen within the Irish community in Paris, which had become increasingly complex on account of rapidly growing numbers of refugees. In France as well as in Ireland, differences were not only due to political matters, but often related to a clash of personalities. However, since Irish *émigrés* were far removed from the serious situation which the home movement had to face, United activities in Paris were mostly lacking the urgency required for hurrying along the Franco–Irish alliance.

The influx of United refugees in the second half of 1797 had fundamentally changed the situation for Irish radicals in France. After Tone had been the sole United agent in the country for almost one and a half years, he now had to share his claim to representation with a number of Irish companions. Without grumbling, he had accepted Edward Lewins as the official United representative in the summer of 1797. Both were cooperating with some of the newly arrived Northerners, such as Lowry, Orr or Tennent and in November, also with Tone's brother Matthew, who had come from Hamburg one month previously. In the course of the second half of the year, discord became noticeable among the United Irish at Paris. A second faction began to take shape. It was led by the 'old, vainglorious Irish alcoholic', Napper Tandy, as he was later called by James Dugan in a devastating appraisal.[51] In fact, Tandy's need for admiration, coupled with an irascible temperament and a vigorous appearance, soon came into effect. While his efforts do not seem to have really influenced French decision-making, he certainly sowed the seeds of discord within the United community in Paris, which polarized after his arrival from Hamburg. He managed to rally a number of supporters around him, including MacMahon, Quigley and Anthony McCann. Without any official authorization from the home movement, Tandy felt entitled to represent Irish

Neuere Geschichte der Freien und Hansestadt Hamburg, 63–5 on French agents in Hamburg in 1798; see Elliott, *Partners in Revolution*, 165–8 on French war aims after the Peace of Campoformio.

51 Dugan, *The Great Mutiny*, 431; *Life of Theobald Wolfe Tone*, II, 452 on Matthew Tone's arrival from Hamburg.

interests and to make his mark on United negotiations in France. Disgusted by Tandy's uncooperative attitude, Lewins and Tone soon dissociated themselves from the veteran radical, who obviously tried to run the show on his own. Tandy did not seem to accept the primacy of his more inconspicuous, but no less honest compatriots. He in fact succeeded in discrediting Lewins at home, where the movement's militants were already pressing for more determined action.[52]

In a meeting of the Irish in Paris in the autumn of 1797, Tandy's camp had openly attacked Lewins and Tone, thus creating an unbridgeable gulf between the two groups. Tandy now seemed to make a serious bid for the leadership. All the indications are that he was trying to win the home movement's blessing regarding a replacement of Lewins. Encouraged by MacMahon and furnished with a message from Tandy, James Quigley left Paris soon after the meeting. Travelling via Hamburg, where Turner seems to have dogged Quigley's heels, and Yarmouth, he arrived in London at the end of the year. There, he resumed his contacts with English radicals. During his stay in the British capital, Quigley was at pains to expand already existing efforts to coordinate British radical circles into a large-scale cooperation of the United brethren in Ireland, England and Scotland. According to Marianne Elliott's detailed account of Quigley's journey, the Irish priest also got in touch with Arthur O'Connor while in England. The latter had left Ireland in a rush some days after a meeting of the United executive shortly before Christmas. Disgusted at the unending dispute over the question of speedy militant action and the moderates' hesitant stance, he had travelled to London. It is unclear whether O'Connor had been given special authority to leave Ireland by his more radical companions within the movement's leadership, but given the rising fortunes of the Society's militants, his mission can be seen as an attempt to hurry along militant policy in Paris and to replace the more moderate Lewins as United ambassador in France. After MacNeven's mission in mid-1797, United militants probably wanted to take matters in hand by dispatching their own agent in order to push through radical demands for an immediate rising. In London, O'Connor eventually met Quigley at the beginning of January, when both radicals agreed on sending off an agent to France to convey information to Tandy.[53]

52 See Elliott, *Partners in Revolution*, 166–72 and Elliott, *Wolfe Tone*, 365–8 on the United Irish in Paris.
53 Nat. Arch. 620/7/74/7, McNally on Quigley's return, 6 February 1798; *Report of the Committee of Secrecy ... Commons* [Ireland], vol. 17, append. XIV, DCCCLXIII, on Quigley's contacts with English radicals; Nat. Arch. 620/18ᴬ/11, on Quigley's journey; *Memoirs and Correspondence of Viscount Castlereagh*, II, 3–5, secret information relating to MacMahon

Owing to his mercantile connections, Edmund O'Finn seemed to be best suited to this mission. As a member of the Munster executive, he had been acquainted with Roger and Arthur O'Connor since the latter's journey to Cork at the end of 1796. He had moved to England with his wife shortly afterwards and had soon engaged in mercantile shipping. Accompanied by his wife and his brother Francis, O'Finn eventually put to sea on board Captain Mumford's smuggling vessel around mid-January. Upon arriving at Rotterdam some five days later, he was arrested as an English subject, at a time when the French had substantially tightened security measures in order to prevent enemy spies from flocking into France. However, O'Finn was soon set free. He was permitted to travel to the Hague, where Delacroix, the former Minister of Foreign Affairs, held the post of French minister to the Batavian Republic. At the Hague, Delacroix gave the Irish agent a warm reception and provided him with passports to France. Travelling via Brussels, the O'Finns finally reached Paris in the following month. There, they lodged in the same hotel with Tandy and some of his associates. Tandy's group was certainly delighted by the Irish messenger, who carried on him detailed plans for an invasion of Ireland and who claimed that 70,000 Irishmen were ready to assist the French. In his talks with French government officials, O'Finn then conveyed his information, although he was hardly in a position to make an objective judgement about the state of affairs in Ireland and just as little about recent developments within the United movement. Since he had been absent from Ireland for more than a year, he could not have been up to date on Irish affairs. He represented rather O'Connor's inflated ideas of militant action, which certainly did not have the blessing of unified United executive. However, although O'Finn merely expounded O'Connor's wishful thinking, his explanations contributed to French views of United activities. News from Ireland was awaited at a time when the Directory and even Bonaparte had already begun to consider another Irish expedition. Due to insufficient communications with Ireland, the French authorities were hardly in a position to assess the Irish situation properly.[54]

After being present at a meeting of the newly created national committee of the United Britons on 5 January 1798, Quigley set out for Dublin, accompanied by the United British delegates, William Bailey and Benjamin Binns.

and Quigley; Elliott, *Wolfe Tone*, 365–8 and *Partners in Revolution*, 172–6, MacDermot, 'Arthur O'Connor', *I.H.S.*, XV (1966), 57–9, Maguire, 'Arthur MacMahon', *Irish Sword*, IX (1969–70), 213, Goodwin, *The Friends of Liberty*, 435–6 and McEvoy, 'Father James Quigley', *Seanchas Ardmhacha*, V (1970), 258–9 on the background of Quigley's journey.

54 Nat. Arch. 620/36/22, 59; 620/66/99; 620/37/1; PRO F.O. 97/241; PRO P.C.I/43/A.153, correspondence and information relating to O'Finn's mission; Elliott, *Partners in Revolution*, 176–8.

Both were to inform the Irish leadership about the state of affairs in Britain and to create the necessary conditions for an alliance of the United men in Ireland, England and Scotland. Shortly after addressing himself to a meeting of United leaders in Dublin, Binns travelled to Cork, where he had been invited by John Swiney to speak to an assembly of the Munster executive. Quigley as well set about initiating the United leaders into the purpose of his mission, among others Lord Edward, whom he met soon after his arrival. Towards the end of January, he proceeded to Belfast in order to convey news to the northern United men. At the beginning of February, Quigley concluded his journey to Ireland and started out for Manchester. There, he resumed contacts with his United brethren and made no secret of the intended mission to France, which was to be headed by Arthur O'Connor. Upon arriving at London around mid-February, Quigley met up again with O'Connor. In the following two weeks, the latter was at pains to make extensive preparations for his journey to France and all the indications are that he intended to leave the country for a length of time. But before taking ship to the Continent, O'Connor, Quigley and three other associates were arrested in Margate/Kent on 28 February.[55]

The Margate arrests put an early end to one of the most spectacular United missions in the 1790s. Since it involved Arthur O'Connor, one of the most enigmatic radical leaders, the following trial attracted a great deal of public attention. Although relatively little actually came to light during the trial, it was enough to focus British government attention on the threat of Irish radicalism. The Margate incident helped much to catapult the United Irishmen from an Irish trouble to a problem jeopardizing British security in times of a major European war. Moreover, the trial became the subject of much speculation, since only Quigley was convicted of high treason and subsequently executed on 7 June. O'Connor escaped the death penalty, because no clear evidence of his guilt could be produced without uncovering important sources of information. His social status as an Irish aristocrat and his good standing with a number of British Whig leaders already elevated him above his co-defendants. He was acquitted, but re-arrested immediately afterwards to answer a charge of treason brought by the Irish government.

Although many particulars of O'Connor's mission are still shrouded in mystery, most historians are agreed that he was intent on superseding Lewins

55 PRO P.C.I/40/A.133, P.C.I/4/A.136, A.139, A.140; Nat. Arch. 620/7/74/7, 620/36/2, 620/18A/11, 620/10/121/96; *Report of the Committee of Secrecy, 21 August 1798 ...* Commons [Ireland], vol. 17, append. XIV, DCCCLXIII; Elliott, *Partners in Revolution*, 178–85, MacDermot, 'Arthur O'Connor', *I.H.S.*, XV (1966), 57–60, McEvoy, 'Father James Quigley', *Seanchas Ardmhacha*, V (1970), 259–67.

as the United Irishmen's representative in France, an assumption which is
also verified by the conversation between Turner and Lord Fitzgerald in
London in October 1797. In this way, the Society's militants in Ireland as
well as Tandy's party in Paris hoped to exert greater pressure for another
French expedition. For them, O'Connor's experience and his persuasive power
must have been the decisive factors for his appointment, to say nothing of
O'Connor's own part in exerting an influence on the decision. Whatever the
intentions behind the mission might have been, Arthur O'Connor, the highly
self-willed power politician, was hardly suited to even out disagreements between the estranged United factions in Paris. There, he certainly would have
created a great deal of unrest among the United Irishmen, not least because
he was a leader of one of the two factions who were at loggerheads in Dublin.
However, O'Connor was prevented from continuing his journey. According
to his own statements, he intended on going first to Hamburg. Indeed, the
addresses later found in his razor case verify the supposition that O'Connor
was planning on staying at the residence of Johann Conrad Matthiessen and
his wife Henriette, whom he had last seen on his journey to the Continent
some two years previously.[56]

In many respects, the early months of 1798 represent a turning point in
the history of the United Irishmen. Due to failures, misconceptions and mis-
judgements, Franco–Irish communications had come to a dead end. French
foreign policy was characterized by a multitude of contrary conceptions. In
Ireland as well as in France, the United leadership was divided into two
increasingly irreconcilable factions. Nevertheless, the United Irishmen had
developed into Britain's outstanding domestic security risk and government
officials in Dublin and London fell over themselves to get the situation under
control. Dublin Castle as well as Whitehall succeeded in recruiting some United
men, most of whom, however, did not belong to the decision-making body
of the movement.[57]

In many ways, Samuel Turner proved to be the most important source of
information. In contrast to his fellow informers, Turner occupied the attention
of high government officials in 1797–8. He was already held in high regard by
December/January, when his first reports from Hamburg reached their destination. But delight at Turner's services was soon marred by disagreement
over the question of how to make use of his information. In December 1797,

---

56 Nat. Arch. 620/36/2, PRO P.C.I/41/A.136, examinations, testimonies and papers of the
    Maidstone trial; Elliott, *Partners in Revolution*, 182–5, MacDermot, 'Arthur O'Connor',
    I.H.S., XV (1966), 58–60, McEvoy, 'Father James Quigley', *Seanchas Ardmhacha*, V (1970),
    260–7 on the trial.
57 See Curtin, *The United Irishmen*, 112–3 on radicals infiltrating the United Irish organization.

Home Secretary Portland expressed the view that 'it is most desireable that he should remain where he is for some time longer ... ', whereas Lord Lieutenant Camden pointed at 'the importance which attaches to Turner's coming forward.' Camden was annoyed by Downshire, who had by-passed Dublin Castle, forwarding Turner's intelligence to the British Foreign Office. On 8 January, Camden complained to Downshire that the latter 'had better communicate with him [the Irish Chief Secretary Thomas Pelham] than with Lord Grenville's office.' A few days later, Downshire reassured Camden that he would 'use every endeavour, as requested, to induce R. [Turner alias Richardson] to do what is right and necessary', and yet, Downshire was not willing to put at risk this important source of information. He continued to pass on Turner's letters to the Foreign Office. For the time being, disagreement between Dublin Castle and Whitehall was put aside, until March, when discussions about Turner flared up again.[58]

Some time in February 1798, Turner returned to London. Little is known about his activities between December 1797 and February 1798, but it must be assumed that he stayed in Hamburg. It is also unclear why he finally proceeded to England. Since he had already arrived at London towards the end of February, he most likely had not been ordered back on account of O'Connor's arrest, and yet, there are grounds for the supposition that he made a contribution to the Margate captures. However, his information was to become crucial for the conviction of Quigley, his fellow Ulster militant, whom Turner had sounded out in Hamburg and Paris.

Soon after Turner's arrival, Camden increased his efforts to exploit the spy's talents in order to prosecute Irish radicals. In a series of letters, the Lord Lieutenant tried to pressurize Whitehall as well as Downshire into agreeing to make use of Turner's evidence in open court. He was convinced that the Hamburg spy could be eminently useful by remaining in the British Isles. Accordingly, Camden urged Downshire most strongly to detain Turner. He argued that 'by Richardson being sent abroad we certainly lose the advantage of his assistance in bringing to light the Irish conspiracy.' Moreover, Camden feared that 'Downshire's friend' would 'very soon be suspected in France', which in turn could ruin British efforts to infiltrate the United movement.[59] But Camden's requests were of no avail. Turner remained in

58 PRO H.O. 100/70/365, Portland to Camden, 16 December 1797; PRONI D.607/F/8, Camden to Downshire, 8 January 1798; Nat. Arch. 620/35/34, Downshire to Camden, 14 January 1798; see Nat. Arch. 620/33/135, PRONI D.607/F/10, PRO H.O. 100/70/113–7, 127, 139–41, 331–2, 335–51, 365, H.O. 100/75/3, 6–10, 11, 15, 30, 71–2, correspondence relating to Turner and his secret intelligence.

59 PRONI D.607/F/79, Camden to Downshire, 4 March 1798; PRO H.O. 100/75/145–6,

London, where he was interrogated by Downshire and Portland. Both of them were opposed to the idea of doing without Turner's services on the Continent, and their efforts to induce him to proceed to Dublin did certainly not sound too convincing. They had already something planned for Turner. Towards the end of March, the Irishman was sent on a fact-finding mission to the Continent. En route for Paris, he travelled via Hamburg and Holland, until he finally reached the French capital on 17 April. On 20 April, Turner met Talleyrand, whom he had last seen on his visit to Paris in September of the previous year. To the foreign minister, he complained about attempts that 'have been made to injure my character here by some Persons equally despicable as malicious.' He continued, 'I mean Lewins and his associates from whom, tho' united Irishmen I pride myself in differing both in sentiment and conduct.' Turner then entered on the purpose of his mission, expressing his intention 'to bring over to the side of the United Irish, what is called the independent interest alias the Country Gentlemen ... , who feared in a Revolution the loss of their Property ...'. Turner's following account of the state of affairs in Ireland must have aroused the interest of Talleyrand. The foreign minister was certainly pleased to hear of a revolutionary minded and property-owning bourgeoisie, which, according to Turner, was willing to pay for French expenses after the intended liberation of Ireland. Moreover, the Irishman pointed to the importance of using Hamburg as a channel of communication with the Irish independence movement. Turner had already come to be regarded as a kind of Irish representative in Hamburg and his good relations with the French minister residing in the Hanse town were also known to Talleyrand. The minister showed himself interested in Turner and promised to lay the memorandum, which the latter had prepared, before the Directory. In the following two weeks, the Irishman had a number of meetings with Talleyrand. Outwardly, the Hamburg agent was at pains to induce the French government to commit itself on the issue of an expedition to Ireland. With this aim in view, he emphasized the importance of conveying news to the Irish radical leaders as soon as possible. He asked Talleyrand to forward information to a Charles Ranken, Esq., whom he named as his intermediary in London. Turner even offered to proceed to the British Isles himself in order to accelerate communications with Ireland. But the French government does not appear to have fully shared Talleyrand's interest in Turner's plans and, for the moment, denied the agent audience with the Directory. The Irishman was stalled until the second week of May, when he was told to bring along a person of integrity

Camden to Portland, 2 March 1798; see also PRONI. D.607/F/93A, Camden to Downshire, 4–14 March 1798 and PRO H.O. 100/75/138–40, 144–7, 150–2, Camden to Portland, 1, 2 and 6 March 1798.

to introduce him to the Directory. Since Abbé Grégoire and Stone, two well-known revolutionary figures, refused to accompany him, Turner's efforts to present his plans at the highest level of French decision-making were frustrated. The Directors pretended to be pressed for time and did not allow him in; Duckett, whom he met in the Directory's antechamber on 8 May, was not admitted either. The next day, Turner left Paris. Via Cuxhaven and Lowestoft, he travelled to London, where he eventually arrived during the night of 17/18 May.[60]

In London, Turner reported on his mission to France. He gave an accurate account of his activities and also of the United Irish community in Paris. He even went into details about the financial situation of each individual.[61] Although he had obviously come in for a lot of criticism among his United companions in France, Turner once again proved to be crucial for the nascent British intelligence network on the Continent. Up to the autumn of 1797, the British were in the dark regarding United activities outside Ireland. Turner's information on their moves, and the consternation about Arthur O'Connor's mission, had eventually made it more than obvious to the authorities that the United–French alliance was threatening the very foundations of Britain and Ireland. It had also become clear that British efforts relating to Hamburg had to be increased in order to gain the upper hand in this crucial city.

Heightening tensions in Ireland and growing hysteria on account of the United–French association jolted the British government into action in the spring of 1798. Increasingly, Hamburg came into focus, not least because of its position between Britain and France. Both antagonists had become aware of Hamburg's strategic importance and both tried to gain advantage from the city, which had developed into a centre of undercover activities by 1798. The missions of Bourdon, Duckett, Parandier and numerous agents of minor importance had already revealed French interests, so that the Senate's spy Lelarge had his hands full with reporting on French activities in Hamburg. Apart from making use of Turner's information, the British were relatively slow to get off the ground. Up to the beginning of 1798, tranquillity surrounded the work of Frazer, the English minister in Hamburg, whose accounts of United activities were only coming in dribs and drabs. After his wife's death in February, Frazer was permitted to return to England in March, but he only

---

60 PRONI D.3030/189, Turner's secret intelligence; Nat. Arch. 620/37/102, Downshire to Cooke, 18 May 1798 and PRO H.O. 100/76/281, Whitehall to Camden, 28 May 1798 on Turner's return; see also Fitzpatrick, *Secret Service under Pitt*, 20–30 on Turner's mission to Paris in the spring of 1798.

61 PRONI D.3030/189 & 190, Turner's intelligence relating to his mission.

left the city on 29 April. He was replaced by Sir James Craufurd, who up to that point had filled the post of secretary to the British legation at Copenhagen. Only at the end of April 1798, did the English foreign ministry actually start to react to the situation in Hamburg. A few days before his departure, Frazer was asked to 'employ some confidential intelligent person for the express purpose of obtaining an accurate account of all the English and Irish now at Hamburg and of endeavouring to discover the nature of their connexions and correspondence there … '. However, it was not until Craufurd took office that new English policies started to be effective. Soon after his arrival in the city, he received clear-cut instructions on how to proceed. With a certain note of nervousness, the Foreign Secretary outlined his ideas and told Craufurd that 'there is no point which is so urgent, as that of your procuring the most accurate Information that can be had respecting the Names and Characters of His Majesty's Subjects arriving or established there. This is more important at the present moment, as I have received such information as leaves no Room to doubt that a constant and active Intercourse is carried on between His Majesty's Enemies and the Rebels in Ireland by the Means of Agents continually passing and repassing, by the way of Hamburgh.'[62] In the following years, Craufurd carried out his task with meticulous care. He kept an eye on radical activities in Hamburg. With precision, he reported on individual English and Irish travellers and hardly anyone escaped his observation. He had begun to recruit some helping hands soon after arriving in the city. On 18 May, he reported progress to Grenville, stating that he had 'already established several Channels', through which he believed to derive accurate and extensive information on the Irish trouble makers. By the summer, he had set up a system of intelligence, involving a number of regular agents and payments in order to acquire information. To the satisfaction of his London superiors, Craufurd soon succeeded in making a considerable change in English policies in Hamburg, which from now on was becoming a dangerous place for United Irishmen.[63]

62 PRO F.O. 33/14/203, Downing Street to Frazer, 24 April 1798; PRO F.O. 33/15/30-1, Downing Street to Craufurd, 11 May 1798; see Ham. Staats. Senat Cl. 1, Lit. Pb, Vol. 8c, Fasc. 2, Nr. 21, for Lelarge's reports on French activities in Hamburg and PRO F.O. 33/13-4 for Frazer's reports.

63 PRO F.O. 33/15/48, Craufurd to Grenville, 18 May 1798; see PRO F.O. 33/15/2, 263, 273, 288 and F.O. 97/240 for government reactions to Craufurd's new policies. See Wells, *Insurrection*, 28-43 on the development of British secret service activities in the years between 1795 and 1803.

VII

In Ireland, things had become tense since the early months of 1798. The Margate incident had created quite a stir among Irish conservatives. Moreover, Camden, who had already begun to unnerve Whitehall officials with over-anxious reports, contributed to the hysteria, which followed the O'Connor episode. As early as 30 March, he wrote to Portland that United activities 'no longer can be considered in any other light, or treated in any other way than that of direct Rebellion … '.[64] Although his sombre prognostications were not taken too seriously in London, they were certainly in line with the feelings shared by a large part of Ireland's protestant population. Since they assumed the radical movement to be an entirely catholic plot, they feared to be swept aside in an Irish Massacre of St Bartholomew. In the first half of 1798, the Irish government was faced with increasing alarm on the part of Irish protestants and catholics alike. By late spring, divisions within Irish society had substantially hardened and the country was in a state of inner turmoil.

At a time when the United Irishmen were struggling to maintain a brittle equilibrium within the Society, the events in the early months of 1798 threw the whole movement into a state of nervous agitation. After the Margate affair had made it clear that the authorities were close on United heels, the Society's militants under Lord Edward seem to have played the determining part in the national executive. But it was not before 12 March that moderate cautiousness was thrown to the winds once and for all. With the help of Thomas Reynolds's information, Dublin Castle had succeeded in arresting many of the Leinster leaders, amongst them most of the moderates. Freed of the moderate or cautious element within the movement's leadership, militant activists now gained the upper hand. Despite the divisions within the Society and the effect of arrests in the North, radicalism continued to gain momentum in the South, where arrests had barely begun. Although the Leinster Society was hit by the Margate incident and the March arrests, the southern movement increased in numbers on the eve of rebellion. The new executive, however, was at pains to set the pattern for a national rising under United control. In the week subsequent to Lord Edward's arrest on 19 May, the United leaders finally gave the go-ahead. Starting on 23 May, various revolts in several of the Leinster counties broke out, followed by a somewhat belated attempt at rising in Antrim and Down in early June. By the end of June, however, when Cornwallis, the new Lord Lieutenant, arrived in Ireland to take the place of Camden, the rebellion had been put down.[65]

64 PRO H.O. 100/75/343–4, Camden to Portland, 30 March 1798.
65 Elliott, *Partners in Revolution*, 189–213, Curtin, *The United Irishmen*, 254–281, McDowell,

On the eve of the rebellion, the United Irish in Ireland as well as on the Continent were very active. Due to events at home, radical migration heightened again in the course of the spring and the summer of 1798. Following the Margate affair and the state of panic it had aroused, United travellers trod more carefully. Utmost secrecy seemed more than reasonable in the face of increasing government watchfulness. The carelessness, which was a feature of earlier journeys to the Continent, was a thing of the past. Henceforward, movements of individual United men were more numerous, and in the spring and summer of 1798, radical migration presented an unclear picture of hustle and bustle, which is also reflected in the Hamburg sources. There, Sir James Craufurd took his new task seriously. Soon after arriving in the city, he had his hands full with reporting on suspicious to-ings and fro-ings. Hardly any move escaped his vigilance, and yet, it is difficult to get an idea of United moves on the Continent, because the welter of details makes it harder to see the connection. Since there is often no clue to the identity of the Irish arrivals, giving a clear account of the situation in Hamburg proves to be difficult. Moreover, no listing of foreigners as such exists and none is possible out of tax records, police records or other official documents in the Hamburg archives. Therefore, we are mostly in the dark about the real development of foreign activities in the city, which certainly exceeded the extent of activities mentioned in the Hamburg sources.

In the months prior to the outbreak of the rebellion, the United Irishmen were busy making final preparations for the forthcoming rising. In early March, Thomas Braughall passed through Altona on his way to Mainz and Frankfurt, where he stayed on the seventh. Nothing is known about the purpose of his journey, but there are grounds for the supposition that Braughall was not merely on a business trip. Some two-and-a-half months later, he was arrested and transported to Kilmainham Goal. Also the Byrne brothers of Dundalk, who had fled Ireland in the summer of 1797, were on the move some time between March and April. In November of the previous year, Turner had reported about the two Leinster United men, whom he believed to have travelled to Frankfurt, before they were eventually arrested at Liège. In the spring, both radicals turn up in Hanover, where John visited his brother Patrick. In April, Patrick seems to have stayed in the British Isles, and all the indications are that he was instructed to convey information to Ireland. However, both brothers had returned to Paris by the autumn of 1798.[66]

Ireland in the Age of Imperialism, 594–644 and Pakenham, Thomas, *The Year of Liberty. The Great Irish Rebellion of 1798*, 11th edn (London, 1978) on the rebellion and the situation in Ireland in the first half of 1798.

66 Nat. Arch. 620/42/22, papers relating to Thomas Braughall; PRO H.O. 100/75/8, Turner's

As May approached, the United Irishmen feverishly tried to get ready for the intended military clash. At the beginning of April, two Irishmen, named Blake and Moore, arrived in Hamburg. Although they did not go unnoticed, the English minister was late in getting on to them. Shortly after reaching Hamburg, they had proceeded to Suhla in Saxony, where they then purchased '6000 fusils and 4000 arquebuses' from the arms trader Guillaume Henri Spangenberg. It is unclear whether the two Irishmen succeeded in making their way back to Ireland. However, the Suhla episode is likely to have been only one of a number of United efforts to arm the Irish republican forces. In the spring and summer of 1798, the correspondence from Hamburg teems with rumours of arms shipments and gun running. Although some reports would probably not bear close examination, it can be assumed that Hamburg served as a trade centre for arms. The United Irishmen were badly in need of weapons, and the city's trading port was certainly the most suitable place to ship them. Hamburg's docks were hardly closely supervised by the port authorities, who did not care about the interconnections of the European war. Thus, the harbour was a hotbed for all kinds of smuggling vessels and shady figures, who did not ask any questions and who could be easily found by those willing to enlist their services.[67]

At the beginning of April, William Bailey and William Hamilton fell back upon the services of the American Captain Mumphort. The latter had conveyed Quigley back to England in late 1797 as well as the O'Finns to the Continent in January. Bailey, who had already accompanied Quigley to Ireland at the beginning of the year, and Hamilton had been two of the Irish members of the London Corresponding Society, which had entered into some form of alliance with their United brethren in Ireland in the early months of 1798. They took ship from Gravesend to Hamburg on 6 April and immediately proceeded to the Hague. There, they had conversations with Delacroix and General Daendals, whom they informed of United plans to rise on 12 June. According to Samuel Turner, Bailey was taken hostage, while Hamilton was permitted to travel to Paris. On his way to the French capital, Hamilton met Lewins in Bruxelles, where the latter promised him to do what he could to secure a passport for Bailey. Hamilton eventually reached Paris on 17 April,

information, 19 November 1797; PRO H.O. 100/76/69, 110–1, Nat. Arch. 620/18^A/11, letters relating to the Byrnes brothers, April 1798, including list of United Irish in Paris, October 1798.

67 PRO F.O. 33/15/37, 39, 55, 125, 132, 135 on the Suhla incident; see PRO F.O. 33/15/219, F.O. 33/16/38 & 65–6, H.O. 100/76/168–9, 230, H.O. 100/77/207, H.O. 100/78/3, P.C.I/43/A.152, Nat. Arch. 620/39/141, 620/18^A/11, PRONI D.3030/208 on arms shippings and gunrunnings in the spring and summer of 1798.

the day also Turner arrived in the city. Bailey was detained in the Hague until mid-May. He then turned up in London, but is reported in Paris some months later. Although it is not clear on whose instructions the two Irishmen undertook their mission, their journey seems to be a desperate attempt on the part of the United Irish to seek French assistance for the intended rebellion. The Irish radicals felt they could not defer a rising any further for a French landing, though they retained hopes of being joined by their comrades-in-arms.[68]

On 18 April, two Irishmen entered Hamburg, who were to become infamous some months later. On arrival, John Murphy and George Orr of Antrim, brother of William, went to see Bourdon, who was on the point of returning to France. According to Murphy's own statement, the two Irishmen told Bourdon 'they were desired to call on him by Coigley and Turner ... Bourdon gave them a good reception. They dined with him, they often saw Duckett ...', who subsequently tried to obtain passports for the two Irishmen's journey to France.[69] Passing themselves off as London merchants, however, Murphy and Orr went on to Leipzig on the twentieth. When they eventually returned to Hamburg at the beginning of June, Craufurd's men latched on to them. The two Irishmen remained in Hamburg until early July, when news about a projected French expedition to Ireland roused them from passivity. They packed their bags 'in great distress, obliged to borrow money, and ran away without paying their lodgings.' Since 'Orr and Murphy could not obtain Passports to go directly to Paris', they first proceeded to the Batavian Republic, where they seemed 'to undergo a sort of probation'. The Irish rebellion had highlighted tensions between France and England. The French were somewhat irritated by the host of Irishmen pouring into France, 'suspecting them all to be *Agents de Pitt*.' But, in the face of innumerable Irish *émigrés* of every shade, they could not prevent some from slipping through their fingers. George Orr and John Murphy eventually slipped through French security checks and reached France some time later.[70]

The French were right to be concerned about the hordes of refugees coming from the British Isles. Also the British government was worried about events in Hamburg, where Irish conspirators were numerous. Apart from

68 PRONI D.3030/190, Turner's account of Bailey and Hamilton; *Life of Theobald Wolfe Tone*, II, 479–80, PRO F.O. 33/15/25, 110, 127, 156 and P.C.I/43/A.152 on the mission; Nat. Arch. 620/18ᴬ/11, Warren's account of the United Irish in Paris, 27 October 1798.
69 PRO H.O. 100/87/334–5, examination of John Powell Murphy, 2 November 1798; see 100/87/310–35 and *Memoirs and Correspondence of Viscount Castlereagh*, II, 6 on the circumstances of Murphy and Orr's stay in Hamburg.
70 PRO H.O. 100/77/222–3, Wickham to Cooke, 10 July 1798; F.O. 33/15/135–6, 138, 200, Craufurd's correspondence relating to Orr and Murphy.

urging Craufurd to watch radical activities in the city, London tried to use the confusion prevailing there as an opportunity to smuggle in further agents in order to expand the intelligence network on the Continent. In dread of being found out, several members of the English radical scene had offered their services to the government in the wake of the Margate affair, and the British authorities willingly accepted their help. One of them was James Powell, a former member of the London Corresponding Society, who had already supplied the government with information about the London Corresponding Society in the preceding months. At the end of April, he was waiting to take ship from Yarmouth. Devoting a lot of his time to grumbling about money, Powell put off his departure in order to settle financial matters first. With regard to his task of watching United activities in Hamburg, however, he showed himself confident in his letters to Wickham, one of the Under-Secretaries of State in the Home Department. On 28 April, he wrote to him 'that George Orr, a united Irishman, with whom I was very intimate in London sailed from here a fortnight ago. If I should be so lucky as to find him out I shall be able to get among the Irishmen immediately.' On 4 May, he eventually boarded a packet boat to Hamburg, after once again reassuring Wickham that there was no reason to doubt a successful completion of his mission. At any rate, Phibbs, as Powell called himself in Hamburg, does not appear to have succeeded in deceiving the United Irishmen about the fact that he was merely a confidence trickster, whose main concern was money. After remaining in Hamburg for some time, he was ordered back to England, where his contacts with English radical circles were of more use to the government.[71]

Although Powell's attempts to infiltrate Irish circles in Hamburg do not appear to have been successful, government efforts to get an idea of radical doings in the city started to gain in effectiveness. In connection with this, the new English minister, Sir James Craufurd, certainly made a great contribution to British advances. Although a diplomat rather than an inspector, his activities had nevertheless all the characteristics of police operations. According to the instructions he had received on taking up his duties, he gave most of his time to the moves of Irish radicals staying in Hamburg. It is thanks to the extremely ambitious Craufurd that some form of intelligence network took shape in mid-1798. The fact that the United Irishmen had developed into an issue occupying British attention to a great extent meant that for Craufurd in contrast to Frazer the issue was central. In the light of heightening tensions

71 PRO P.C.I/41/A.138 and P.C.I/42/A.143, Powell's letters to the government; PRO F.O. 33/15/189, Craufurd about Powell, 26 June 1798. See Emsley, Clive, 'The Home Office and its Sources of Information and Investigation 1791–1801', *English Historical Revue*, XCIV (July 1979), 553–4 and Goodwin, *The Friends of Liberty*, 445–6 on Powell.

between France and Britain, events in Hamburg had made it necessary to adopt a new attitude towards the city; and Craufurd proved to be an ideal tool to translate British ideas into action. Soon, the new English minister got a foothold in Hamburg, attending to his task with great zest.

The outbreak of the Irish rebellion in the second half of May drastically changed the situation in Hamburg. In the two years prior to 1798, some twenty United men had reached Hamburg. Whereas United numbers in the city had already increased in the months prior to the rising in Ireland, amounting to twenty arrivals in the first half of 1798 alone, Craufurd was now faced with droves of Irish refugees flocking into Hamburg. Even allowing for the fact that Craufurd's suspiciousness even fell on carefree travellers from the British Isles who no less than radicals had perforce to use Hamburg in war time as the gateway to Europe, the number of reports on suspected Irish radicals is large. The numbers of Irish arrivals multiplied in June and in the following months. In England, Wickham assumed most of them to be only on their way through Hamburg, before eventually hastening to France in order to become involved in an intended expedition to Ireland. While for many Irishmen Hamburg served as a halting-place, as in the instance of Orr and Murphy, some refugees preferred to stay in the city. This is confirmed by numerous accounts of radical activities in Hamburg. In the summer of 1798, many revolutionary clubs and associations sprang up in Hamburg, mostly consisting of French and Irish *émigrés*, but also of English and Scottish members. Since foreign groups were connected with local liberal circles, Hamburg presented a confusing picture of radical associations. This in turn gave cause for concern and speculation both for the city's authorities as well as for the English government. The Irish attracted special attention. They appear to have been occupied with establishing contacts with their United brethren in Ireland and France. Already by June, they had set up some sort of an Irish committee that was closely cooperating with French republican circles residing in Hamburg. In the first half of July, the Irish were busy in making preparations for the forthcoming anniversary of Bastille Day, which they deemed worthy of celebrating.[72]

It is impossible to give a clear account of the activities of the numerous nameless Irish refugees, who sought their salvation in flight to the Continent

---

72 PRO F.O. 33/15/22, 172, 190–3. 200, 204, F.O. 33/16/16, 96 on radical associations coming into existence in the summer of 1798 (including Irish activities); PRO F.O. 33/16/56–8, P.C.I/3117 and Ham. Staats. Senat Cl. 1, Lit. Pb, Vol. 8c, Fasc. 2, Nr. 21 (Lelarge's reports of 16 June and 8 July) on the Irish committee; PRO F.O. 33/15/219–20; Ham. Staats. Senat Cl. 1, Lit. Pb, Vol. 8c, Fasc. 2, Nr. 21 (Lelarge's reports of 20 & 22 July) and Grab, *Demokratische Strömungen in Hamburg und Schleswig-Holstein*, 219 on Irish preparations for Bastille Day.

in the wake of the Irish rebellion, but it is plainly recognizable that the rising had a catalytic effect on radical migration from the British Isles. Starting in 1796, United travellers had begun to tread a path to Hamburg. In the year leading up to the rebellion, Hamburg had witnessed a renewed increase in United immigration, but it was not before the autumn of 1798 that events finally reached crisis point.

CHAPTER 5

Duckett, Tandy and the United
Bone of Contention, 1798–9

Although there was obviously a storm brewing in Ireland, the Irish rebellion found the Directory unprepared for the event. Since April 1798, a large part of the French forces had been deployed in a military campaign in Egypt under the country's most enigmatic general, Napoleon Bonaparte. Moreover, the French government had long shown complete disregard for a specific expedition to Ireland, and on the eve of the rebellion, Irish affairs were a single aspect of more comprehensive English invasion plans. In the summer of 1798, news of the Irish rising, brought over by growing numbers of United refugees, finally awakened the Directors from their slumbers. Ireland came to the fore in French military plans again. In Hamburg, the United issue reached its climax in the following year. Sparked off by the United Irish question, a clash of interests between Britain and France erupted in Hamburg some months after the Irish rebellion. With justification one could maintain that the United Irishmen contributed much to the European crisis, which originated in Hamburg towards the close of 1798.[1]

Encouraged by reports of early rebel victories, French authorities thrusted forward in favour of sending help to Ireland as soon as possible. This turned out to be difficult at a time when the bulk of French forces was employed in Egypt, Central Europe and Italy. In the weeks following the outbreak of hostilities in Ireland, Bruix, the French Minister of Marine, who had been entrusted with conducting the Irish preparations, was at pains to scrape together sufficient troops, money and equipment for another invasionary attempt. Like Hoche some one-and-a-half years earlier, Bruix was not only confronted with major logistic and strategic obstacles, but also with the tortuous paths of French decision-making. The Irish business had never really enjoyed unqualified acceptance among French authorities. Also in the summer of 1798, numerous

1 Elliott, *Partners in Revolution*, 214–7 on French war plans with regard to Ireland.

difficulties stood in the way of an immediate expedition to Ireland, which simply could not be conjured up out of nothing.

I

Bruix showed himself determined to lend his full backing to the Irish project. Apart from his efforts to get an expedition under way, he also tried to prepare the ground for a successful outcome of the forthcoming enterprise. With this aim in view, he decided to send an agent to the British Isles. He fell back upon William Duckett, who had already proved his worth under Bruix's predecessor Truguet. After leaving Hamburg for Paris towards the end of April, he had remained Léonard Bourdon's right-hand man until June, when Bruix determined to use the Irishman for his own ends. On 1 July, the Minister of Marine informed Joubert, commander of the French forces in Holland, about the intended mission. Accordingly, Joubert was instructed to hand over 24,000 francs to Duckett, who was expected to arrive at the Hague some five or six days later. Joubert was also told to do everything within his power to enable the Irishman to continue his journey to Hamburg without disruptions. In his letter, Bruix emphasized the importance of Duckett's task of supporting the Irish rebellion. According to Elliott, the Irishman's mission was to stir up 'a mutinous tendency' among the Irish in England's armed forces. In the light of Duckett's experience as an agent of the Ministry of Marine, this seems a likely explanation. However, Bruix's letters to Joubert do not reveal any clear-cut instructions for the agent, who seems to have received a *carte blanche* in order to keep the Irish on the simmer.[2]

On 10 July, Duckett reached the Hague from Paris. According to the orders he had been given by Bruix, Joubert had already made the necessary preparations for the Irishman's mission. He furnished him with 24,000 francs and a French passport in the name of Jean Dubois. The following day, Duckett set out. Arriving in Bremen on the fifteenth, he immediately continued his journey eastwards. He was accompanied by his younger brother Sidney, who had been working as a language teacher in Bremen up to that point. In all probability, William had asked his brother to support his efforts, as he had done on a

---

2 Elliott, *Partners in Revolution*, 218; NLI pos. 210/81–5, Bruix's correspondence with Joubert; PRONI D.3030/189, Turner's account of his meeting with Duckett on 8 May in the Directory's antechamber; see chapters 3 and 4 of this study on Duckett's involvement with the Ministry of Marine in 1797–8; see Elliott, *Partners in Revolution*, 218–20 and Servières, Georges, 'Un Épisode de l'Expédition d'Irlande. L'Extradition et la Mise en Liberté de Napper Tandy (1798–1802)', *Revue Historique*, XCIII (1907), 57–9 on Duckett's mission.

number of occasions in the years before. Passing through Rotenburg an der Wümme in the electorate of Hanover on 17 July, William Duckett was put under arrest by the French *émigré* Monsieur DePelleport, one of Craufurd's henchmen. The Frenchman erroneously assumed William to be another Irish agent named Keating, but soon realised that he had even made a better catch. As Bourdon's secretary in Hamburg, Duckett had attracted a great deal of British attention and had been a constant source of irritation ever since.[3] DePelleport handed Duckett over to Captain Hinüber, Commander of the Hanoverian Grenadiers and of the garrison of Rotenburg, who then transferred the Irishman to Verden, some 25 miles south-east of Bremen. There, Scheither, general in command of the local garrison, immediately set about informing General Walmoden at Hanover and also the English minister at Hamburg about the incident. Excited about the news, Craufurd lost no time in rushing to Verden in order to push through Duckett's extradition to Britain. On 18 July, he wrote three letters to General Walmoden, the duke of Brunswick, and the Regent of Hanover, in which he accused Duckett of being a dangerous rebel and demanded his delivery into British hands for reasons of justice. But General Scheither had already decided to send the French agent under escort to Hanover. Since Duckett had vehemently insisted on his rights 'as a French Citizen and Commissary of the Directory to be set immediately at liberty', the Hanoverian general found himself in an awkward situation.[4] Therefore, he resolved to rid himself of the Irishman and to transfer him to his superiors in Hanover. Eager to prove his worth, the ambitious Craufurd set out for Hanover on the twentieth in order to bring his influence to bear on the matter. Neither the French nor the English government had intervened, and yet, the affair seemed to develop into an extremely explosive subject, since Craufurd as well as Duckett stoutly held to their respective claims. Regency authorities in Hanover did not want to get their fingers burnt over Duckett. Maintaining it to be an entirely military affair, they decided to leave the decision up to the duke of Brunswick, as the supreme commander of the circle of Lower Saxony. He in turn declined original jurisdiction over the matter. The

3 NLI pos. 210/85–8; PRO F.O. 33/15/237–8, account of Duckett's examination; F.O. 33/15/233, Craufurd to Grenville, 19 July 1798; see chapter 3 of this study on Sidney Duckett and his involvement with his brother William in 1796; see PRO F.O. 33/15/52, 54, 70, 119, 214, 217, Nat. Arch. 620/18^A/11 and also Ham Staats. Senat Cl. 1, Lit. Pb, Vol. 8c, Fasc. 2, Nr. 21, Lelarge's report of 23 March for references to Duckett, March–July 1798.

4 PRO F.O. 33/15/237–8, account of Duckett's examination; F.O. 33/15/233–6, 239, 241–2, 244–7, 250, Craufurd's letters to Grenville (19 July 1798), to General Walmoden, to the duke of Brunswick and the Regent of Hanover (all 18 July 1798) & German account of Duckett's examinations.

dispute was referred to the court of Berlin for a decision. According to the duke of Brunswick, the Prussian king, in his capacity as the leading monarch of the circle of Lower Saxony, was to have the final say in the affair. But Prussia did 'not think of interfering in the internal concerns of the Electorate of Hanover.'[5] There was no limit to the complications of eighteenth-century Germany with its numerous states and city states and just as many tortuous jurisdictions. Responsibility for Duckett was shifted back to Hanover again.

Fortunately for the Regency, France and England had avoided a fuss over the matter. London and Paris were restrained in their responses to the doings of the two main antagonists, Duckett and Craufurd, both of whom had displayed unauthorized behaviour. On 27 July, Downing Street brought Craufurd back into line. He was reprimanded with the assertion that the detention of Duckett 'cannot be attained without too far committing the neutrality of that Electorate' and that 'the farther conduct must be left to the persons employed by His Majesty in His Hanoverian government'.[6] After lending his support for the Irishman's extradition with grim determination, Craufurd had to return to Hamburg at the end of July. Reluctantly, he had to withdraw from Duckett, who was detained in Hanover until the beginning of September. For Duckett as well as the Hanoverian authorities, the affair took a turn for the better in the summer of 1798. Although the Regency of Hanover got off lightly this time, the episode indicates the troubles German small and city states could get into. Keeping to a policy of neutrality proved to be extremely difficult amidst a conflict involving the leading powers of Europe. Some months later, the United Irish business was also to become a touchstone for Hamburg's neutrality.[7]

William Duckett was set free in early September and started out for Hamburg. In order to elude Craufurd's grasp, he immediately proceeded to Altona, taking up lodgings at the house of Heiligenstädt, one of the city's best-known republicans. In Altona, William joined his brother Sidney, who had been left alone by the Hanoverian authorities in July and who had subsequently hastened to Hamburg to convey news to the French consulate.[8]

5   PRO F.O. 33/15/277, Craufurd to Grenville, 31 July 1798; F.O. 33/15/248, 253–7 and 258–62, Craufurd to Grenville, 20 & 23 July 1798 and various papers relating to Duckett's arrest.

6   PRO F.O. 33/15/274, Downing Street to Craufurd, 27 July 1798. See Elliott, *Partners in Revolution*, 219 on British and French reactions to the Duckett affair.

7   PRO F.O. 33/15/279 and 33/16/10, 53–6, Craufurd's letters respecting the Duckett affair, 31 July, 10 August and 7 September 1798; see also NLI pos. 210/87–98, letters of the French government and the Duckett brothers relating to the episode.

8   NLI pos. 210/86–8, Sidney Duckett's letter, Altona, 28 July 1798; PRO F.O. 33/16/53–6, Craufurd to Grenville, 7 September 1798; see 33/15/48, 190–1, 200 on Heiligenstädt.

Shortly after his arrival at Altona, William Duckett bitterly bewailed the
Hanoverian occurrence in a letter to Bruix, expressing his disappointment
about the lack of French support during his detention. Giving way to his
marked tendency towards dramatising, he described his 'misfortune' in great
detail. He also informed Bruix about his intention to stay on in Altona in order
to report on Irish moves in the city. Duckett knew full well that his mission
had fallen through and that there was no point in continuing his journey,
since English authorities had become aware of him.[9]

Craufurd was still dogging the agent's heels and nothing seems to have
made him change his mind about the Irishman. He had kept an eye on Duckett
ever since he had returned to Hamburg. On 24 September, Craufurd reaffirmed his determination to put Duckett under arrest. Getting hold of the
Irish agent had developed into an obsession with him, much to the annoyance
of his superiors in London. Tired of the English minister's *idée fixe*, Downing
Street reasoned him out of arresting Duckett. 'With respect to Duckett', the
foreign minister indicated on 16 October,

> it appears ... that greater Benefit is likely to result to the King's Service,
> at present, from his Continuance at Hamburgh, than from his being ar-
> rested there, and sent to this Country as a Prisoner. I have therefore to
> signify to you His Majesty's Pleasure that you take no steps whatever for
> apprehending him, but that you have him carefully watched, and employ
> such Persons for that Purpose as may appear the most capable of gaining
> his Confidence, and thereby discovering any designs with the Execution
> of which he may be entrusted, or with respect to which he may be con-
> sulted.[10]

Craufurd then assured Grenville that 'there is scarcely a single step which
he [Duckett] has taken since he has been at Hamburgh with which I am unacquainted.' In the following years, he did not let Duckett out of his sight.
As a matter of fact, starting with the Hanoverian episode, it was largely thanks
to Craufurd that the Irish agent was condemned to ineffectiveness in his last
years in Hamburg.[11]

William Duckett remained in Altona, busily reporting back to Paris. In the
months subsequent to the Hanoverian affair, he continued to show a lively

9 NLI pos. 210/92–8, Duckett to Bruix, 17 September 1798.
10 PRO F.O. 33/16/100, Downing Street to Craufurd, 16 October 1798; 33/16/88, Craufurd
   to Grenville, 24 September 1798; see also 33/16/96, Craufurd to Grenville, 28 September
   1798, on Duckett.
11 PRO F.O. 33/16/103, Craufurd to Grenville, 23 October 1798; see also 33/16/122–5 and
   141 for Craufurd's reports on Duckett in late 1798.

interest in France's Irish policy and there is no doubt that Ireland's freedom was his main concern. Apart from reporting on Irish activities in Hamburg, Duckett made several proposals respecting a landing in Ireland. Stating that Ireland would still accommodate a substantial rebellious potential, he urged the French government to prevent Irish disturbances from simmering down. Over and over again, he asked to be allowed to proceed to Ireland in order to render assistance to the republican movement. French authorities, however, had lost interest in their agent. Since Craufurd had blown the Irishman's cover, Duckett was of no use to the French for undertaking secret missions of importance. The Directory kept putting off Duckett, telling him to stay on in Hamburg, where he would be of good service to France. In the autumn of 1798, Duckett's numerous letters to the French government exude both a genuine enthusiasm for the Irish cause and reveal his growing frustration about his superiors in Paris. He felt cast aside and trapped in Hamburg. The incident in Hanover had been the beginning of the end of his career as a French under-cover agent. Realising that his influence was on the wane, he gradually retired from political matters, setting greater store by his private life. He remained in Altona until around the year 1800, when he got married to Frederica Georgina Vollmeister. Shortly afterwards, he moved back to France and settled down in Paris, where he earned his living as an English teacher and author of lyric poetry. William Duckett died in 1841. Although often viewed with suspicion by his fellow countrymen, he was a staunch, yet eccentric supporter of Irish nationalism, whose French-tinged republicanism contributed much to United diplomatic advances in France in the crucial years between 1796 and 1798.[12]

II

French naval preparations after the outbreak of insurrection in Ireland were relatively slow to get off the ground. Despite Bruix's efforts, it was not before July 1798 that some kind of invasion plan took shape. Accordingly, four expeditions gathering in Holland, Rochefort, Brest and Dunkirk were to head for different places on the northern coast of Ireland. They were 'to divide the attention of the defence forces, and were eventually to join with the rebels in one army.' However, the expeditions still only existed on paper, and

12 NLI pos. 210/98–131, including Duckett's correspondence, September–December 1798; Nat. Arch. 620/11/130/45 and Kennedy, 'William Duckett', in Baylen/Gossman, *Biographical Dictionary*, 138–9.

in the following two months, French authorities were brought down to earth with a bump.[13]

In the run-up to the expeditions, the Directory was occupied with including United *émigrés* in French naval schemes. Some United Irish in France had already abandoned hopes of seeing their native country again, before an Irish rebellion and subsequent French naval preparations reawakened interest. The hectic rush prevailing among the Irishmen in Paris is illustrated by Samuel Turner's detailed report on what was his third fact-finding mission to France. He appears to have left England some time after the outbreak of rebellion in Ireland, possibly instructed to sound out the intentions of the United men in the French capital. He arrived in Paris to find the Irish *émigrés* in a state of frantic nervousness. The prospect of an Irish invasion had once again highlighted existing divisions within the Irish community in Paris. These differences had become irreconcilable by July, when most United men tried to push themselves to the fore, offering their services for the forthcoming expedition. Tandy, in particular, made a serious bid for the leadership. After 'having quarrelled with Lewins, and Tone [he] called a meeting of United Irishmen in conjunction with Muir, Madget, and Stone. At the meeting a division took place ... ', which subsequently had an effect on the make-up of the expeditions. The Directory tried to show consideration for the situation within the Irish community and accordingly split up the United Irishmen into three different groups. 'Tandy was appointed General', his staff being composed of 'those that sided with him' at the meeting. According to Turner, Tandy's group left Paris around mid-July and proceeded to Dunkirk, where General Rey, the military commander of the expedition, had already commenced preparations. Among those setting out for Rochefort on 21 July were Bartholomew Teeling, Matthew Tone and a man named Sullivan, the latter possibly being one of the Sullivans, who had arrived in Hamburg around mid-May. They were to be under General Humbert, who had won fame for himself in the Vendée under Hoche. Some days later, Theobald Wolfe Tone and some of his associates were sent to Brest in order to join the main force under General Hardy.[14]

---

13 Elliott, *Partners in Revolution*, 220; see also Guillon, *La France et l'Irlande*, 366–70 for French naval schemes.

14 PRONI D.3030/212, Secret information from Hamburg, 16 August [1798]. The author of this note is not named. Regarding the tone, the chronological and logical context, all the indications are that it was Turner. This opinion would also be in line with Fitzpatrick, *Secret Service under Pitt*, 73. In connection with this, see PRO H.O. 100/78/52–3, Wickham to Castlereagh, 9 August 1798 and PRONI D.607/F/432, Richardson to Richardson, 27 September 1798. This letter, the fact concealed by the author's irony or his Newry humour, is by Turner himself. There is no mistaking his handwriting. See

While in Paris, Samuel Turner was sworn 'into the Secret Committee for managing the affairs of Ireland and Scotland in Tandy's place'. Apart from Turner, it only consisted of Madgett and Muir, two of Tandy's closest associates. According to George Orr, Turner himself had 'refused to have anything to do with any of the expeditions' and soon left Paris. Travelling via Lille and Bruges, he reached the Hague some time later. There, he communicated with General Joubert, the French commander in Holland, and Ahearn, before leaving for Germany. After passing through Cuxhaven on 8 August, Turner eventually arrived at Hamburg a few days later.[15] Although he 'had done [him]self completely up', he was not given a chance to rest. Shortly after reaching Hamburg, he had to do his reports for his 'friends' in England and Ireland, who were desperate for any piece of evidence to convict the rebel leaders of the late insurrection. In the meantime, his name had been inserted in the Fugitive Act (38th Geo.III, ch.80), an Act of Attainder against those, who had fled the country, being charged with high treason, and who had not surrendered by a certain time.[16] Much to the annoyance of most Whitehall authorities, the matter had been 'pressed by Persons whom would not dissuade without drowning him [Turner] with suspicion', Castlereagh regretfully informed Wickham. He went on, 'I trust however no bad consequences can arise from his name being included, it will rather cover him from observation.'[17] Looking at Turner's immediate future in Hamburg, the new Irish Chief Secretary saw the situation quite right. By the autumn of 1798, Turner appears to have shed his overanxious persecution mania, which was a feature of his negotiations with Irish and English authorities in the year before. With a certain note of self-satisfaction, he wrote under cover to Sir James Craufurd at the end of September. 'I hope the person at *the Hill* remains ignorant of my engagements. With a little of your assistance, I hope to play the old boy a trick.' In fact, Turner remained in Hamburg after his third fact-finding mission to France and continued to 'play the old boy a trick' in the following years.[18]

PRO F.O. 33/15/54–5 for information on Sullivan. See also Elliott, *Partners in Revolution*, 216–20 on the United Irish in France on the eve of the expeditions.

15 PRONI D.3030/212, Secret information from Hamburg, 16 August [1798] (Turner's account); *Memoirs and Correspondence of Viscount Castlereagh*, I, 409, Secret intelligence by George Orr, enclosed in Wickham's letter to Castlereagh, 25 October 1798; PRONI D.607/F/432, Richardson to Richardson, 27 September 1798.

16 PRONI D.607/F/432, Richardson to Richardson, 27 September 1798; Madden, *The United Irishmen*, 2nd ser., 2nd vol., 521 and 3rd ser., 1st vol., 326 on the Fugitive Bill.

17 PRO H.O. 100/78/325–6, Castlereagh to Wickham, 10 September 1798; see PRO H.O. 100/77/260–1, 264–6, 276–7, 288–90, 317–9 for the correspondence between Whitehall and Dublin Castle relative to the disclosure of secret sources. See Elliott, *Partners in Revolution*, 208 for a further account.

18 PRONI D.607/F/432, Richardson to Richardson, 27 September 1798.

Meanwhile, the ball had started rolling in France. French naval preparations had been dragging out until the beginning of August, when still little seemed to have moved. Those responsible for provisioning the expeditions were not only faced with major logistic and organizational difficulties, but had also problems in raising the necessary money for the intended campaign. Since the young Republic had been at war for more than six years, it is hardly surprising that the country's economy was showing signs of fatigue by 1798. Obviously annoyed about the ponderous preparations standing in the way of an immediate expedition to Ireland, General Humbert had begun to fit out three frigates on his own responsibility. By making a supreme effort and by getting round normal military procedures, he managed to raise some 1000 men, arms and uniforms. Set on getting started as soon as possible, he cast off on 5 August. Since he could not have cared less about existing schemes, Humbert's premature departure thus made a nonsense of French plans of a concerted campaign. After slipping through the English naval blockade, Humbert's ships, however, landed at Killala Bay, Co. Mayo on 22 August. Despite the initial enthusiasm displayed by large parts of Connaught's rural population, many of whom were eager to join the French troops, and in spite of early Franco–Irish victories at Killala and Castlebar, Humbert's expedition soon came to an end. On 8 September, he was defeated by Cornwallis's crown forces at Ballinamuck, Co. Longford.[19]

Tandy and his crew, the bulk of which consisted of Irish *émigrés*, were still waiting for instructions in Dunkirk at the end of August. Some two and a half months after the devastating defeat of the Wexford rebels at Vinegar Hill, time hung heavy on their hands. Nevertheless, Tandy, the would-be military hero, was still keen on making his mark, when he was finally given the go-ahead at the beginning of September. Together with 200 men, he set sail for Ireland on board the fast-sailing corvette the *Anacréon*, leaving behind his ex-associates Alexander Lowry, Arthur MacMahon and Edmund O'Finn, who had dared to contradict their high-handed general. Tandy's well-documented expedition reached Rutland Bay on the Donegal coast on 17 September. There, they heard of Humbert and his mission, which had ended in disaster some nine days before. Although Tandy is said to have been in a state of inebriation for the most part of the voyage, he realized that venturing a clash with powerful crown forces was pointless. Since English ships had stayed close on his heels ever since the *Anacréon* had cast off from Dunkirk, Tandy and Rey decided to sail away from the Donegal coast as soon as possible in order to elude their pursuers. On the eighteenth, they left Rutland and set on a northerly course,

19 Elliott, *Partners in Revolution*, 221–31 and Guillon, *La France et l'Irlande*, 370–407 on
    Humbert's expedition.

knowing full well that taking the direct route to France would hold too many dangers. The following day, the expedition passed the Orkneys off the northern coast of Scotland. After clashing with several English vessels shortly afterwards, the disabled *Anacréon* headed for the Norwegian coast and eventually berthed at Bergen on 21 September. For the duration of the repairs on the ship, the crew stayed in Bergen. At the beginning of October, the various members of the expedition dispersed and went their own ways.[20]

The devastating defeat of Napoléon's fleet at the battle of Aboukir Bay on 1 August 1798 had jolted the French into action against England. After the failures of Humbert and Tandy, the dispatch of a third invasionary force to Ireland appears like a desperate attempt at deriving some benefit from the Irish crisis after all. The Directory had managed to raise ten ships and some 3000 men, which were to be under the *Chef de Division* Bompard. The expedition, including Theobald Wolfe Tone, eventually left Brest in the middle of September. En route for the north of Ireland, Bompard's ships had to fend off numerous British attacks and only reached the coast of Donegal some three-and-a-half weeks later. Entering a bay off Lough Swilly, the French fleet soon found itself trapped by the vessels of Admiral Warren. After a short but fierce fight, Bompard had to surrender on 12 October. Theobald Wolfe Tone was taken into captivity, transported to Dublin and eventually committed suicide in mid-November.[21]

The disastrous failure of the French expeditions in 1798 brought United set-backs to a climax. Starting with growing reprisals in Ulster in the year before, the Irish government had pressed the northern Society hard. By the spring of 1798, Dublin Castle had deprived the Ulster United Irishmen of a great number of top leaders, who had emerged after the re-establishment of the Society in 1795–6, and had weakened its capacity or resolve to respond to events. In the South, arrests had barely begun, when the Leinster Society was hit by the Margate incident, the March arrests and Lord Edward's capture. In cooperation with Dublin Castle, London had begun to put emphasis on infiltrating radical circles, and had even succeeded in smuggling in a United leader, namely Samuel Turner, into Hamburg. Starting towards the close of 1797, hardly any United Irishman in Hamburg escaped London's watchfulness, which was all the more important, as United agents, like refugees, almost exclusively travelled via Hamburg up to the end of 1798. By mid-1798, the British had a fairly clear idea of United moves and the Irish radicals'

20 PRO P.C.I/43/A.152, Turner's letter from Hamburg, 28 December 1798; H.O. 100/ 79/321–3, 332, intelligence from Hamburg; TCD MSS. 5967/3–4, Corbet's account; Coughlan, *Napper Tandy*, 124–48 and Elliott, *Partners in Revolution*, 232–4.
21 Guillon, *La France et l'Irlande*, 407–13 and Elliott, *Partners in Revolution*, 234–7.

alliance with France. Thus, the actual launch of French expeditions to Ireland did not come as a surprise to the authorities in London and Dublin. However, the devastating failure of the Irish expeditions in the summer of 1798 also weakened the cause of the United Irishmen in France, since the French came to realise that conquering Ireland was not as easy as the Irish radicals had claimed it would be. Henceforward, United agents were to have a hard time of it with the French authorities, who were simply more sceptical about Irish missions than they used to be before the expeditions. United diplomatic relations with France, which Tone had got under way with great difficulty in 1796, cooled down substantially after his death. Tone's unhappy fate, however, did not end the matter. The painful aftermath of the Irish expeditions was soon to be felt in Hamburg.

III

Events in Ireland and France threw Hamburg into a state of agitation. In the late summer of 1798, there was no end to the line of Irish arrivals, when further refugees reached the Elbe in the wake of the suppression of rebellion in Ireland. While some twenty United men had reached Hamburg in the period from January to June 1798, the number of Irish arrivals tripled in the second half of the year. From July to December 1798, about sixty arrivals were recorded, and yet, only about twenty of them are known by name and biographic detail. Hence, it is quite difficult to keep track of the many Irishmen reaching Hamburg after the rebellion, since there is simply no clue to their identity. It must be assumed, however, that most of them did not stay in the city for any length of time, and only some twenty to thirty Irishmen at most appear to have been present at various points of time in the second half of 1798.

On 13 August, Lady Pamela Fitzgerald arrived and moved in with her stepsister Henriette Matthiessen, *née* de Sercy. Accompanied 'by a Mr Murphy, a Parson', she had left Ireland at the end of May, while her husband was still fighting for his life in his Newgate prison cell. She and her three little children had travelled to London to stay with her mother-in-law and also Lord Edward's sister Lucy. Lady Pamela eventually set out for Hamburg one month later on account of a bill of attainder, whereby she was enjoined not to stay in Britain any longer.[22] In the following years, the 'beautiful and unfortunate creature', as Tone described Lady Pamela on 20 June 1798, was to remain in

22 Campbell, *Edward and Pamela Fitzgerald*, 140–5 and 198–205, including Lady Lucy's diary from 2 March–8 June 1798; Fitzpatrick, *Secret Service Under Pitt*, 76.

Hamburg, where she was to be found 'among the most dangerous' of her countrymen. In 1800, she entered into an unhappy marriage with Pitcairn, the American consul residing in Hamburg, which, however, was soon dissolved. Lady Pamela stayed on in the city for some more years, before she eventually settled down in France.[23]

In most instances, Irish migration to the Continent in the second half of 1798 did not centre on such enigmatic characters. The United Irishmen's rank-and-file also sought safety in flight. Among the numerous arrivals in Hamburg in August were the Dublin United men George Grey and Lyndon Bolton, the latter a yeoman and an 'inactive United Irishman', according to his wife. Both were still reported to be in the city by 1799. Bolton remained in Hamburg until 1803 and he was certainly not as 'inactive' as his wife claimed him to be. In the years leading up to 'Emmet's Rebellion', his name turns up on many occasions, showing that he had a hand in United affairs on the Continent.[24] In the late summer and the autumn of 1798, however, Bolton and Grey were joined by Thomas Campbell, the United poet (*The Exile of Erin*), Dennis O'Neill, Durnin, and the Meath United rebel Corr, who was to turn up again in Paris some time later, and also by shiploads of refugees who had left Ireland after their involvement with Humbert.[25] Apart from Turner, Duckett and the O'Finns, the latter of whom had reached the city some months earlier, Hamburg's Irish community consisted of a motley crowd of post-rebellion refugees. Some of the late arrivals already regretted having left Ireland, for instance Lyndon Bolton, whose situation was certainly not exceptional. 'At present here', he wrote on 4 November 1798, 'I am God knows in a miserable Way living in a Garret without friends or Acquaintance, at a great Distance

23 *Life of Theobald Wolfe Tone*, II, 508–9; PRO H.O. 100/85/48, Whitehall to Castlereagh, 11 January 1799, on Lady Pamela. See Madden, *The United Irishmen*, 2nd edn, 2nd ser., 475–551, Campbell, *Edward and Pamela Fitzgerald*, 205–32, Harkensee, II, *Madame de Genlis*, 43–6 for information on Lady Pamela and her stay in Hamburg.

24 Nat. Arch. 620/41/2, Jane Bolton's letter, 2 November 1798; see also PRO F.O. 33/16/44, 66, 144–6, 33/17/131, 33/19/238, 97/241, PRONI D.607/F/432 (Turner's account, 27 September 1798) and Nat. Arch. 620/40/113, 620/11/130/26, 620/11/130/43, various reports on Grey, but especially on Bolton, 1798–1803.

25 See Madden, *The United Irishmen*, I, 1st edn, 313 and *Memoirs of Miles Byrne*, ed. his widow, II (Paris, New York, 1863), 48–50 on Thomas Campbell; see PRO F.O. 33/16/169–70 (Craufurd to Grenville, 20 November 1798), 33/17/101–4 and Elliott, *Partners in Revolution*, 269 on Corr; see Nat. Arch. 620/40/113, PRO H.O. 100/86/183 and *Memoirs and Correspondence of Viscount Castlereagh*, II, 230–4 on O'Neill; see PRO F.O. 33/16/141–2, 33/17/126, 33/19/79–80, Craufurd's letters, November 1798–August 1799, and Fitzpatrick, *Secret Service under Pitt*, 290–8 on Durnin. See NLI pos. 198 (Archives Nationales, Fonds AF.III 57/224), letter from Altona, 6 vendémiaire an 7 (27 September 1798) relative to a ship arriving with numbers of United refugees.

for six Months without any Assistance to my family.[26] The problems of money and a certain kind of rootlessness, some 1000 kilometres away from their respective homes, were to be stumbling-blocks for many a United *émigré* in the following years.

Quite a few Irish refugees were not content with waiting for better times. The members of the Irish committee, who had first got together in June, were busy paving the way for a 'great activity between Ireland and the various committees' residing in Hamburg.[27] They had begun 'to correspond on the one hand with Ireland, on the other with the Irish Committee at Paris', as Craufurd was horrified to find on 7 September.[28] After returning from Hanover, also William Duckett, apparently a member of the Hamburg United committee, was at pains to get in touch with his United brethren at home. With the help of Captain Doyle, a native of Rush, whose smuggling vessel operated frequently between Hamburg and Ireland, he seems to have succeeded in establishing contacts with Joseph Holt, who was still hiding out in the Wicklow Mountains in the autumn of 1798. Duckett was still obsessed with revolution in his native country and continued to stand up for a French involvement in Ireland in the following months. The authorities in London, however, who had got wind of Duckett's efforts, gave an order to seize Doyle's ship towards the close of the year. As a matter of fact, the subsequent seizure confirmed their suspicions. Experience had shown that a watchful eye should be kept on Hamburg and its ships, which seemed to be a dangerous bridge between Ireland and its rebellious *émigrés*.[29]

In Hamburg, United matters met with approval on the part of the city's liberal circles. Subsequent to the rebellion, Irish affairs were on everybody's lips. Apart from contacts with resident French republicans, with whom they apparently had close associations, United *émigrés* cooperated with Hamburg's

---

26 Nat. Arch. 620/41/13, Lyndon Bolton's letter from Hamburg, 4 November 1798; PRO F.O. 33/15/137, 200, H.O. 100/79/332 and 100/87/326 on the O'Finns; see PRO F.O. 33/16 on Craufurd's reports in the autumn of 1798.

27 PRO F.O. 33/15/202, Craufurd to Grenville, 3 July 1798.

28 PRO F.O. 33/16/56, Craufurd to Grenville, 7 September 1798.

29 NLI pos. 210/108–10, Duckett to the Directory, 25 vendémiaire an 7 (16 October 1798) and Nat. Arch. 620/11/130/45 on Doyle; see PRO F.O. 33/16/104, 141, 180, 203, H.O. 100/79/132–3, 100/85/61, 82, 124 and *Memoirs and Correspondence of Viscount Castlereagh*, II, 102–4, 193–4 on Duckett and Doyle. See NLI pos. 210/110–22 for Duckett's correspondence with Paris, October–December 1798 and NLI pos. 210/117–8 on Duckett and the Hamburg committee of United Irishmen. See PRO F.O. 33/15/137, 207, 212, 219; 33/16/6–10, 38–42, 64–6, 90–2, 134, Nat. Arch. 620/18ᴬ/11, 620/39/41 and PRONI D.3030/200 for reports on suspicious activities and connections with regard to the Hamburg ships, June–November 1798.

Philanthropic Society, which was exposed to heavy criticism ever since its involvement with Bourdon. As a matter of fact, the Philanthropists were eventually banned by the Senate in November, after the imperial court at Vienna
had made a strong protest about the Society's continued existence. However,
together with German, French or other foreign groups, Irish *émigrés* were involved in all kinds of activities, committees and meetings. Apart from establishing a specific Irish objective, these oddly assorted amalgamations appear
to have been a melting pot for all sorts of anti-English feelings. The 'avowed
object of their association [The Philanthropic Society]', as one informant reported to London, 'is to reform Kingdoms and states. Their councils and
debates are pointedly calculated for making the good subject of England un-
easy ... and to excite ... to Rebellion.'[30] In the second half of 1798, the
Hamburg sources teemed with reports on suspicious associations and radical
agitators, amongst whom Irish affairs enjoyed a certain degree of popularity.

Starting with Turner and especially Craufurd, the British authorities were
ever vigilant for Irish activities in Hamburg. Craufurd's countless reports were
read with interest by government officials in Dublin and London. Over and
over again, Craufurd's letters were copied for the internal use of various
government sections dealing with United matters. At the height of the Irish
rebellion and the following invasion scare, the authorities gave up a lot of
time to the 'Hamburgh papers' and the handling of arriving pieces of secret
information. By the summer and autumn of 1798, the British intelligence
system was running at full steam.[31]

The British government had been in the picture about Tandy's moves from
his departure from France in early September up until his arrival in Bergen.
Already in mid-October, Downing Street urged Craufurd to watch out for
Tandy and his associates, who had left Bergen on the second. Supposing that
the Irishmen would pass through Hamburg, Craufurd was instructed to 'concert with the Senate of Hamburgh the necessary measures for apprehending

30 PRO P.C.I/3117, letter from Hambro', 20 July 1798; see F.O. 33/15/172-3, 190-3,
    204-7, 220, 291-5, F.O. 33/16/20-3, 96, P.C.I/3117 (letters from Hambro', 10 July-10
    August 1798) and Ham. Staats. Senat Cl. 1, Lit. Pb, Vol. 8c, Fasc. 2, Nr. 21 (Lelarge's
    report of 22 July 1798) on radical associations and Irish activities; see P.R.O. F.O. 33/15/
    190-1, 200-2, 214, F.O.33/16/56, 112-3, 145, P.C.I/3117, NLI pos.210/117-8 and Ham.
    Staats. Senat Cl. 1, Lit. Pb, Vol. 8c, Fasc. 2, Nr. 21 (Lelarge's reports of 16 June, 3, 8,
    12, 20 July, 27 October 1798) on the Irish committee and its associations with French re-
    publicans, the Philanthropic Society and other groups. See Grab, *Demokratische Strömungen
    in Hamburg und Schleswig-Holstein*, 219-23 and Wohlwill, Adolf, *Hamburgische Beiträge zur
    Geschichte der Jahre 1798 und 1799* (Hamburg, 1883), 57-64 on the Philanthropic Society.
31 See PRO H.O. 100/77-9, F.O. 33/15-6 and *Memoirs and Correspondence of Viscount
    Castlereagh*, I-II for information on the British intelligence system in the second half of
    1798.

them, as being charged with high Treason, and for sending them to England under the Custody of such proper persons as you may select for that purpose. This object being of great importance, you will omit no pains for its being effectually carried into Execution.'³²

It was also thanks to the helping hands of John Powell and George Orr that London stayed hard on Tandy's heels. After leaving Hamburg in July, they had joined the Dunkirk expedition, which eventually brought them to Norway towards the end of September. In Bergen, both men were desperate to get away from Tandy and his friends, with whom they were having nothing but trouble ever since departing from Dunkirk. They managed to clear out shortly after arriving in Norway, applied to Greig, the English consul in Bergen, telling 'him they had been deluded with that Expedition'. Greig, who obviously believed in their hypocritical lies, thereupon arranged a passage for Orr and Murphy. On board the American ship the *Filona*, the two Irishmen eventually reached England around mid-October. They immediately proceeded to London and lost no time in conveying news to Wickham in a number of detailed, but enormously spiteful reports.³³

It is against this background that the first refugees from Tandy's expedition drifted into Hamburg at the beginning of November 1798. After leaving Bergen at the close of September, Thomas Burgess, Anthony McCann, two of the 1797 *émigrés*, and William Corbet set foot in the city on 3 November. The latter, an ex-student of Trinity College from Cork, had left Ireland towards the end of May, at the height of the Irish rebellion. Accompanied by his brother Thomas, he had sailed from Dublin to Trondheim, Norway, from where he had proceeded to Copenhagen. After passing through Hamburg around July, the Corbets had eventually reached France some time later. Subsequently, the two brothers had separated, Thomas joining the Brest expedition and William making his way to Dunkirk.³⁴ Upon reaching Hamburg, Corbet, Burgess and McCann applied to Marragon, the new French minister,

32 PRO F.O. 33/16/106, Downing Street to Craufurd, October 1798; see *Memoirs and Correspondence of Viscount Castlereagh*, I, 331, 397–410 for the exchange of information relating to Tandy's moves prior to his arrest in November.

33 PRO H.O. 100/87/335, examination of John Powell Murphy; see H.O. 100/79/59, 61, 69, 321–3 and 100/87/310, 318–335, 351–4 for Murphy and Orr. See also Coughlan, *Napper Tandy*, 123–49 for further information on Tandy's expedition, including Orr and Murphy's involvement.

34 PRO F.O. 33/16/142 for the arrival of the three Irishmen; Nat. Arch. 620/38/253, PRO F.O. 33/16/96, PRONI D.3030/302 and 212 (Turner's information, 16 August [1798]) on the journey of the Corbet brothers in the summer of 1798; see Healy, F.J., ed., 'A Famous Franco–Irish Soldier: General William Corbet', *Journal of the Ivernian Society*, III (1910–1), 239–44 on Corbet.

for passports in order to continue their journey to France. They also told him about the forthcoming arrival of Tandy and several of his associates. Marragon, however, refused to issue the Irishmen with passports, but offered them some money to cover their expenses in Hamburg.[35]

Some days later, also Hervey Montmorency Morres experienced difficulties in obtaining a passport from the French representation in Hamburg, which had been urged to exercise restraint with regard to granting entries to Irish refugees some three months before. While staying in Dublin in March 1798, the Tipperary United Irishman had been 'appointed to the Adjutant-Generalship of Munster' but was subsequently prevented from returning to Tipperary. He went into hiding in Dublin and Westmeath before eventually leading a small rebel force on its way to join Humbert's troops in early September. In the weeks following Humbert's defeat, he had managed to get to Dublin and subsequently escaped to England on 22 October. On 7 November, Morres reached Hamburg, where he soon got in touch with the local committee of United Irishmen. This in turn referred him to Lady Pamela Fitzgerald, who was very popular with United refugees and the French authorities alike. Her position as the widow of an highly esteemed Irish rebel leader and, last but not least, her breathtaking beauty had already made her a social attraction in Hamburg's Irish and francophile circles. Lady Pamela did not deny Morres her help. Furnished with a letter of introduction she had written on his behalf, the Irishman called on Marragon around mid-November. In the meeting, he expressed his wish to go to France. According to Marragon's report to Talleyrand, he claimed to have 'important matters to communicate' to the French government, but said that he would wait for some Irish commander of the late expedition, with whom 'he hope[d] to make the journey' to France. Bearing in mind that Morres did not take part in any of the expeditions, this statement shows clearly the mood of excitement among the United Irish in Hamburg on account of the forthcoming arrival of Tandy. But Marragon declined to provide the Irishman with a passport, as he had already done in the instance of Burgess, McCann and Corbet. Morres and his compatriots had no choice, but to await Tandy, who would surely remedy the matter.[36]

35 Servières, 'Un Épisode de l'Expedition d'Irlande', *Revue Historique*, 53; see also PRO P.C.I/43/A.152, Turner's letter, 28 December 1798 on Corbet, McCann and Burgess.

36 *Memoirs and Correspondence of Viscount Castlereagh*, II, 96–8, Marragon to Talleyrand, 29 brumaire an 7 (19 November 1798); see ibid., 94–6 and 98–100, Morres's memorial to Bruix and Lady Pamela's letter of introduction; see Servières, 'Un Épisode de l'Expedition d'Irlande', *Revue Historique*, 53 on the August instructions concerning Irish entries; see Wells, *Insurrection*, 129 and 132 and Elliott, *Partners in Revolution*, 229 on Morres and his activities prior to his departure from Ireland.

In the meantime, Napper Tandy was approaching Hamburg. Accompanied by his Adjutant-General James Bartholomew Blackwell, a naturalised Frenchman who had emigrated from Ireland in the 1770s, he had left Bergen by land on 2 October, a few days after Corbet, Burgess and McCann. En route to France, Tandy and Blackwell passed through Christiana (Oslo) on 12 October, the same day Corbet and his friends stayed in the city. But unlike their comrades, Tandy and Blackwell took their time for the continuation of the journey, knowing full well that the British authorities were still after them. They reached Copenhagen only on 16 November, some two and a half weeks after Corbet, Burgess and McCann had already arrived in Hamburg.[37] Disguised as two American merchants, Bleifest (Blackwell) and Jones (Tandy), the alias Tandy had already used on his last visit to Hamburg in the previous year, the two Irishmen set foot in the city on the evening of 22 November. They took rooms at the Wappen von Amerika (American Arms), where they were soon joined by Mr Robe of Holland (Corbet) and Mr Peters of Ireland (Morres).[38] It is unclear where Burgess and McCann were at that time, but they appear to have gone their separate ways, since there is no mention of them in connection with their compatriots subsequent to their meeting with the French minister some two and a half weeks before. The following day, however, Tandy and his friends went to see Marragon to make the necessary arrangements for the continuation of their journey to France. But once again, the French minister had to cold-shoulder the Irishmen. Despite his rank as a French general, Tandy's reputation does not seem to have got as far as Marragon, since he showed himself ill-informed about the Irishman in his letter to Talleyrand of the same day. It was not before 25 November that the French foreign ministry instructed its Hamburg representative to lift the restrictions placed on Irish entry to France. Thus, without having achieved anything, Tandy and his comrades left the French representation, apparently decided on setting out for France at any rate. There is reason to believe that Marragon, who had already showed himself dissatisfied with the French refusal of entry in a preceding letter to Talleyrand, encouraged the Irishmen to continue their journey nevertheless. The same evening, however, Tandy, Blackwell, Corbet and Morres were invited to have supper with 'Messrs. T____ & D____' at the home of Lady

37 *Memoirs and Correspondence of Viscount Castlereagh*, I, 400–3, James Greig to Evan Nepean, Bergen, 2 October 1798; Ham. Staats. Senat Cl. 1, Lit. Pb, Vol. 8d, Fasc. 15b1, Inv. 3, passports of Corbet and Blackwell; see Cox, Walter, 'James Bartholomew Blackwell', *Cox's Irish Magazine and Monthly Asylum for Neglected Biography* (January 1809), 32–4 and Madden, *The United Irishmen*, 1st vol., 3rd ser., 73–6 on Blackwell.

38 *Hamburgische Adreß-Comtoir Nachrichten*, 26 November 1798, announcement of the arrival of Jones, Bleifest, Pieters and Robe, who subsequently took rooms at the *Wappen von Amerika*; PRO F.O. 33/16/174, Craufurd to Grenville, 24 November 1798.

Pamela Fitzgerald. All the indications are that those initials stand for the names of Turner and Duckett, as assumed by the historians, Fitzpatrick, Ní Chinnéide and Coughlan.[39] The two Hamburg agents 'continually' associated with each other, according to Turner himself. Moreover, both were in close touch with Tandy's party while in Paris as well as with Lady Pamela in Hamburg, to say nothing of Blackwell's contacts with Duckett since their student days at the Irish College in Paris. Thus, there are many grounds for the supposition that the four Irishmen had an informal get-together with their old friends Turner and Duckett, as well as with their charming hostess Lady Pamela, before they eventually returned to their hotel around three or four o'clock in the morning of 24 November.[40]

Upon arriving at the Wappen von Amerika, the Irishmen got ready to leave for France. They had fixed their departure for Holland for the twenty-forth, according to Blackwell's letter to his wife, dated 3 frimaire an 7 (23 November 1798). In the letter, he informed her that he and his friends had to proceed with utmost caution 'in order to avoid falling into Mr John Bull's hands, who is looking for us since our departure.' On top of keeping his wife up-to-date, Blackwell seemingly had to settle yet another affair. Among the papers later found upon the Irishmen, there is an unfinished letter in Blackwell's handwriting, the completion of which appears to have been prematurely prevented during those early hours of the twenty-forth. He must have left Lady Pamela's home in a state of emotional confusion, now trying hard to maintain his composure. Churned up, he got a guilty conscience and wrote, 'there, dear Madam, let us have none affliction in the common of two.' Blackwell was obviously at pains to reason his female addressee out of a liaison, the beginnings of which had left him utterly bewildered. To all appearances, the supper party at the home of the charming Lady Pamela did not stop at political talks.[41]

39 T.C.D. MS. 5967/3–4 & 25, Corbet papers, including his *The Conduct of the Senate of Hamburgh (La Conduite du Sénat de Hamburg devoillée aux yeux de l'Europe)*, written in 1807 and Tandy's account, written a few days before his death on 24 August 1803; *Memoirs and Correspondence of Viscount Castlereagh*, II, 96–9, Marragon's letters to Talleyrand, 29 brumaire an 7 (19 November 1798) and 3 frimaire an 7 (23 November 1798); Servières, 'Un Épisode de l'Expédition d'Irlande', *Revue Historique*, 53 on Talleyrand waiving restrictions for those Irishmen returning from the expeditions; see Fitzpatrick, *Secret Service Under Pitt*, 76–80, Ní Chinnéide, Níle, *Napper Tandy and the European Crises of 1798–1803*, O'Donnell Lecture (Galway, 1962), 3–8 and Coughlan, *Napper Tandy*, 151–2 for accounts respecting the course of events between November 22nd and 24th.

40 PRONI D.607/F/432, Turner describing his association with Duckett; Swords, *The Green Cockade*, 64 on Duckett and Blackwell.

41 Ham. Staats. Senat Cl. 1, Lit. Pb, Vol. 8d, Fasc. 15b1, Inv. 3, papers found upon the four Irishmen, 24 November 1798, including Blackwell's letters.

Meanwhile, Craufurd swiftly set to work. He had been waiting for Tandy and Blackwell to arrive since the end of October. Some months after his hapless involvement in the Duckett episode, he wanted to do better this time. With the help of Samuel Turner, who seems to have provided the necessary information on the Irish fugitives, he moved against Tandy and his associates in the early morning of Saturday, the twenty-forth.[42] Some hours before, he had communicated with *Prätor* Klefeker, the city's chief magistrate, who had refused to comply with Craufurd's demand for the immediate extradition of the Irishmen. But Klefeker had been prepared to meet the Englishman halfway. He had approved of arresting Tandy and Blackwell and placing them under the authority of the city of Hamburg. After receiving word of the Irishmen's return to their hotel, Craufurd accompanied the *Bruchvogt* (chief of police) and his guard to their hotel at the Rödingsmarkt. At five o'clock in the morning, they entered the Wappen von Amerika, where Tandy and his associates were making final preparations for their journey to France. It is unclear what precisely happened on the Irishmen's arrest, but it can be presumed that only Tandy and Blackwell offered active resistance. Moreover, Blackwell vehemently complained about this violent intrusion on his rights as a French officer, but his furious protests were to no avail. Also Corbet and Morres had to bow to their fates, although Craufurd was certainly not interested in them. The English minister had not planned to have them 'arrested not thinking it of importance but it happened by accident they being in the house with Tandy', as he claimed later that day.[43]

While the four men were transported to separate prisons, Craufurd once again urged the *Prätor* to hand over the Irishmen before possible French intervention. But the *Prätor* reaffirmed that he had no power over such important decisions and declared that matters would fall under the jurisdiction of the

42 PRO F.O. 33/16/111 & 169, Craufurd's wait for Tandy, 30 October & 20 November 1798; Coughlan, *Napper Tandy*, 152, Ní Chinnéide, *Napper Tandy and the European Crises*, 8–9 on Turner and the Tandy affair. There is no clear evidence of Turner's involvement, but it must be assumed that Craufurd would not have been able to proceed as swiftly and decisively as he did without the agent's help.

43 PRO F.O. 33/16/(174–)180, Craufurd's account of the arrest, 24 November 1798; Ham. Staats. Senat Cl. 1, Lit. Pb, Vol. 8d, Fasc. 15b1, Inv. 1, Senate's minute-book; see Wohlwill, *Neuere Geschichte der Freien und Hansestadt Hamburg*, 214–5, Ní Chinnéide, *Napper Tandy and the European Crises*, 9, Servières, 'Un Épisode de l'Expédition d'Irlande', *Revue Historique*, 54, Coughlan, *Napper Tandy*, 152–4, Harder, Karl Wilhelm, *Die Auslieferung der Vier Politischen Flüchtlinge Napper Tandy, Blackwell, Morres (Morris) und George Peters im Jahre 1799 an Großbritannien unter Widerspruch von Frankreich* (Leipzig, 1857), 8–9 for the arrest. Despite its age, Wohlwill's book, written in 1914, still offers the most concise account of the Tandy affair, including extensive research in the Hamburg, Berlin, Vienna and Paris archives.

Senate. A few hours later, events took a turn for the worse for the city's authorities. Accompanied by the French consul Langau, Marragon called at the house of *Bürgermeister* (burgomaster) von Sienen at noon. There, the two Frenchmen registered a protest against the arrests, describing them as an 'act of violence' and a 'violation of human rights'. The city fathers would have no right to detain the Irishmen, who, in their capacity as French officers, would have to be set free immediately. In a threatening tone, the two Frenchmen demanded the reversal of 'that error', which had incurred France's wrath and which on no account could be accepted. Von Sienen, however, did not show himself impressed by this French attempt at intimidation, explaining that decisions would be up to the Senate now. Thus, Marragon lost no time in writing a letter of protest to the Senate, but only insisted on the immediate release of Tandy and Blackwell, without including the names of the other two prisoners. It was not until 23 January 1799 that the French minister officially put in a claim for Corbet and Morres.[44]

In a matter of hours, Hamburg's city fathers found themselves in an extremely awkward situation. The extraordinary sitting of the Senate, which was called that same day, eventually decided to put off the ministers of England and France for the time being and to turn to the representatives of Prussia and Austria for help. In the following weeks, the Senate was confronted with a deluge of French and English notes as both powers persisted in their demands regarding the Irish prisoners. In their endeavours not to fall out with either side, the city's authorities became entangled in the conflict between the two antagonists. A communication to Craufurd, dated 28 November 1798, well illustrates Hamburg's dilemma. In the letter, the Senate regretted that it could not comply with England's demand for the extradition of Tandy and Blackwell, since 'their quality as English subjects is disputed and thus the legality of their confinement. The city finds itself exposed to a great danger in consenting to their extradition. ... The Senate feels obliged to consider this affair as undecided and wants to remain impartial in not giving way to either demands of the two belligerent powers, the one and the other friends of this city.'[45] But those 'friends' of Hamburg did not let up. France and England continued to put heavy pressure on the Senate in the following months, accompanied by diverse menaces and admonitions. Craufurd, for instance, who showed his

44 Ham. Staats. Senat Cl. 1, Lit. Pb, Vol. 8d, Fasc. 15b1, Inv. 7a, negotiations with France, including Marragon's letter to the Senate of 4 frimaire an 7 (24 November 1798); see also Inv. 1, Senate's minute-book for the course of events, 24 November 1798.

45 Ham. Staats. Senat Cl. 1, Lit. Pb, Vol. 8d, Fasc. 15b1, Inv. 6, negotiations with England, including the Senate's letter to Craufurd, 28 November 1798; see Inv. 7a for the Senate's correspondence with the French.

personal sympathy for the city fathers' dilemma on a number of occasions, was soon instructed to go ahead in the most determined manner and not to rest until Tandy and his friends were placed in the custody of England. The caution that both powers had shown in the handling of the Duckett episode some time previously was thrown to the winds altogether at the close of 1798.[46]

England as well as France knew full well that there was more at stake than the lives of the unfortunate Irish prisoners. Starting in the autumn of the year, London had pursued a policy of rapprochement towards Prussia, which had pledged itself to be neutral and had guaranteed north German neutrality ever since the Peace of Basel in April 1795. Now, the Tandy affair seemed to offer an ideal opportunity to tip the scales in favour of a new conservative coalition. But Prussia did not dissociate itself from its neutral stance in 1798–9. In the face of heavy threats on the part of England and France, Berlin kept a low profile throughout the crisis, thus leaving Hamburg to its own devices at a time when support was most needed. With no decision in sight, the matter dragged on. By the spring of 1799, when Hamburg's city fathers still stood uneasily between English and French claims, the conflict revolving around the Irish prisoners widened into a far more complicated affair. In agreement with English plans to woo Berlin into a conservative coalition including Moscow, Russia also intervened. In the second half of March, the Russian Tsar delivered an ultimatum to the Senate, whereby he demanded the immediate extradition of the four prisoners to England as well as a prompt ban on all revolutionary clubs in the city. On the expiry of the ultimatum on 1 April, when the Senate had still not shown any sign of response, Tsar Paul I placed an embargo on all Hamburg ships in Russian ports and, moreover, ordered the expulsion of all Hamburg representatives from his country. In a letter to the Russian minister in Hamburg, dated 26 April 1799, Paul I gave expression to his anger about the free German city. Hamburg, he stated, 'has become a den of malcontents, and a refuge of all sorts of vagabonds, who want to evade justice, and who, in order to get only a piece of bread, are prepared to do anything.' Shortly afterwards, Russia broke off diplomatic relations with Hamburg. On 30 April 1799, Mouravieff, the Russian minister, received instructions to leave the city, and immediately proceeded to Altona. Since Marragon had already moved to Altona some four days before, Hamburg found itself in a highly precarious situation by the end of April.[47]

46 PRO F.O. 33/16/243–5, Downing Street to Craufurd, 11 December 1798; see 33/16/ 174–260 on Craufurd's correspondence with the Foreign Office, 24 November–end of December 1798.

47 Historical Manuscripts Commission, *Report on the Manuscripts of J.B. Fortescue, Esq., preserved at Dropmore*, V (London, 1906), 33, Tsar Paul I to Mouravieff, 26 April 1799 (see also pages 32 and 48–9 for other pieces of the Russian correspondence relating to the

At the same time, also the British government started to tighten the rein on Hamburg. Spurred on by early military victories of the newly created second conservative coalition, which by now included England, Russia and Austria, London saw it necessary to make use of present French difficulties in order to put an end to north German neutrality. Since the fortunes of war seemed to have deserted France, there was hope that Berlin would show itself willing to alter its neutral course and join the conservative side. In connection with this, the dispute over the four Hamburg prisoners might prove to be the deciding factor in the crucial diplomatic contest for north German military assistance. It was against this background that England issued the *Report from the Committee of Secrecy* in March 1799. Section 8 of this much publicised government paper dealt with revolutionary activities in Hamburg and devoted a lot of space to France's efforts to use foreign radicals residing in the city for its own ends. In particular, the report shed light on Hamburg's importance as a crossroads for communications between France and the disaffected United Irish:

§ 8 *Societies at Hamburgh.*
In Addition to this Mass of Treason, in Great Britain and in Ireland, Your Committee find, that, for the Purpose of more convenient Communication between France and Ireland, a Committee of United Irishmen has been formed at Hamburgh. That Place has long been the Receptable of those disaffected Persons who have fled from Great Britain or Ireland, either from Apprehension of the Consequences of the treasonable Practices in which they have been engaged or for the Purpose of assisting the Conspiracies carried on against their respective Countries; and with the latter View it has been the Centre of a Correspondence, which has long subsisted among the British and Irish Societies established at that Place, as well as in London and Paris; and this Correspondence with Great Britain and Ireland, has frequently been covered by the Pretence of Commercial Transactions, or of communicating Intelligence for the public News-paper. Hamburgh has also been the resort of the disaffected of every other Country, whose intrigues are constantly directed to the object of spreading the principles of Jacobinism in Holstein

Hamburg affair); Ham. Staats. Senat Cl. 1, Lit. Pb, Vol. 8d, Fasc. 15b1, Inv. 8, negotiations with Russia; see also Inv. 1, 5, 6, 7a, 9 and 10 for the international crisis; Wohlwill, *Neuere Geschichte der Freien und Hansestadt Hamburg*, 216–25, Harder, *Die Auslieferung der Vier Politischen Flüchtlinge*, 11–55, Ní Chinnéide, *Napper Tandy and the European Crises*, 11–5, Servières, 'Un Épisode de l'Expédition d'Irlande', *Revue Historique*, 55–62 and Elliott, *Partners in Revolution*, 258–66 on the diplomatic background of the European crisis, November 1798-spring of 1799.

and the north of Germany, and generally in all the northern parts of Europe. Many emissaries, English, Scotch, and Irish, have been dispatched from time to time from Hamburgh to Great Britain and Ireland, and to various parts of the continent, as circumstances required. There has recently been established at Hamburgh, Altona, and the neighbourhood, a society called *The Philanthropic Society*, for the purpose of correspondence with the republicans of all Countries, upon the Plan of the Corresponding Societies established in Great Britain and Ireland; and whose avowed Object is the Reform of all Kingdoms and States. The leading Members of this Society, who direct all the rest, compose a Committee of about Twenty Persons, British, French, Dutch, and Germans. The members of the subordinate Societies at Hamburgh and Altona are all under the Control of the Committee or principal Society before-mentioned. This Committee constantly corresponds with Great Britain and Ireland, and all Parts of Germany. It has Secretaries skilled in different Languages, and corresponding Agents in different Towns, particularly in London. It may become a formidable Engine in the Hands of the French Directory, and it appears to be making considerable Progress; but there is Reason to hope that it has at length attracted the Notice of the Governments of those Places.[48]

With its secret committee report, the English government turned the spotlight on Hamburg in the spring of 1799. Although the paper's accuracy left a great deal to be desired – the 'Philanthropic Society' for instance had long been banned – it carried Hamburg's embarrassment to extremes. But rather than deciding the ongoing tug of war concerning the four Hamburg prisoners as well as the question of north German neutrality, 'it simply intensified the existing stalemate by terrifying Prussia into total inaction ... ' and by getting 'Hamburg to follow her example ... '.[49] London, however, did not give the city a chance to rest. In April, England sent warships to the mouth of the Elbe which, according to English government announcements, was to prevent possible French military intervention. On 5 April, Craufurd was informed about the principal reason for England's interference with Hamburg's neutrality. 'Rather than suffer Hamburgh to become a Station from which the Irish Rebels may with impunity carry on their treasonable Designs', he was given to understand, 'His Majesty is determined to incur the Inconvenience, whatever it may be, of placing that Port in a state of Blockade, and of trans-

---

48 Report from the Committee of Secrecy, 15 March 1799', in *Journals of the House of Commons of England*, vol. 54 (1798–99), 341.
49 Elliott, *Partners in Revolution*, 263; see also ibid., 258–9 for the secret committee report.

ferring the Commerce of His Subjects to other points equally well adapted for that purpose. I have already apprised you, that it is not the Importance of the Individuals that is here in question, but the point whether Hamburgh is, or is not a place, where the King may claim and enjoy the Rights and Advantages of an impartial Neutrality, notwithstanding any Menaces of His Enemies.'[50] Thus, Foreign Secretary Grenville had designs on forcing Hamburg as well as Berlin into a corner. While he knew of Hamburg's dilemma, Grenville was convinced that only this show of strength would tip the scale in England's favour. 'I conclude from it', he wrote on 18 April 1799, 'that Messieurs les Hamburgeois are not a little afraid of all these great protectors, and I cannot much blame them for it. The Senate has written to me to beg to leave to send Napper Tandy and his colleagues about their business, but I am adamant.'[51] After watching United activities in Hamburg for more than two years, London did not want to stand by and do nothing as in the years before. It put its full weight behind the extradition of the Irish prisoners to gain the upper hand in the Hamburg affair. The free German city had developed into a diplomatic theatre of war, with the Irish prisoners as a mere pawn in the contest for supremacy in north Germany. In the spring of 1799, however, while the Senate was still unable to force itself to take a decision, the four Irishmen stayed in the dark in their Hamburg dungeons.

Soon after their arrest on 24 November 1798, the Irish prisoners were the talk of the town. The Tandy affair highlighted existing divisions among the Hamburg burghers, thus reflecting the variety of sentiments as to the fundamental alignment of the city's policy. Craufurd was quick to realise that using the barometer of public opinion for his own ends might be of benefit for English claims. In early December 1798, he engaged Johann Wilhelm Archenholtz, a well known publicist and editor of the *Minerva*, to write a pamphlet relative to the arrest of the Irishmen, for which the German received ten pounds some time later. In his highly pro-English article, dated 6 December, Archenholtz criticised Hamburg's city fathers. Why had they not handed over the Irish prisoners before those were claimed by the French? Since the Irishmen had not passed themselves off as French officers, France would have no right to demand their release. While Archenholtz went into details about the nobility of British warfare, he warned against incurring Britain's wrath. Unlike France, it would present no problem for England to destroy Hamburg as well as its commercial foundations. Therefore, he declared himself strongly in favour of the immediate extradition of the four

50 PRO F.O. 33/18/12–3, Cleveland Row to Craufurd, 5 April 1799.
51 Historical Manuscripts Commission, *Report on the Manuscripts of J.B. Fortescue*, V, 14; see Wohlwill, *Neuere Geschichte der Freien und Hansestadt Hamburg*, 233.

prisoners in order to preserve Hamburg's economy from harm.[52] Archenholtz's partisan pamphlet soon became the subject of much criticism, and a paper was published in response. The author of *Einige Bemerkungen* pulled Archenholtz's arguments to pieces, describing his article as 'useless' and 'pointless', since it was obviously directed towards influencing Hamburg's decision-makers.[53] While the international dispute dragged on, various Hamburg residents continued to show a lively interest in the Irish prisoners. Thus, French republicans debated about the steps to be taken in behalf of the Irishmen. In concert with local liberals, such as Chapeaurouge or Unzer, several meetings were held throughout 1798–9. Also Samuel Turner took part in the discussions. The Hamburg sources reveal that he was still in close touch with French authorities in Hamburg and Paris as well as with Irish and English dissidents in the French capital, among those Joseph Orr, Thomas Corbet, Thomas Paine or General Clarke, the future Duc de Feltre. Although he certainly played no small part in the arrest of the Irishmen, Turner pretended to be deeply sympathetic over their unfortunate fate. He wrote two letters to Blackwell and *Prätor* Günther to the effect that he confirmed his intention to do everything within his power to alleviate the situation of the Irish prisoners. Turner's hypocritical letters, which survived in the *Hamburger Staatsarchiv*, show further proof of the Ulsterman's showing as a double agent, who knew how to poke his nose into everything.[54]

While the Tandy affair had wide repercussions at a local as well as an international level, the four Irishmen remained in captivity. Descriptions of the circumstances of their detention are varied, but mostly based on Corbet and Tandy's *Conduct*, written several years after their stay in Hamburg. English-speaking studies, in particular, fail to take account of the prisoners' papers in the *Hamburger Staatsarchiv*, thus giving unrestricted credit to the showmanship of Corbet and Tandy.[55] According to Corbet's *Conduct*, he himself

---

52 *Betrachtung eines Hamburger Bürgers über die Verhaftung einiger Irländer allhier* (Hamburg, 1798); see PRO F.O. 33/18/218, account of secret service expenses by Craufurd for Archenholtz's engagement.

53 *Einige Bemerkungen über die unter dem Titel: Betrachtungen eines Hamburger Bürgers über die Inhaftierung einiger Irländer allhier, erschienene Schrift* (Hamburg, 1798).

54 Ham. Staats. Senat Cl. 1, Lit. Pb, Vol. 8c, Fasc. 2, Nr. 21, Lelarge's reports of 8 December 1798, 26 January, 1, 9, 16, 22 February, 18 May 1799 relative to the French republicans' interest in the Irish prisoners, including letter on Roberts (Turner's alias) of 16 February 1799; Ham. Staats. Senat Cl. 1, Lit. Pb, Vol. 8d, Fasc. 15b1, Inv. 3 & 4, Turner's letters of 15 April & 4 June 1799; see also PRO P.C.I/43/A.152, Turner's letter, Altona, 28 December 1798, and Fitzpatrick, *Secret Service Under Pitt*, 31–4 for his contacts.

55 TCD MS. 5967, Corbet's *The Conduct of the Senate of Hamburgh* (1807), including Tandy's account, written a few days before his death in August 1803; Ní Chinnéide,

was 'thrown into a dungeon, where the water reached nearly to [his] knees ... ', shortly after his arrest on 24 November. Corbet bitterly bewailed the severeness of the cold and the appalling conditions in which he had to spend the first forty days of his imprisonment. He was subsequently moved from prison to prison, but conditions only differed with regard to the degree of the dreadfulness he had to endure. Corbet, as well as Morres and Blackwell, made several bids for freedom, all of which were foiled thanks to the help of Samuel Turner. Going into detail about his last attempt to escape from his prison cell, Corbet voiced his suspicion, stating that 'the same traitor who had formerly deranged my plans, discovered all to the English minister Crawford, who immediately gave orders to have our guards changed and that those of the different posts of Hamburgh should be doubled, which contin- ued even to our departure.' Turner did not fail to lend a willing ear to his compatriots and their confidential information. He subsequently conveyed news to Craufurd, who in turn sent word to the Senate of the Irishman's plans. Corbet, however, remained in captivity. Some eight years later, he forced out into the open the 'infamous outrages done to that great nation [France] ... by mercenary Magistrates, bribed by the Gold of England ... '.[56]

Although his slightly propagandistic *Conduct* has to be taken with a pinch of salt, it has to be conceded that Corbet had a rough time in Hamburg. The Senate's 'Account of Expenses for Prisoners' verifies the assumption that Corbet did not fare as well as Tandy and Blackwell, both of whom were given preferential treatment by the city fathers. Moreover, he seems to have spoiled things for himself with the men on guard by 'venturing all kinds of impu- dences', as one of the sentinels reported to his superiors. In the course of his imprisonment, numerous complaints about Corbet reached the Senate, and one is led to believe that the Irishman was partly responsible for the regrettable circumstances he had to endure.[57] While conditions for the other Irishmen had already vastly improved, the Senate does not appear to have lightened Corbet's burden by the beginning of 1799. In the early months of the year,

Napper Tandy and the European Crises, 9–14, Coughlan, *Napper Tandy*, 154–6, Elliott, *Partners in Revolution*, 261–3. Coughlan and, to a lesser extent, Elliott's accounts of the Hamburg prisoners are, for the most part, based on Ní Chinnéide, who, however, makes little use of the sources of the *Hamburger Staatsarchiv*.

56 TCD MS. 5967/4–12, Corbet's account of his imprisonment. See Fitzpatrick, *Secret Service under Pitt*, 79 for Turner's betrayal and Ham. Staats. Senat Cl. 1, Lit. Pb, Vol. 8d, Fasc. 15b1, Inv. 6, on Craufurd giving notice of the intended escape.

57 Ham. Staats. Senat Cl. 1, Lit. Pb, Vol. 8d, Fasc. 15b1, Inv. 3, account of expenses for the Irish prisoners & letters relative to the prisoners, including Lieutenant Laurence's let- ter on Corbet, 25 February 1799.

he kept bombarding the Senate with a deluge of letters, furiously protesting against the 'inhumanity' and the 'cruelty' with which he was treated. Furthermore, he retailed his distress to the city fathers at the 'Corrupted Air' in his cell, which was 'so unwholesome that the Sentinels almost daily fall down, to all appearances dead & are with difficulty recovered', as he reported on 27 March 1799. He continued, 'The Sentinel for several weeks had orders not to let me sleep. Their cruelty at one time forced me to endeavour to get possession of a Sword and thus end an existence, they rendered insupportable. This they have represented falsely as an attempt to make my escape.' Corbet, by the way, was to describe the same incident as an attempt at escape in his highly dramatic *Conduct* several years later. On closer examination, Corbet's marked tendency towards a rather liberal interpretation of truth becomes plainly recognizable. On 24 March, only three days before he wrote the above-quoted letter to the Senate, he addressed his thanks to *Prätor* Günther. 'I acknowledge with gratitude', he stated, 'the kind Attention and Civility I have received from you since your Praetorship commenced'. Not in the slightest, does his respectful letter to Günther reveal the weariness of life Corbet expressed a few days later. Only shortly afterwards, the Irishman bothered Günther with less polite news. 'I must at present look upon you as the most deadly Enemy I have in the World', he started, 'the injuries you have done to me are irreparable. The rapid Decay which my Health has undergone these last days leaves me no hope of ever recovering that Excellent Constitution which I enjoyed till destroyed by the Neglect I have experienced since your Praetorship commenced. I no longer apply to you to be removed to another Prison. It is too late. My only Hope at present is that Death will soon free me from its Horrors.' In fact, it was not too late for Corbet in that spring of 1799. Thanks to the new *Prätor* Günther, who had taken the place of Klefeker in February, conditions appear to have been made tolerable for the Irish prisoners, and Corbet stopped sending letters to the Hamburg authorities by the early summer of the same year.[58]

While Corbet was changed from prison to prison, not least because of his attempted break-outs, his fellow prisoners spent most of their time in the dungeons of the police station near the Gänsemarkt. There, Blackwell wrote a number of letters to various French authorities in Germany and France, all of which were subsequently intercepted by the Hamburg police. In this way, however, he tried to draw attention to the situation of the Irish prisoners. In one of these letters, dated 15 germinal an 7 (4 April 1799) and addressed to Jean Debrie, French minister plenipotentiary at the Rastadt negotiations,

---

58 Ham. Staats. Senat Cl. 1, Lit. Pb, Vol. 8d, Fasc. 15b1, Inv. 4, Corbet's letters; see TCD
    MS. 5967/8–9 for Corbet's account of his attempt at escape.

Blackwell bewailed his wretched fate. 'The situation of my feelings is also easy to grasp, difficult to describe', he informed Debrie, 'here in irons and doomed to inaction, in a moment when my comrades and friends march and fight against loathsome hordes of slaves of coalising tyrants.' Blackwell never failed to express his loyalty to the Revolution, let alone the great services he claimed to have rendered France. Thus, he also wrote to Langau on 29 prairial an 7 (17 May 1799) to the effect that he complained about 'the free and neutral city of Hamburg betraying a citizen, an officer, whose only fault it is to love liberty and hate the government of England.' In a turgid and often French-coloured style of writing, Blackwell presented himself in a favourable light and also provided his fellow prisoners with enthusiastic exhortations to hold out. 'I say from my heart Erin-go-Bragh', he tried to cheer up Tandy on 11 May. The distinguishing feature of his letters is the intrepid persistence with which he maintained his political convictions, and yet, one simply can not avoid being filled with wonder in the face of Blackwell's eccentric patriotism. At any rate, he did not become lost in plaintive correspondences with Hamburg's city fathers, whom he scarcely addressed at all. The Senate had already started to improve conditions for Blackwell towards the end of 1798, and in the late spring of the following year, he had been granted a teacher of German to lighten his lot. As time progressed, however, also Blackwell poured his distress to Günther on 21 thermidor an 7 (8 August 1799). After a captive state of almost nine months, he gave vent to his dejection, writing 'that my feelings are so triste and so irksome, caused by my suffrances, on mind and on body, that I am far from being in a state of engaging myself in poetic fictions. Everybody here suffers illegally in irons of a prison which is unlucky and I think deplorable.' The deprivations of his confinement started to wear down Blackwell, who seemed to be at the end of his tether by the summer of 1799.[59]

Tandy's letters are missing in the *Hamburger Staatsarchiv*, according to an entry in his file dated 1980, so that surveys on his imprisonment have to rely merely on his own account of the Hamburg affair, written shortly before his death in August 1803. Like Blackwell, however, also Tandy was given preferential treatment by the Senate. He had stayed in a tiny dungeon in the first few hours after his arrest, before being transferred to a watchhouse on the ramparts. There, he was chained up for ten days, but subsequently moved to the police station near the Gänsemarkt, where he had to wait out the remainder of his stay in Hamburg. Thanks 'to the French Minister who had claimed [him] as a French Officer', Tandy enjoyed certain privileges towards the end of 1798. Compared with his fellow prisoners, he lived in relative

59 Ham. Staats. Senat Cl. 1, Lit. Pb, Vol. 8d, Fasc. 15b1, Inv. 4, Blackwell's letters.

comfort in a tolerable room, with a proper bed, good food as well as wine, and was also provided with English periodicals and books, according to Morres. With an English-speaker at his disposal, Tandy was in the happy position of having an advocate, who conveyed his wishes directly to the authorities. Moreover, he was looked after by an officer, who came to enquire about his health every day. 'Their visits produced a good effect', Tandy wrote later, 'it prevented the Hamburghers, who are naturally a dirty people, from smoking and spitting in my room as they used before.' Thus, Tandy was comfortably off with regard to prison conditions, and despite of his advanced age (he was over sixty in 1799), he got through his confinement relatively well.[60]

Morres had to be content with less comfort while in Hamburg. In his first letter to Günther, dated 19 March 1799, he only asked for a 'lock of my wife's hair', which was in the waistcoat that had been confiscated from him on his arrest. This he described as 'the greatest imaginable favor I can ask' and stated that 'it will be a comfort, and happiness for me, in my melancholy prison, an enjoyment beyond expression.' A few weeks later, a ray of hope made him snap out of his melancholy. At the beginning of April, Craufurd took trouble over Morres's well-being, asking permission of his London superiors to effect the release of Morres and Corbet, since they had not been claimed by the French Republic. He assured Grenville that the Senate would be 'ready to deliver them up whenever I may demand them.' Craufurd, however, was soon warned against 'taking any steps whatever respecting those persons.' Portland himself had intervened, declaring the two Irishmen 'in every respect unworthy of His Majesty's favour' and 'highly deserving of the utmost exemplary punishment that the Law can inflict.'[61] Corbet and Morres's case was put aside again. On the whole, Morres himself was restrained in his comments about his situation in the early spring of 1799, but became thereafter absorbed in adventurous plans. This can be explained by the fact that his (as well as Corbet's) health had 'much suffered', according to the report of a medical examination of the Irishmen. By April, Morres was in a terrible state of nerves, which obviously impaired his perceptive faculties.[62] On 12 April, he asked 'for the permission to be banned into a neutral country', but confirmed that he 'will always be ready to serve his motherland against all

60 TCD MS. 5967/25–30, Tandy's account of the Hamburg affair. See Ham. Staats. Senat Cl. 1, Lit. Pb, Vol. 8d, Fasc. 15b1, Inv. 4, Morres on Tandy.
61 PRO F.O. 33/18/35–6, 46, 115–6, Craufurd to Grenville, 9 April 1799, Downing Street to Craufurd, 19 April 1799, Portland to Grenville, 13 May 1799. See Ham. Staats. Senat Cl. 1, Lit. Pb, Vol. 8d, Fasc. 15b1, Inv. 6, Craufurd's efforts on behalf of Morres and Corbet.
62 PRO F.O. 33/18/132, 133, 147, report of the surgeon, 1 May 1799, Morres to Günther, 22 April 1799, Craufurd to Hammon, 14 May 1799.

external and internal enemies' and that he would like to talk to Craufurd about 'all these things'. Starting in April, the balance of Morres's mind became disturbed. His letters to Günther, for the most part written in German by a helping hand whose name is not mentioned, present a confusing picture of manic-depressive fits, contemplative moods and crazy notions of how to get out of his hopeless situation. 'I have this day requested to be delivered up to England in order to stand my trial', he informed Günther on 13 July 1799, 'death is preferable to be buried alive as I am; and I have more to hope from the British Government at this moment, than from the humanity of my keepers. It will be a comfort for my very family to know me free from torments of mind and body which I am now exposed to, and nearly no longer am able to bear.' On several occasions, Morres made it manifest that he was prepared to do everything to escape from his endless suffering. After hearing about several Irishmen being transported from Waterford to Emden in order to join the Prussian army, he wrote to Günther on 9 September 1799, 'I, too, wish to serve the Prussian monarch, and herewith offer my services to Your Royal Majesty.' He urged Günther to talk to the Prussian legate on his behalf, but emphasized that 'nobody, on no account, should be allowed to ask me to ever serve against my Motherland, and neither, at the present moment, in a time of war, against France ... '. A few weeks later, he repeated his request. Morres, however, was not taken at his word, but released from his agony in a different way.[63]

While the Senate was still trying to wriggle out of its dilemma in the spring and summer of 1799, the Hamburg affair took a new turn. By the middle of the year, the fortunes of war had turned against France which, over and above that, was shaken by Jacobin as well as Royalist insurrections. The armies of the Second Coalition were making a good showing 'and, by August, the French were driven back once more behind their own frontiers.'[64] In the same month, after much hesitation, the Prussian court had finally made up its mind. Although the French armies were in retreat, and Berlin declared against taking sides with either of the great powers, leaving the decisions to the Senate, the Prussian king nonetheless gave a clear indication of his opinion that the prisoners should be delivered up to England.[65] Thus, a decision by Hamburg's city fathers became easier by the late summer of 1799, when, in the face of present French difficulties, the Senate forced itself to take a decision after

63 Ham. Staats. Senat Cl. 1, Lit. Pb, Vol. 8d, Fasc. 15b1, Inv. 4, Morres's letters.
64 Ní Chinnéide, *Napper Tandy and the European Crises*, 14; see Sutherland, D.M.G., *France 1798–1815. Revolution and Counterrevolution*, 2nd edn (London, 1988), 308–35 on France in 1799.
65 Ham. Staats. Senat Cl. 1, Lit. Pb, Vol. 8d, Fasc. 15b1, Inv. 10, negotiations with Prussia.

having put off one for more than ten months. On 27 September, the Senate sent word to Craufurd of its decision to hand over the Irishmen, which was eventually translated into action in the early morning of 1 October.[66]

The four prisoners were transported to England on board the HMS *Xenophon*, but were finally transferred to Ireland in November to stand their trial. In the meantime, the four Irishmen had been in the public eye for a year. Their extradition had eventually caused an uproar on the part of the many sympathizers they had attracted. The British authorities had lost interest in actually finishing off the Irishmen on the scaffold, all the more as also most European powers supported their cause. Thus, Tandy was sentenced to death, but finally set free at London's behest and subsequently shipped to France on board the *Favourite Nancy*. On 14 March 1802, he reached Bordeaux, where he was given the red carpet treatment, which certainly fit in very well with his predilection for histrionics. His three friends, however, were released or allowed to escape and eventually reunited in France in the course of the same year.[67]

For the Senate, the extradition did not end the embarrassment that had been caused by the Irishmen. While the conservative powers tried to restore their connections with Hamburg (Russia, for instance, had terminated its embargo and re-established diplomatic relations in the course of the next weeks), the French government took appropriate steps to have its revenge on the city. In the meantime, Reinhard had succeeded Talleyrand as foreign minister on 20 June 1799. France's former minister at Hamburg, who had always been favourably disposed towards the city, had received a letter, dated 27 September, whereby the Senate informed Reinhard about its intention to deliver up the Irishmen, and at the same time, offered apologies for the intended extradition. The French foreign minister, however, returned the letter unopened, commenting that 'nothing could possibly justify the extradition of citizens Tandy and Blackwell and their companions.'[68] On 8 October, the French government denounced the extradition, accompanied by a decree to the effect that the Directory instructed its representatives to leave the free German city; Hamburg officials in France were ordered to depart from their respective residences within the next twenty-four hours and were given eight days to quit the country. Moreover, an embargo was put on all Hamburg

66 Ham. Staats. Senat Cl. 1, Lit. Pb, Vol. 8d, Fasc. 15b1, Inv. 16, records relative to the extradition of the Irish prisoners.
67 Ní Chinnéide, *Napper Tandy and the European Crises*, 18–22 and Coughlan, *Napper Tandy*, 170–228.
68 Ham. Staats. Senat Cl. 1, Lit. Pb, Vol. 8d, Fasc. 15b1, Inv. 7a, Senate to Reinhard, 27 September 1799 and Reinhard's reply, 19 vendémiaire an 8 (11 October 1799).

ships in French ports in order to cripple the city's economy. Meanwhile, Napoléon's return from Egypt on the 9 October raised French hopes that the popular general would finish off the Second Coalition. Soon after arriving in France, he had become involved in an anti-Directoral conspiracy, which eventually led to the coup d'état of 18 brumaire (9 November 1799) and to the foundation of the Consulate. By the time Hamburg's second note of apology, dated 13 December, reached France, Bonaparte had already established himself as the head of the new government. The Senate's 'grovelling letter', as it was later described by the German historian Laufenberg, was a 'crude attempt to play off the new government against the old by means of a blatant distortion of the truth and a smart-bold argumentation of fabulous stupidity.' Bonaparte's famous and oft-quoted reply, however, was harsh in the extreme.[69]

> We have received your letter, gentlemen, it does not justify you. Courage and virtue preserve states, cowardice and dissoluteness ruin them. You have violated hospitality. That would not happen among the barbarous hordes of the desert. Our fellow citizens will forever reproach you for this. The two unfortunates that you delivered up will die most famously, but their blood will do more harm to their persecutors than an army could possibly do.[70]

Although Napoléon's attempt at intimidating the free German city caused a stir, his wrath was short-lived. He knew full well that Hamburg's neutral merchant fleet and the city's trade relations were of vital importance for keeping up French commercial links. In the face of the country's isolation within Europe, Napoléon would have been ill-advised to cut one of the most important threads of France's economic life. The embargo was lifted on 13 nivôse (3 January 1800). Thanks to Hamburg's eager negotiators in France, diplomatic relations between the Hanse town and the Republic were restored in the course of the next two years. Thus, the Tandy affair had kept Hamburg in suspense from the autumn of 1798 until the spring of 1802, when Reinhard finally arrived in the city for the second time to take up again the post of French minister at Hamburg.[71]

69 Laufenberg, *Hamburg und die Französische Revolution*, 83; Ham. Staats. Senat Cl. 1, Lit. Pb, Vol. 8d, Fasc. 15b1, Inv. 7a, negotiations with France; Servières, 'Un Épisode de l'Expédition d'Irlande', *Revue Historique*, 62–7, Ní Chinnéide, *Napper Tandy and the European Crises*, 14–7, Harder, *Die Auslieferung der Vier Politischen Flüchtlinge*, 55–69 and Sutherland, *France 1789–1815*, 331–2.

70 Ham. Staats. Senat Cl. 1, Lit. Pb, Vol. 8d, Fasc. 15b1, Inv. 7a, Napoléon to the Senate, 9 nivôse an 8 (30 December 1799).

71 Ham. Staats. Senat Cl. 1, Lit. Pb, Vol. 8d, Fasc. 15b1, Inv. 7b, 7c, 19, 20, Hamburg's

The Tandy affair had created a stir throughout Europe. Even in England, there was controversy about the issues of Hamburg's neutrality and the English interference with the city's interests. On 1 November 1799, the *Morning Chronicle* brought up the question whether 'the measure was proper in itself, and not as the Government of France loudly asserts in its Manifesto, contrary to the Law of Nations.' The author of 'The Question of Napper Tandy' reached the conclusion that for 'so-called state offences (e.g. High Treason), for the punishment of which we believe, the sanctuary of a foreign territory has rarely if ever in modern times, been violated. Treason against one society is often, as in the present calamitous times, encouraged and protected by another; and it has often happened, that from the nature of civil broils, the most virtuous characters in community have fallen under the denomination of rebels, and been obliged to escape the vengeance of the successful party by flying to a foreign country.' Thus, 'the right of giving asylum to Suppliants accused of High Treason has rarely if ever, in modern times, been very sternly disputed.' Condemning England's interference, however, did not necessarily mean standing up for Hamburg, which was belittled as a 'feeble neutral state'.[72] Hamburg's role in the Tandy affair mostly met with disapproval. Although the extradition of the Irishmen did not have lasting repercussions on the city, it nevertheless left an unpleasant taste. While relations with France were soon sorted out, the Hamburg episode had certainly an effect on the city's importance as a place of refuge for the Republic's disciples. Starting with the arrival of Craufurd, London laid greater emphasis on harassing the Irish *émigrés*, because the free German city had developed into the most important co-ordinating point between Ireland and its French ally by 1798. By that time, the United Irishmen had already been playing up England for two years, so that London was determined to finish off the Irishmen in Hamburg. In connection with the change in Britain's Hamburg policy, Duckett's arrest in Hanover only served as a half-hearted prelude to the show of strength, which London made some months later. Nonetheless, Duckett's arrest as well as the Tandy affair acted as deterrents to the United Irishmen, who had already been set back by the suppression of rebellion in Ireland and the failure of the French expeditions.

negotiations with France, 1799–1802; Servières, 'Un Épisode de l'Expédition d'Irlande', *Revue Historique*, 67–8, Harder, *Die Auslieferung der Vier Politischen Flüchtlinge*, 68–71 and Ní Chinnéide, *Napper Tandy and the European Crises*, 17–8. Ní Chinnéide's conclusion that the embargo was withdrawn in April 1801 is not in accordance with the Hamburg sources (and neither with Servières or Harder), which reveal that the embargo was lifted in January 1800.

72 *Morning Chronicle*, 1 November 1799. See also Ham. Staats. Senat Cl. 1, Lit. Pb, Vol. 8d, Fasc. 15b1, Inv. 21, the French press on the Tandy affair.

CHAPTER 6

New Wanderers and the
'Exiles of Erin', 1799–1802[1]

The international crisis revolving around the Hamburg prisoners was followed by a decisive break in the pattern of United migration to and from the
Continent. In the wake of the suppression of the Irish insurrection and the
failure of the French expeditions, United migration to the Continent had
reached its climax towards the end of 1798. Thereafter, Irish radical wanderers
decreased in numbers, a fact which was particularly noticeable in Hamburg,
once the undisputed stopping-off place between Ireland and France. To a certain degree, the city lost its political importance for the United Irishmen, and
yet, one should not be blind to the fact that most important United missions
in the years subsequent to the crisis of 1798–9 did enter Hamburg. This can
only partly be explained by the deterrent effect of the Tandy episode. Crediting
the Tandy affair as the sole reason for the drop in United arrivals in the free
German city would be an oversimplification of events. In fact, the decrease
in the numbers of Irish *émigrés* in Hamburg corresponded with a waning
wanderlust of the United Irishmen which, in turn, was due to changed circumstances within the home movement as well as to the presence of a new government in France. At a time when peace was in the offing, the general political
climate in Europe was not apt to further United–French relations. In the early
years of the nineteenth century, the end of the Second Coalition became
apparent, and French foreign policy-makers did not seriously contemplate
elaborating new plans for another descent on Ireland. Hamburg's importance
for the United Irishmen, however, should not be measured in terms of the
number of reports on Irish *émigrés*. Accounts of United activities in the city
suffer substantially from the fact that the French diplomatic mission was dis-

---

1 Poem by Thomas Campbell, who arrived in Hamburg in 1798, see *Correspondence of Charles,
First marquis Cornwallis*, ed. Charles Ross, II (London, 1859), 362.

banded in April 1799. It was not before the spring of 1802 that France fully re-established diplomatic relations with Hamburg, which to a certain degree took away the Irishmen's incentive to head for the free German city. Moreover, Craufurd, who had been ever vigilant for Irish radicals, left Hamburg in December 1799 and only returned towards the close of the following year; in December 1801, he eventually packed his bags for good. His replacement, and in turn his successor, did not see themselves as men from the secret service, and turned their attention to their diplomatic tasks. In the absence of Craufurd, reporting on United Irishmen in Hamburg was in eclipse.

I

Popular disaffection kept Ireland on the simmer in the months following the insurrection. In some parts of the country, bands of *banditti* continued to create unrest throughout the winter of 1798–9, the impetus behind their activities ranging from agrarian grievances, to loyalist sentiments, and French-coloured republicanism. While Ireland was still in a state of turmoil after the rebellion, the tide was on the turn for the United Irishmen. Those leaders in the Dublin prisons, who had not fallen victim to the bloody clashes and subsequent executions, had come to an arrangement with the Irish government. Under the aegis of Arthur O'Connor, William James MacNeven and Thomas Addis Emmet, the so-called state prisoners had showed themselves willing to give evidence on the internal affairs of the United Irishmen since the Society's foundation in 1791 in order to prevent further executions from being carried out. Moreover, they had in mind to save their own skin by getting the government to agree to their banishment to a foreign country. However, although the 'Kilmainham Treaty' had been signed and sealed by the beginning of August 1798, they achieved only partial success. O'Connor, MacNeven, Emmet and about seventeen other top United leaders were transported to Fort George, Scotland, in the spring of 1799, where they were to be held captive until the end of the war.[2] Several hundred state prisoners of lesser importance were sent abroad in the course of the following years. In accordance with the Banishment Act, which had resulted from the Kilmainham negotiations, many United men were set free and allowed to leave for countries not at war with Britain. In an endeavour to rid themselves of their awkward malcontents, British authorities

2 *Memoirs and Correspondence of Viscount Castlereagh*, I, 353–72, Memoir of the State Prisoners; PRO P.C.I/3117 and 3526, McDowell, *Ireland in the Age of Imperialism*, 655–67 and Elliott, *Partners in Revolution*, 208–10 and 243–5 on the state prisoners and the Irish situation in the aftermath of the rebellion of 1798.

even thought of shipping some prisoners to Hamburg, but soon discarded the plan. 'Under the circumstances attending the arrest of Napper Tandy and his associates, both the duke of Portland and Lord Grenville are anxious that no persons of that description should be sent publicly to Hamburg, at least, not till after the result of this affair shall be known', Wickham informed Castlereagh on 10 January 1799. In fact, it was not before September 1799 that some 310 United prisoners were deported to the north German coastal town of Emden in order to join the Prussian army. At the end of the year, Dublin Castle appeared to have disposed of its difficulties, if it had not been for the Fort George prisoners, who continued to be a thorn in the flesh of the British authorities.[3]

Although shattered by a succession of heavy set-backs, the United Irishmen survived the events of 1798. Deprived of its leadership, a new generation of United leaders rose from the ashes of the rebellion. Men, such as Robert Emmet, William Putnam McCabe or George Palmer, most of whom had been of secondary importance prior to the Irish insurrection, came to the fore, subsequently playing a decisive part in rebuilding the crippled Society. In the aftermath of the rebellion, however, the old leaders in the Dublin prisons still set the tone in the period of transition, which followed the summer of 1798. Although relatively little is known about the details of their co-operation with the new leaders, the state prisoners had a hand in the reconstruction of the United movement. Furnished with the directives of Arthur O'Connor, Thomas Russell and their colleagues, the new leaders put a different complexion on United matters, this time placing greater emphasis on tightening the Society's structure. In the light of the movement's infiltration by government spies, which had contributed to the downfall of the original leadership on the eve of the insurrection, the post-rebellion leaders reorganised the Society from scratch. The re-formed United Irishmen were to avoid a ramified hierarchy of committees and subcommittees, which could be easily penetrated by secret agents. Decision-making powers were to be in the hands of a few persons to preclude United leaders from getting bogged down in fruitless debates on general principles. The Society had to be put on a stricter and more exclusive basis, even though this meant a voluntary numerical curtailment. The lower ranks of the movement would have to be constituted in the instance of a French landing, which was to be the crucial prerequisite for another attempt at a rising. Therefore, securing French assistance took precedence over the

---

3 *Memoirs and Correspondence of Viscount Castlereagh*, II, 86–7, Wickham to Castlereagh, 10 January 1799; PRO H.O. 100/88/98–113 for the wording of the Banishment Act; McDowell, *Ireland in the Age of Imperialism*, 676–7 for United prisoners in the Prussian service.

creation of a mass movement. Since the new leaders thought it prudent to keep their intentions secret, little news of United affairs became public knowledge. Thus, Dublin and London knew little of United moves in the years after the insurrection. In the course of 1798, established sources of information began to dry up. John Edward Newell had already stopped operating as a government spy in the early months of the year; followed by Thomas Reynolds, whose information had led to the March arrests and who had subsequently blown his own cover by giving evidence in open court. Leonard McNally was not taken into the new leaders' confidence; and also Samuel Turner's star was on the decline in the aftermath of the rebellion. If it had not been for the Belfast United Irishman James McGucken, government officials would have been destitute of efficient help from within the movement. Dublin and London, however, mostly remained puzzled about the post-rebellion Society, since McGucken did not penetrate into the highest echelons of the United Irishmen. For the most part, the authorities were also faced with a riddle with regard to United activities abroad. Due to the new leaders' obsession with secrecy, United travellers henceforth trod more carefully on the Continent than their predecessors.[4]

II

In the early months of 1799 there were Irish efforts to revive the crippled communication between Ireland and France. With this aim in view, an Irishman named O'Reilley reached Hamburg from Copenhagen in February. Around the middle of the same month, he set out for Paris, but he is reported to have stopped off at Amsterdam only as late as 12 March. According to Craufurd, O'Reilley hoped to set out soon 'with the expedition which is preparing at the Texel for Ireland.' While O'Reilley's hopes were certainly a misinterpretation of French intentions, he in fact returned to the British Isles to carry news to the disaffected. By mid-April, he was in London, after staying in France 'on business from the London Corresponding Society', as one 'repentant Member of the L.C.S.' informed the duke of Portland on 2 May. Very little is known of O'Reilley. It is unclear whether he can be identified as Terence O'Reilley, mentioned in Byrne's *Memoirs*, or Richard O'Reilley, described by Marianne Elliott. The British authorities, moreover, lost track of him after his visit to London in April/May.[5] At any rate, his efforts signify the

4 Elliott, *Partners in Revolution*, 243–51; PRO P.C.I/44/A.155, Madden, *The United Irishmen*, 2nd ser., 1st vol., 144–311 and 1st edn, 1st vol., 205–332 for the post-rebellion Society, the state prisoners and government espionage.
5 PRO F.O. 33/17/126 & 245–8, Craufurd to Grenville, 12 February & 12 March 1799;

determination of the Irish to secure French military assistance after the set-backs of the previous year. In connection with this, Duckett's old friend Sidderson passed through Hamburg in the first half of March. Like Duckett, he had been a student at the Irish College in Paris and had also been a member of the 1793 propaganda mission to Ireland. Around mid-March 1799, he was again on the way to Ireland, from where he was to 'correspond with Duckett', as Craufurd assumed. Though the circumstances of his mission are unclear, there is no doubt about the political implication of his journey.[6] In the following month, another United messenger arrived in Hamburg. Although the young Hanoverian Lescham [Lischam] said that he was 'employed to go to England to procure a man to superintend the great manufactory of Wedgewoodware at Paris', he aroused Craufurd's suspicion. While in Hamburg, Lescham had talked carelessly about French plans for a descent on Ireland in the near future. Moreover, the observant English minister found out that Lescham had been 'frequently at Muir's' while staying in Paris for the last two years, and further that the Hanoverian was in possession of letters from some of the Irish at Paris to their friends in Ireland. Thus, by the time Lescham reached England, Craufurd's superiors had taken steps to intercept him. His apprehension in London in early May confirmed Craufurd's suspicion: Lescham was found to be in possession of letters from Lewins and several other United Irish in France.[7]

United activities in the spring of 1799 seem to point to a belief among Irishmen that a French expedition was imminent. While their communications are somewhat confusing, it is apparent that the United brethren in Ireland and France were at pains to revive the Franco–Irish alliance. The free German city remained the preferred crossroads between Ireland and France, as indicated by numerous reports that reached Dublin and London in the first half of 1799. A confused uneasiness prevailed in Britain with regard to French intentions as well as to the nature of the co-operation between France and the United Irishmen.[8] The government's nervousness is reflected in the arrest of Jan

P.C.I/44/A.158, secret information, 2 May 1799; Memoirs of Miles Byrne, III, 188–9 and Elliott, *Partners in Revolution*, 347–8.

6 PRO F.O. 33/17/245–6, Craufurd to Grenville, 12 March 1799. See Swords, *The Green Cockade*, 108–17, Elliott, *Partners in Revolution*, 59 and chapter 3 of this survey on the propaganda mission of 1793, including Duckett and Sidderson.

7 PRO F.O. 33/18/60–1, Craufurd to Grenville, 19 April 1799; Nat. Arch. 620/18^A/11, Wickham to Castlereagh, 7 May 1799.

8 PRO H.O. 100/85/281–3, 100/86/317, 365, 100/87/67–8; P.C.I/44/A.155, A.158, A.161; Nat. Arch. 620/18^A/11, *Memoirs and Correspondence of Viscount Castlereagh*, II, 132, 165–8, 193–5, 200–1, 206–7, 229–30, reports on Hamburg and rumours of a French expedition, January-August 1799.

Anders Jägerhorn in March, some two months before also Lescham was apprehended. The Swede had been an unknown quantity in 1797, when he had met Lord Edward Fitzgerald in London, but he attracted the authorities' attention on his business trip to the British capital in 1799.[9]

London tried hard to get an idea of United–French activities in 1799. Apart from various agents on the Continent, Captain d'Auvergne, Prince of Bouillon, for instance, put the British government in the picture about French naval movements from his base on the Channel Islands.[10] Joseph Pollock, who had already been of good service to the government by inducing Samuel Turner to change sides in mid-1797, kept his ears to the ground in London; and James McGucken was at pains to pick up information from the new United leaders in Ireland, to say nothing of well-tried informers like Francis Higgins and Leonard McNally, who, however, appear to have outlived their usefulness by the end of the century. Moreover, British authorities succeeded in enlisting Captain Mumphort's support for their efforts to infiltrate the United Irishmen. In the last two years, Mumphort had carried United emissaries to and from the Continent, among others James Coigley, the O'Finns, William Bailey and William Hamilton. By the spring of 1799, he had sold his services to the British government, and in May, he was already on his way to France to sound out the United Irishmen in Paris. On arriving in the French capital on 19 June, Mumphort set about making use of his old contacts, namely Bailey and Hamilton, offering to convey news to Ireland. But the United Irish in France had already set to work on their own initiative. Some five days before, an Irishman named O'Mealy had left Paris in order to travel to Ireland. Furnished with dispatches from Lewins, Bailey and Hamilton, he had been commissioned both to update the United men at home and to gather information on the state of affairs in Ireland. On hearing about O'Mealy's mission, Mumphort immediately followed his trail to London. The Irish messenger was not unfamiliar to Mumphort, who had transported O'Mealy to and from France on several occasions, but he was forced to realise that the United agent had already penetrated through to the north of Ireland. Although Craufurd reckoned on O'Mealy coming to Hamburg in October, there is no clue to his whereabouts after Mumphort had lost sight of him in the summer of 1799.[11]

9 *Memoirs and Correspondence of Viscount Castlereagh*, II, 242–65, PRO P.C.I/44/A.158 on Jägerhorn's arrest. See chapter 3 of this study for Jägerhorn's mission to Britain in 1797.

10 *Memoirs and Correspondence of Viscount Castlereagh*, I, 250, 373, 382, II, 104–5, 162–7, 266–9, 297–8, 376–8; PRO H.O. 69/26–30, W.O.I/921–4 for examples of Bouillon's information; see Fitzpatrick, *Secret Service Under Pitt*, 38–9 on Bouillon. See PRO W.O.I/396–7, various agents on the Continent.

11 Nat. Arch. 3332/1, Mumphort's secret information, 24 July 1799; PRO F.O. 33/19/201, Craufurd to Grenville, 19 October 1799; see *Memoirs and Correspondence of Viscount*

Startled by rumours of a possible French invasion of Ireland, England was on the alert for United activities in the spring and summer of 1799. In the preceding years, the British secret service had greatly benefitted from its foreign agents. Intelligence of United activities at home had often been obtained by keeping a vigilant eye on the Irish radicals abroad. Subsequent to the suppression of the rebellion, however, the new United leaders tried to prevent the easy infiltration by government agents by remodelling the Society's organization. For the most part, the British government failed to bring its efforts into line with the changed conditions within the home movement. The overall picture of United decision-making remained blurred.

Little was known about the circumstances of the dispatch of William Putnam McCabe and George Palmer, but it must be assumed that they were instructed to petition the French government for another expedition to Ireland. According to Joseph Pollock in London, the two United men left Ireland in the first half of December 1798. They sailed from Dublin to Liverpool on a packet boat and subsequently made their way to London. On arrival, the two agents got in touch with United Irish circles, which had survived the events of 1798. They had meetings with Valentine Lawless, the key United intermediary on the British mainland since the end of 1797, John Bonham and William Dowdall. The three United leaders in London had been arrested at the height of the insurrection scare at the end of May 1798, together with McGucken, but had been released again several months afterwards. In the years to come, the Irish radicals in London kept in touch with their United brethren in Ireland and continued to serve as a crucial bridgehead for United agents on their way to and from the Continent.[12] McCabe and Palmer stayed in London for some time. At the beginning of February, they were 'on the point of setting out from London' for Hamburg, together with William St John Mason, another United messenger, who had recently arrived in the capital. According to Craufurd's reports, the Irish agents attempted to sail for the north German coast in March, but could not get further than Heligoland and subsequently returned to the British mainland. There, they must have received word of the Irish state prisoners' transfer to Fort George in the second half of March. McCabe and Palmer started out for Scotland some time after the disruption

Castlereagh, II, 359–62 & 371–2 for Mumphort's enlistment. See chapter 4 of this study for Mumphort's activities in 1797–8.

12 Nat. Arch. 620/7/74/1–2, secret information from Pollock, 2 January 1799; PRO H.O. 100/66/415, 100/76/304, 309, 100/77/90, 93; Wells, *Insurrection*, 153–6 and McDowell, *Ireland in the Age of Imperialism*, 480 on Lawless, Bonham, Dowdall and McGucken. See Wells, *Insurrection*, 162–77 and Elliott, *Partners in Revolution*, 252–8 on the connections between the United Irishmen in Ireland and England after the rebellion.

of their journey to the Continent to interchange ideas with the arrested United leaders. They managed to make contact with Arthur O'Connor, who provided them with a letter to the Directory. They remained in Britain until later that summer, when they eventually continued their journey. Accompanied by the United agent George Wilkinson and most likely also William St John Mason, McCabe and Palmer reached Hamburg under the assumed identities of Craig and Wilson at the beginning of August 1799. The Irishmen had left O'Connor's letter in England in the hands of a good friend for reasons of security. In Hamburg, they did not encounter any difficulties in procuring travel permits for their journey to France. On account of McCabe's earlier association with her husband, Lady Pamela took it upon herself to support the Irish messengers. She introduced them to Parandier, the French agent, who promised to do the Irishmen a service. By mid-August, they had left Hamburg for Paris.[13]

At the time the Irishmen finally arrived in Paris, France was in a state of turmoil. Due to military defeats by the armies of the Second Coalition, and to royalist and Jacobin upheavals, the Directory was on the decline by the late summer of 1799. The opposition to the government had grown substantially throughout the year, and when Napoléon eventually returned from Egypt on 9 October, the anti-Directoral coalition fêted him as its providential liberator. The coup d'état of 18 brumaire (9 November 1799) finally brought down the Directory one month later. A provisional Consulate was set up, including Napoléon, Abbé Sieyès and Roger Ducos, but before long Bonaparte established himself as the sole ruler of the French nation. It was against this background that McCabe and Palmer reached Paris some time after their departure from Hamburg around mid-August; and the political instability in France must account for the fact that their stay in the country is shrouded in mystery. Reports on Hugh O'Hanlon, another of the new United leaders, and his letter to the Directory, dated 15 July 1799, but little else, have survived in the Paris archives.[14] There is some possibility that this was also due to the changed

13 Nat. Arch. 620/7/74/8 & 23, Pollock's information, 7 February & 26 April 1799; PRO F.O. 33/17/101–4, 126 and 33/19/50, 56–7 & 71, Craufurd's letters, 5 & 12 February and 6, 15 & 23 August 1799; P.C.I/44/A.161, secret information from Cleland, August 1799. Although Cleland does not mention McCabe's name, all the indications are that McCabe is the person referred to. See PRO P.C.I/3583, examinations of William St John Mason and Michael Farrell, 1 & 2 November 1803 and Nat. Arch. 620/11/130/45, secret information, 6 October 1803, various pieces of information on William St John Mason. See Elliott, 'The "Despard Conspiracy" Reconsidered', *Past and Present*, 75 (1977), 49–50 for Elliott's account of the mission of McCabe and Palmer.

14 Sutherland, *France 1789–1815*, 308–35 for the situation in France in 1798–9; Elliott, *Partners in Revolution*, 249 on O'Hanlon.

situation within the United Irish community in Paris. Lewins's claim to sole representation had done nothing to simplify Franco–Irish negotiations; it rather distorted Irish affairs in France, since he failed to pay heed to the changed nature of the United business. The terms of the instructions he had received in 1797 were outdated in 1799, when most of his former colleagues had disappeared from the scene. In the years following the insurrection, Lewins increasingly alienated himself from his United compatriots by showing a complete disregard for the concerns of the post-rebellion principals. Unacquainted with the new situation within the home movement as well as with its emergent leaders, Lewins appears to have outlived his usefulness by the time McCabe and Palmer arrived in France.[15]

Towards the close of 1799, William Putnam McCabe returned to Hamburg. There, he was soon tracked down by Craufurd, who was on the point of leaving the city for England to settle his private affairs. On the day of his departure on 6 December, the English minister gave a report on McCabe. In this letter, he also gave notice of William Bailey's arrival in the city on the fourth, adding that Bailey as well as McCabe had received passports from the French Foreign Ministry for their journey to Ireland. It was McCabe, however, who was deputed by his countrymen in France to obtain the recall of Lewins as Irish plenipotentiary in Paris as well as the nomination of another. Under the feigned identity of an American merchant Craig, McCabe also functioned as a bearer of important letters to the 'chiefs in Ireland'. Giving credence to Craufurd, the Irish radicals in France attempted to win over the United leaders in Ireland to the appointment of McCabe as the successor of Lewins. In the light of Lewins's conduct in Paris, a cause of dispute with some of the new United leaders, Craufurd's report helps to elucidate the circumstances of McCabe's stay in France; Lewins's place at the centre of Franco–Irish negotiations in Paris may have made direct access by McCabe to French government officials impossible, and hence made new instructions from Ireland essential.[16] At any rate, McCabe had returned to Ireland some weeks later, when he was reported to be in Belfast. On 8 January 1800, Castlereagh informed John King about McCabe's arrival from Paris, also stating that he carried news of a French fleet, which was ready to sail for Ireland from Brest. In the following months, McCabe was obviously at pains to gather information on the state of United affairs. Although Dublin Castle was provided with reports on McCabe on several occasions, the British authorities could not get hold of him. By the end of the autumn of 1800, he had left Ireland and had

15 Elliott, *Partners in Revolution*, 265–73 on Lewins and the United Irish in France in the years following the rebellion.
16 PRO F.O. 33/19/255, Craufurd to Grenville, 6 December 1799.

returned to France by the close of the same year, possibly instructed to induce Lewins to step down from his post as United plenipotentiary in Paris.
However, while McCabe's missions are certainly indicative of United dissatisfaction with Lewins, the Society's new leaders were, first and foremost, concerned with winning French favour for another expedition to Ireland. Lewins,
who still knew how to pull strings in France, could be important for the new
leaders, too; and thus, he continued to head up the United Irish in Paris.[17]

In the summer of 1800, the Irish in Paris were still waiting for news from
McCabe. He had left the country towards the close of the preceding year,
when United efforts to secure a French invasion had petered out on account
of the prevailing crisis in France. After the coup d'état of 18 brumaire, the
United men in the French capital had pinned their hopes on Napoléon, ex-
pecting that he alone could give a renewed impetus to Irish affairs. As McCabe
was a long time in coming, they decided to send two agents to Ireland to update negotiations with their United brethren at home. Towards the end of
July 1800, Thomas O'Meara and Edward Carolan reached Hamburg, where
they then halted for about a fortnight. Soon after their arrival, Craufurd's
replacement, James Glennie, had become aware of their presence in the city;
and it must be assumed that it was Samuel Turner, who drew Glennie's attention to the Irishmen's moves. In a report to London on 5 August, the
British representative informed his superiors that O'Meara was on the point
of setting out for England 'with the first fair wind in the *Elizabeth* Captain
Ehlers'.[18] Also Turner had kept his ears to the ground and dropped London
a hint of the Irishmen's mission soon afterwards. Subsequently, government
agents followed the trail of Carolan and O'Meara, who were put under surveillance immediately after their arrival at Gravesend. Upon reaching London
around mid-August, the two United men decided to separate. While O'Meara
remained in the British capital, Carolan started out for Ireland on his own.
There, he was to have conversations with Robert Emmet and William Bailey,
the latter of whom had passed through Hamburg on his way to the British
Isles in December of the previous year. According to the intelligence from
Hamburg, Carolan was to confer with his United brethren on a forthcoming
French expedition to Ireland. Carolan's mission caused great uneasiness among
the Dublin Castle authorities, who simply did not like the idea of United

17 PRO H.O. 100/93/3, Castlereagh to King, 8 January 1800, 100/94/242, Cooke's letter,
    29 November 1800; Nat. Arch. 620/10/121/125-6 and 620/10/118/4, McNally's infor-
    mation, 10 June, 5 September 1800, 23 January 1801, 620/9/98/9-11 and 620/49/111,
    various pieces of information on McCabe. See also Madden, *The United Irishmen*, 3rd ser.,
    1st vol., 296-357 on McCabe.
18 PRO F.O. 33/20/227, Glennie to Hammond, 5 August 1800, 33/20/199, Glennie to
    Hammond, 25 July 1800.

agents 'travelling around Ireland, and spreading news of French assistance.' 'Upon the whole', Marsden wrote to John King, Under-Secretary of State in the British Home Department, on 18 August 1800, 'I should be inclined to prefer having Carolan apprehended upon some pretence which should not expose our friend at Hamburgh, whom on no account I would risk.' Although Whitehall had already put Murphy on Carolan's trail, the United agent continued his journey to Ireland without serious difficulties. While O'Meara was arrested in London on 21 September, Carolan slipped past the traps the authorities had set for him. In the following months, he was still rumoured to be in Ireland, but he appears to have left for Hamburg by February 1801.[19] The circumstances of Carolan's mission clearly indicate Dublin's difficulties in infiltrating the re-formed United organization. The authorities had only shallow knowledge of the close circle of new United decision-makers.

By the time Carolan finally returned to the Continent, three other United agents had already got through to France: William Putnam McCabe had headed back for France towards the close of 1800, preceded by Robert Emmet and Malachy Delaney, who had arrived on the Continent in August. Subsequent to Bonaparte's takeover, the new United leaders in Ireland applied all their energies to win the French over to another invasion attempt. After passing through Hamburg in late August, and Holland, Emmet and Delaney were eventually permitted to enter France some time later. Although the French authorities showed themselves reasonably impressed by the Irishmen's conceptions of a new Franco–Irish alliance, United excitement about the prospect of another expedition soon petered out. In the course of the following year, the Irish radicals had to realise that Bonaparte did not seriously contemplate sending a fleet to Ireland. The Irish business had become a minor issue in French war plans; previous declarations of intent for an invasion of Ireland had vanished into thin air by 1801, when the situation in Europe had altered for the better for Bonaparte. Already in 1799, the Second Coalition had begun to crumble. Annoyed by the British occupation of Malta, Russia had deserted the conservative alliance in October 1799, and soon afterwards joined the Northern Coalition for the protection of neutral trade, including Sweden, Denmark and Prussia. When Austria finally signed the Peace of Lunéville on 8 February 1801, thus agreeing to French dominance over northern Italy and the left bank of the Rhine, Britain was on its own as the only remaining con-

---

19 PRO H.O. 100/94/159–60, Marsden to King, 18 August 1800; see also 100/94/143–4, 165–70 & Nat. Arch. 620/49/38–59, 620/10/121/128–36, 620/18/14, 620/10/118/5, various pieces of information on the mission of Carolan and O'Meara; PRO F.O. 33/21/60, Craufurd to Grenville, 17 February 1801. See Elliott, *Partners in Revolution*, 274–5 for another account of the mission.

servative power at war with France. But that was not all. While Bonaparte had gone from strength to strength in the early years of the nineteenth century, Britain was forced to maintain its hold on the Continent against the Northern Coalition. At the end of March 1801, Prince Charles of Hesse, Commander-in-Chief of the Danish armies in the Duchies of Holstein and Schleswig, occupied Hamburg, and subsequently ordered the sequestration of British property in the city. Although the order was not carried into effect, Britain reacted against this attempt at intimidation with Nelson's bombardment of Copenhagen in the beginning of April. In May, Danish troops withdrew from Hamburg; the situation eased off soon, and yet, Britain's delicate position in Europe had become all too apparent. By the summer of 1801, the British government under the new Prime Minister Addington had shed its reluctance to make peace with the French Republic, a step that had still been inconceivable under his predecessor Pitt in the previous year. In August, a preliminary treaty with France was signed at Leoben, followed by the Peace of Amiens, which eventually put an end to the Second Coalition in March 1802. Irish efforts to secure a French invasion, however, were ill-starred in the early years of the nineteenth century. Since United negotiations with France stood or fell by the course of the war, Irish plans had not much chance of materialising after the rebellion of 1798. While Bonaparte's takeover had raised United hopes of profiting from the change of government in France, the powerful general did not take any serious interest in the Irish fight for freedom. In the years subsequent to his return from Egypt in 1799, he gave precedence to the consolidation of his position in the field of home affairs, which he hoped to bring about by containing his European war-time enemies. By 1801–2, United schemes were incompatible with Napoléon's plan of campaign. These were directed at reaching a peace agreement with England rather than provoking an escalation of the war by intervening in Ireland.[20]

III

Throughout 1799, the Tandy affair kept Hamburg in suspense. Whereas the crisis had arisen from the annoyance about subversive elements in the city,

---

20 Nat. Arch. 620/11/130/26 & 43 on Emmet's mission; Elliott, *Partners in Revolution*, 273–81 on the mission of Emmet and Delaney as well as France's Irish policy after Napoléon's takeover; Sutherland, *France 1789–1815*, 347–51 on Napoléon and the European war, 1799–1802. See Wohlwill, *Neuere Geschichte der Freien und Hansestadt Hamburg*, 247–52 on the Danish occupation of Hamburg in 1801 and PRO F.O. 33/21/168–290 for Craufurd's reactions to it.

it overshadowed the activities of foreign radicals in Hamburg. Preoccupied with the precedent Tandy and his three friends had created, the English authorities paid less attention to the doings of refugees from the British Isles. Craufurd, who had been the key figure in the British effort to track Irish radicals on the Continent in the previous year, kept secret service activities just ticking over in 1799. However, whilst Irish *émigrés* in northern Germany were certainly forced to tread carefully in view of the impressive show of strength displayed by the great powers of Europe, the Tandy affair did not prevent Irish refugees from arriving in Hamburg. Although United migration dropped after the Hamburg crisis, one should not equate this decrease in numbers with a fundamental change in the pattern of radical migration. Hamburg and especially Altona continued to serve as a main point of entrance to the Continent subsequent to 1798, not least because of the lack of a suitable alternative. Nonetheless, Irish *émigrés* kept a low profile in the years following the Tandy affair. Due to an increased obsession with secrecy on the part of the Society's new leaders, coupled with changed circumstances in Hamburg, the city lost some of its importance as the United nerve centre for the exchange of information on the Continent. The bustle, which had surrounded United activities in Hamburg until far into 1799, had come to an end by the turn of the century.

The overall picture of the Irish in Hamburg in the years after 1798 is rather blurred. Nothing is known about the fate of the United Irish committee, nor do we learn much of any political activities on the part of the United men in the city. Many of them moved off to Altona on account of the hysteria that the Tandy affair had aroused. In fact, the one-time Danish part of today's Hamburg appeared to have a certain attraction for those Irish *émigrés*, who wanted to play it safe in the following years. Since many of the Altona archives were destroyed in early 1945, when British bombs hit the train that was taking the records to safety, it is difficult to get an idea of United activities in Altona. Although all the signs are that there was a substantial number of Irish *émigrés* in Altona as well as Hamburg throughout the early years of the nineteenth century, there was no permanent nor coherent community of United Irishmen as such. Due to fluctuations in the composition of the Irish group at Hamburg, one is tempted to describe it as a constant coming and going of Irish refugees rather than a settlement. Nevertheless, Hamburg and Altona accommodated a number of United *émigrés* in the years subsequent to the Irish rebellion, some of whom also stayed for longer periods in what was to be their provisional place of exile.

United survivors of the rebellion still sought salvation in fleeing Ireland in the early months of 1799, when accounts of an increased 'Emigration to England of a lower class than usual at the Season' reached the authorities in

Dublin and London.[21] Irish refugees continued to trickle into Hamburg throughout the autumn and winter of 1798–9, most of whom arrived from the British mainland. By now, the group of Irish in the city reflected various stages of United emigration: Turner, Duckett, and in a qualified sense also Anthony McCann, had been residing in Hamburg since 1797. In the following year, they had been joined by George Grey, Lyndon Bolton and Thomas Campbell, who had fled Ireland shortly after the suppression of the Irish rebellion. In November and December 1798, Durnin, Corr from Meath, and Dennis O'Neill from Wexford had arrived in the city, to say nothing of Lady Pamela Fitzgerald, Morres, Corbet, Blackwell and Tandy, the four Hamburg prisoners, and also of the numerous Irish refugees, whose names turn up in the Hamburg letters. Despite a fall in fresh arrivals (some eighty exiles had reached the city in 1798), some thirty Irishmen took refuge in Hamburg in 1799, and yet, because of the lack of detail, there is no clue to the identity of half of them.

After the Wexford uprising, also William Barker escaped to safety in the months following the rebellion. He had been seriously wounded in the battle of Enniscorthy, as a result of which his arm was amputated. He was arrested shortly afterwards, tried and sentenced to death, but narrowly escaped execution. According to Miles Byrne's *Memoirs*, William's brother Arthur 'succeeded in having Mr Barker provisionally released on account of his bad state of health.' Arthur Barker then 'hastened to get him, his wife and child conveyed away into some safe hiding place, until a neutral ship could be engaged to take them abroad.' William Barker and his family eventually succeeded in fleeing the country and subsequently sailed on a vessel to Hamburg. There, he immediately informed the French minister of his arrival, asking him for passports to travel further to Paris. Barker had to remove to Altona to await the Frenchman's decision, but was soon given the go-ahead to proceed to France, where, some years later, he told Byrne about his escape from Ireland.[22] Another United Irishman, Hampden Evans, reached Hamburg in the spring of 1799. He had 'been allowed under the Banishment act to proceed to Hamburgh', as Castlereagh reported to Wickham about the 'old Gentleman of large Fortune' at the end of March. In the second half of April, he turned up again in one of McGucken's accounts concerning Hamburg, but does not seem to have stayed in the city for any length of time. It is unclear when he left Hamburg,

21 Nat. Arch. 620/46/91, John Shaw's account of the situation in Cork, 26 March 1799; see also 620/46/101, PRO H.O. 100/86/13–4 for other reports on the emigration from Ireland in the first half of 1799.
22 *Memoirs of Miles Byrne*, ed. his widow, 1st vol. (Paris, New York, 1863), 174–8 for Byrne's conversation with Barker in 1803. See also Nat. Arch. 620/11/130/45, secret information, 6 October 1803, for Barker.

before he eventually moved to France. At any rate, he still resided in the Paris region some ten years after the Irish insurrection of 1798.[23]

In the course of the following months, the United Irish in Hamburg were joined by two of the principal leaders of the Leinster rising. Garret Byrne of Ballymanus and Edward Fitzgerald of Newpark had taken part in the battles of Arklow, Vinegar Hill and other bloody clashes throughout the summer of 1798, before they eventually surrendered in the second half of July. They had entered into negotiations with the government as early as the beginning of July, but only gave themselves up some three weeks later with the proviso that they were allowed to leave for any part of Europe not at war with Britain. Although both were subsequently included in the Banishment Act, they were held captive in Dublin for the remainder of the year. At the beginning of 1799, they were permitted to quit the country, and set out for England. Knowing full well that their arrangement with the authorities in Ireland left them with a rather limited freedom of action, Byrne and Fitzgerald tried to be as inconspicuous as possible. But their contacts with the Irish in Bristol, where they had taken up residence after arriving from Ireland in January, soon aroused the suspicion of local police officials. While Whitehall made inquiries about the two Irishmen in a letter to Cornwallis, dated 20 March, the English authorities did not take the time to wait for the Lord Lieutenant's answer, which was eventually sent off on 25 March. On the twenty-second, Fitzgerald and Byrne were arrested at Bath, some fifteen miles outside Bristol, by James Rooke, Lieutenant General of the Severn District. On 8 April, the two Irishmen bitterly bewailed their apprehension in a letter to Dublin Castle. Stating that there must have been some misunderstanding, they wrote, 'we are certain we have not committed any act deserving censure, and cautiously avoided the slightest appearance, that possibly could give offence except that of breathing the free Air.' Thanks to some influential friends in Ireland and England, Fitzgerald and Byrne were released in the second half of April, but it was decided that the two Irishmen should breathe 'the free Air' at some distance from the British Isles. By 30 April, they had moved off to Yarmouth to take ship for Hamburg.[24]

---

23 PRO H.O. 100/86/232, Castlereagh to Wickham, 30 March 1799; 100/88/98–113, Evans and the Banishment Act; P.C.I/44/A.155 for McGucken's information; see Elliott, *Partners in Revolution*, 345–6 & 352 on Evans in France.

24 PRO H.O. 100/66/441, Edward Fitzgerald and Garret Byrne to Unknown, 8 April 1799; see Nat. Arch. 620/39/113, Madden, *The United Irishmen*, 2nd edn, 4th ser., 550–64, *Memoirs of Miles Byrne*, I, 18–305, Pakenham, *The Year of Liberty*, 97, 160–76, 202–317 and Cullen, L.M., 'The 1798 Rebellion in Wexford: United Irishman Organisation, Membership, Leadership', in Whelan, Kevin, *Wexford: History and Society* (Dublin, 1987), 248–95 for particulars of Byrne, Fitzgerald and their involvement in the Irish rebellion of

It is unclear when Edward Fitzgerald and Garret Byrne eventually reached Hamburg. There is no mention of their names in the letters of Sir James Craufurd, and the Irishmen are first referred to in the autumn of 1799 in a correspondence between Dublin Castle and Whitehall. On 25 October, Byrne had applied for permission to return to Ireland, and he found Cornwallis a willing listener. The Lord Lieutenant as well as his secretary Edward Baker Littlehales approved of Byrne's petition, but left it up to the British government to decide on the question.[25] The two Irishmen's effort at actively seeking to return to Ireland, however, seems unusual. Unlike other petitioners, such as Archibald Hamilton Rowan and William Sampson, who had either fled or had been arrested before the outbreak of rebellion, Fitzgerald and Byrne had been participants, even field commanders of sorts, in the actual insurrection. None of the other United leaders who had been actively involved in the bloody clashes in the summer of 1798 pursued the same course, and the fact that Fitzgerald and Byrne were not reported on or mentioned by the British minister in any way during their stay in Hamburg acquires significance on that score. Silence about them in Hamburg may be the counterpart of their success in a comparatively sympathetic response to their representation in Dublin and London. Interestingly, also Edward Hay said little about Fitzgerald in his *History of the Insurrection of the County of Wexford* of 1803. When asked about his cousin, he 'preserved a silence', according to Luke Cullen, since he obviously did not want to prejudice the two Irishmen's attempt to return.[26]

Fitzgerald and Byrne kept putting the Irish government in mind of their situation. Travelling through Altona, the earl of Carysfort, a Wicklow landowner, was confronted with the two Irishmen and their expressions of a yearning for their native Ireland. 'I met here Garret Byrne of Ballymanus, in the county of Wicklow, one of the most guilty, most mischievous, and most powerful of the Irish rebels. He claimed acquaintance with me as his neighbour, and I find he is extremely desirous of being allowed immediately to return to England', Carysfort informed Lord Grenville on 25 July 1800.[27] While Britain was at war with France, the authorities in England and Ireland refrained from taking back the rebels they had repudiated in the aftermath of the Irish insurrection. There

---

1798; see PRO H.O. 100/66/417, 421, 441, 447, 100/88/197, 203–4, Nat. Arch. 620/56/25, 620/7/76/5 and PRO P.C.I/44/A.155 for the correspondence relating to Byrne and Fitzgerald, their arrest and stay in England in 1799.

25 PRO H.O. 100/87/248–50, correspondence relating to Byrne's petition, including Byrne's letter from Hamburg, dated 25 October 1799.

26 Hay, Edward, *History of the Insurrection of the County of Wexford* (Dublin, 1803) and TCD MS. 1472/191 on Hay and Fitzpatrick.

27 Historical Manuscripts Commission, *Report on the Manuscripts of J.B. Fortescue*, VI 278, Carysfort to Grenville, 25 July 1800.

was much fear of the malcontents of 1798 resuming their subversive activities at the beginning of the nineteenth century, when the bogey of Irish radicalism still acted as a deterrent. Thus, Hardwicke, the new Lord Lieutenant, opposed a proposal to allow Fitzgerald and Byrne to come back to Ireland in the summer of 1801, arguing that 'their return at present might produce discontent, as well as some inconvenience in regard to the Precedent it would establish in other cases.'[28] When the Peace of Amiens eventually put an end to the European war in March 1802, the situation of the Irish exiles brightened somewhat. Byrne and Fitzgerald's constant memorialising now seemed likely to bear fruit. General Moore, one of their addressees, who had already lent them his support on their surrender in July 1798, approved of the two Irishmen's petition. Referring to their request for 'the benefits from their property', Moore claimed that 'it does not seem unreasonable', and correspondingly, he put in a good word for Fitzgerald and Byrne in a letter to Cornwallis on 1 September 1802. Cornwallis, who had been relieved of his duties as Lord Lieutenant of Ireland in the spring of 1801, had continued to support the two Irishmen's cause and even turned out to be their most sympathetic advocate. He was prompt to react to Moore's communication. On 5 September, he wrote to Alexander Marsden, one of the under-secretaries of State in the Irish Civil Department, expressing his 'wish to have them allowed to return to England.' He pointed to the fact that the terms of Fitzgerald and Byrne's surrender were that they were to leave the Dominions and that 'those Gentlemen could not be permitted, consistently with the Public safety, to return either to Great Britain or Ireland, during the continuance of the war.' Since hostilities between Britain and France had ceased, there would be no objections to the Irishmen's return. Dublin Castle eventually picked up the matter some three weeks later, when also Hardwicke pronounced himself in favour of the two *émigrés'* petition. 'It does not appear that any inconvenience can arise to Ireland, from these persons being permitted to enjoy the benefits of their capitulation', he informed Pelham, who had succeeded to the duke of Portland's position as Home Secretary in 1801. But Hardwicke acknowledged that a final decision would have to be made in London.[29] By October 1802, the question of Fitzgerald and Byrne's return appeared to have been all but settled. The British government was in agreement with the Dublin authorities about the two Irishmen. 'It does not however seem to be necessary that their return should be postponed to the passing of such a pardon, but notice may be given to them of his Majesty's gracious intention to grant them such pardon, and they

28 PRO H.O. 100/106/190, Hardwicke to Pelham, 24 August 1801.
29 PRO H.O. 100/119/36–40, General Moore to Cornwallis, 1 September 1802, Cornwallis to Marsden, 5 September 1802, Hardwicke to Pelham, 27 September 1802.

may be informed that they may in the mean time return in safety to this Country', Sir George Shee, Under-Secretary in the British Home Department, wrote to the Irish Chief Secretary William Wickham on 15 October 1802. Considering that Byrne and Fitzgerald had confessed to be guilty of high treason, 'nothing short of a Pardon under the Great Seal of Ireland or Great Britain, can effectuate their object of enabling them to return in Security ... ', Shee referred to the juridical problems of the possible presence of the two exiles.[30] The subtleties of the law kept the authorities occupied in the following months. While Cornwallis tried to assert his influence in favour of Fitzgerald and Byrne, the British Home Department was still puzzling over the conditions for the Irishmen's return. Although the authorities had not come to a conclusive decision, Shee wrote to Edward Fitzgerald on 29 January 1803 to the effect that he promised the Irishmen to remove all remaining obstacles in the way of their return. Instructed by Pelham, Shee informed Fitzgerald that 'his Majesty has been graciously pleased to direct that a pardon be prepared for you and Mr Byrne. His Lordship does not see any objection to your coming to England as soon as you may think fit ... '.[31] A fortnight later, Shee communicated to Marsden that 'Lord Pelham thinks there can not be any objection to fulfilling the original capitulation according to its letter by granting the Pardon on condition that Byrne and Fitzgerald should not pass into Ireland.'[32] Thus, it was decided that the Irish exiles should not see their native country again. The authorities in London were merely prepared to meet the two Irishmen half-way, laying down that they were allowed to proceed only as far as England. Fitzgerald and Byrne were far from being gratified at this concession. They did not accept London's offer, and remained in Hamburg in the following years.

Little is known about the circumstances of Fitzgerald and Byrne's stay in Hamburg. Luke Cullen's account, which later served as a basis for Madden's *The United Irishmen*, contains one of the most extensive descriptions of their Hamburg days. It should, however, not be taken at face value, since Cullen's sources of information were mostly drawn from Ireland; and one can not help thinking that his description suffers from a certain degree of subjectivity. Cullen's account reads

30 Nat. Arch. 620/63/46, Shee to Wickham, 15 October 1802, including opinion of Attorney General Perceval, 12 October 1802.
31 PRO H.O. 100/112/50, Shee to Edward Fitzgerald, 29 January 1803; see 100/112/51, 100/119/42–51, Nat. Arch. 620/67/23, correspondence relating to Fitzgerald and Byrne's return, January 1803, mainly letters to and from Cornwallis and Shee, including letter from Fitzgerald to Cornwallis, 11 January 1803.
32 PRO H.O. 100/119/34, Shee to Marsden, 15 February 1803.

In Hamburg they continued to live in close intimacy and friendship, having long shared the same dangers, the same prison after their surrender, they shared the same fate in exile they left their own land together, and they never returned to it. Mr Fitzgerald's health, which was much shattered after his campaign and imprisonment, was much restored in Hamburg. He then frequented some good company, particularly with French and Danish and many Polish families. But in Hamburg and Altona, for he resided in both, the British Government had its faithful agents there – a Turner and Duckett were blamed for a communication. Mr Fitzgerald and his friend, Mr Byrne, were surprised and all their friends in the above cities, to find themselves restricted under very severe penalties by the honest Burghers of Hamburg, to a ride of ten miles from a certain point within the city. This was exceedingly offensive to them both, and Fitzgerald scarcely ever rode out after. This might be said to be the first step towards his dissolution. His boyish spirit was often sought to be restored by drinking. Indeed both friends fell into the same error.[33]

It is debatable whether such 'severe penalties' were inflicted on the two Irishmen, since nothing is known about legislative measures of that kind, but Fitzgerald and Byrne undoubtedly did not have it easy in Hamburg. 'Living in a hovel on the verge of the City', as Garret Byrne informed his sister Fanny on 30 May 1800, they appear to have gone through a hard time in exile. The few surviving letters from Hamburg exude profound frustration and depression in the face of a hopeless situation. 'It is a Devil of a Climate', Byrne further complained about the unpleasant conditions he had to endure. But apart from the awkwardness of the circumstances in Hamburg, the two Irishmen bewailed the loss of their life's work. While in England, they had already pointed to the fact that 'the decree of the cabinet ... to banish us to the continent, is peculiarly distressing to us, at this time, for ... the almost total destruction of our property during the rebellion by being Burned and taken away ... '. In Hamburg, Byrne picked up the matter again. 'I believe in my soul', he wrote to his sister Fanny on 11 April 1800, 'that all Edward's Tenants and mine would be gratified in hearing of our being starved here, a circumstance they must suppose will be the case, if they don't pay us, for what can we do in a Country where we don't Even understand the Language.'[34] Due to their mental hardships as well as to the unpleasant Hamburg climate, the Irishmen's state of health deteriorated in the early years of their exile. As

33 TCD MS. 1472/191, Cullen's version for Madden, *The United Irishmen*.
34 Nat. Arch. M5892A–5 (III–IV), Garret Byrne to Fanny Byrne, 11 April and 30 May 1800; PRO H.O. 100/66/441, Fitzgerald and Byrne's letter from England, 8 April 1799.

already indicated by Luke Cullen, especially Fitzgerald was badly affected by
the wretched conditions he was exposed to. According to a physician he had
consulted, Fitzgerald was 'in that State of Health as to require a Southern
Climate.' The physician further added 'that unless he is moved soon, his life
is in a very precarious state indeed.'[35] But since all their efforts to return to
Ireland failed, Fitzgerald did not see his native country again. On Cullen's
authority, he died in Hamburg around the year 1807. Byrne's fate, however,
is shrouded in mystery. Opinions vary about his later years. Although accounts
in the National Archives seem to suggest that he visited Ireland at the close of
1803, he very likely never returned to Ireland. He appears to have spent the
concluding years of his life in exile. In his recent study on 'The Byrnes of
Ballymanus', Conor O'Brien lists a number of leases of part of the Ballymanus
lands, suggesting that Byrne stayed in England from around 1806 until 1821.
O'Brien concedes, however, that it 'has not been possible ... to establish ex-
actly where Garrett died but it is highly unlikely to have been Hamburg in
any event.' According to Madden's enquiries, Byrne died in either France or
Germany in the early 1830s. Nevertheless, 'the date as well as the location
of Garrett's death ... ' remains ' ... a matter of considerable confusion.'[36]

Fitzgerald and Byrne were no isolated case in the aftermath of the rebellion
of 1798, when a number of United exiles chose Hamburg as their temporary
place of refuge. In the year subsequent to the two Irishmen's arrival at
Hamburg in 1799, Archibald Hamilton Rowan reached the free German city.
After Tone's departure at the turn of 1795–6 and Tandy's journey to the
Continent in 1797, he had remained in America. Residing in Wilmington,
some thirty miles to the south-west of Philadelphia, Rowan had withdrawn
from politics and had gone into business. In the long absence of her husband,
Mrs Rowan had 'used all the interest in her power to procure permission for
her husband to quit America, and go to any country not at war with Great
Britain.' She had contacted John Fitzgibbon, the Irish Lord Chancellor, as well
as Lord Lieutenant Cornwallis, both of whom indeed put in a good word for
Rowan.[37] In the latter half of 1799, Anne H. Rowan was eventually informed

35 PRO H.O. 100/119/42–5, letter from Fitzgerald's physician, Altona, 7 December 1802,
    enclosed in Cornwallis to Pelham, 26 January 1803.
36 TCD MS. 1472/191, Cullen on Fitzgerald's death; Nat. Arch. 620/13/181/8, Col.
    Acheson's letters relating to Byrne, 19 January & 10 February 1804; TCD MS. 873/304–7,
    Madden's enquiries about Byrne. See O'Brien, Conor, 'The Byrnes of Ballymanus', in
    Hannigan, Ken & Nolan, William, eds, *Wicklow: History and Society. Interdisciplinary
    Essays on the History of an Irish County* (Dublin, 1994), 327–9 on Byrne's fate after the
    Irish uprising of 1798.
37 *Autobiography of Archibald Hamilton Rowan*, 354; see ibid., 278–357 for information on
    Rowan's stay in America; see Nat. Arch. 620/13/162/1–4, 620/47/141, PRO H.O.

about the Irish government's decision in favour of her husband. 'I am directed to acquaint you', Chief Secretary Castlereagh wrote on 9 September 1799, 'that in consequence of the favourable report made by the Lord Chancellor, of Mr Rowan's conduct since he resided in America, he will be secured (as far as his Majesty's government is concerned) in the refuge which may be granted to him in Denmark or elsewhere, as long as he continues to demean himself in such a manner as not to give offence.'[38] But it was not before the following summer that Rowan eventually set out for Europe. After five years in America (Rowan had arrived in America on 15 July 1795), he left the New World on board the brig *Sally* in the second week of July 1800. He had come to an arrangement with his wife, by which it was agreed that he should proceed to Hamburg, where he was to be joined by his family some time later.[39]

On 17 August 1800, Rowan reached his destination in the north of Germany. A few days subsequent to his arrival in Hamburg, he waited on the English minister, whom he showed Castlereagh's letter to the effect that Rowan had got permission to reside in Denmark. Rowan, however, was given a cold reception after stating his intention to settle down in Altona. The English minister told him that Castlereagh's letter 'did not authorise me to expect those attentions usually reciprocal between British subjects and their minister. As this occasioned my determination to leave Hamburgh, that emporium of merchandise and mischief, I went to Lubec, where I remained six months.'[40] In Lübeck, Rowan was unable to procure a suitable house for himself and his family. In the meantime, his wife had made preparations to meet him after hearing of his arrival on the Continent. According to his *Autobiography*, 'at last he was induced to think of Altona, where there were many English, and some Irish residents, and a number of French emigrants of rank. There, he rented and furnished a handsome house. Having letters of introduction to many opulent merchants, both German and English, he soon found himself with his family in the midst of a pleasant society. From Sir G. Roembald, who succeeded Sir James Crawford at Hamburgh, he received every mark of kind and polite attention. Here he remained till the year 1803.'[41]

100/87/53, 100/89/111, 158–60, 193 and *Correspondence of Charles, First marquis Cornwallis*, II, 382 on the correspondence relating to Rowan's return, 1798–9.

38 *Autobiography of Archibald Hamilton Rowan*, 355.
39 Ibid., 356–64.
40 Ibid., 365. See PRO F.O. 33/20/243, Glennie's letter on Rowan's arrival.
    Lübeck, a German Hanse town on the East Sea, is situated some forty miles to the north-east of Hamburg.
41 *Autobiography of Archibald Hamilton Rowan*, 366–7; see PRO F.O. 33/21/462–8 and 33/22/40, 139–48, Rumbold, the new English minister, on Rowan, 15 December 1801, 19 March and 10 August 1802.

While Rowan stayed in Altona, some of his friends in Ireland and England made exertions to procure his pardon. Among his advocates were public figures of high standing, such as Richard Griffith of Millicent, a leading Kildare politician, Thomas Pelham, Thomas Steele, the British Paymaster-General, and John Fitzgibbon, whose death in early 1802 robbed Rowan of one of his most important benefactors during the time of his exile.[42] His friends in England proved to be particularly helpful in the early years of the nineteenth century, and they finally succeeded in bringing about a decision in 1803. In May 1803, Rowan was permitted to proceed to England, but was prohibited from setting foot in Ireland. On hearing of the English government's ruling, Lord Lieutenant Hardwicke had expressed strong objections to Rowan's return to England. Whereas he had supported Fitzgerald and Byrne's petition, he did not show approval of Rowan's case. In a letter to Wickham on 7 June 1803, he pointed to the 'inconveniences which will attend such a measure at this particular moment and the impression which it will inevitably make upon the minds of the loyal part of the community.' In the following days, he urged Wickham to do everything to prevent Rowan's pardon. On several occasions, he emphasized that 'a strong objection arises to it from the particular character of the man … ', since Rowan's 'ardent mind' would keep him from remaining a quiet subject.[43] Hardwicke's vehement opposition was of no avail. After residing in the north of Germany for almost three years, Rowan had already arrived in London on 16 June 1803. A few days later, Wickham tried to calm down Hardwicke. 'I regret this business most exceedingly', he wrote to the Irish Lord Lieutenant, 'but the thing being done we must represent it, I think, as done on motifs which cannot be made publick, but which in the mind of Govt. have rendered the measure necessary.' It is unclear which motifs the Irish Chief Secretary was referring to, but London's decision was certainly a bitter pill to swallow for Hardwicke. In his reply to Wickham of 24 June, he once again distanced himself from the Rowan affair, and stated that he would 'clear [him]self from any share in it.' He also gave vent to his annoyance in letters to Pelham and the British Lord Chancellor, Lord Eldon, but Hardwicke was faced with a *fait accompli*.[44] Meanwhile, Rowan had taken up residence in 53 Dean Street, Soho/London, from where he tried hard to reverse his outlawry by procuring a pardon under the great seal of Ireland. Initially, his efforts

42 See *Autobiography of Archibald Hamilton Rowan*, 352–5 and 368–73, PRONI T.2627/ 5/E/220 for some examples of their efforts.

43 PRONI T.2627/5/E/190, 196, 197, Hardwicke to Wickham, 7, 12, 17 June 1803; see King to Wickham, 8 June 1803.

44 PRONI T.2627/5/E/198, 202, 205, 207, Wickham to Hardwicke, 19 June 1803, Hardwicke's reply, 24 June 1803, as well as Hardwicke's letters to Pelham and Lord Eldon, 24 & 25

met with difficulties, possibly due to Hardwicke's opposition. Eventually, fortune favoured him and he was allowed to return to Ireland in 1806. Rowan settled down on his father's estates in the county of Down, where he lived on until 1834.[45]

Another of the Hamburg petitioners of the early years of the nineteenth century was William Sampson, a barrister from Londonderry, who had been one of the Society's legal advisers and contributor to the *Northern Star*. In March 1798, he had been among the numerous United leaders arrested by the government. He was kept in custody until the autumn of the same year, when he was finally allowed to take advantage of the Banishment Act. In early October 1798, Sampson received word from Castlereagh to the effect that he was permitted 'to take his passage from the port of Dublin, to any port in the kingdom of Portugal, without hindrance or molestation.'[46] After an Odyssey of almost half a year, he eventually arrived in Portugal at the beginning of March 1799; he then left the country for France by the summer of the same year. From there, he soon contacted the Irish authorities in Dublin in order to draw their attention to his situation. In the meantime, his wife Grace had written to Cornwallis, whom she tried to mollify. But the Sampsons' efforts to smooth things over with Dublin were of no avail in the summer of 1799, and in the following years, his endeavours to get permission to return to Ireland failed.[47] By the close of 1801, while he was still staying in Paris, he recognised that residing in France was not likely to further his plans of seeing his native country again. 'The intensity of the war with England', he later stated in his *Memoirs*, 'made a state of neutrality and independence more difficult to be preserved – and the sincerity of my disposition allowed of no disguise. I applied therefore for a passport, which I obtained, not without difficulty, to go to Hamburg.'[48] After passing through Rotterdam, the Hague and Amsterdam,

June 1803; see *Autobiography of Archibald Hamilton Rowan*, 372–4 on Rowan's return to England.

45 PRONI T.759 & T.823 and *Autobiography of Archibald Hamilton Rowan*, 374–80 on his efforts to procure a pardon while in England; Ibid., 380–448 on the concluding years of Rowan. See Madden, *The United Irishmen*, 2nd edn, 2nd ser., 174–227 for Madden's account of Rowan's life.

46 *Memoirs of William Sampson* (New York, 1807), 45; see McDowell, *Ireland in the Age of Imperialism*, 385, 532, 557, 569 and 601 for Sampson's involvement with the United Irishmen until 1798.

47 Nat. Arch. 620/47/10A, Grace Sampson to Cornwallis, 8 May 1799, PRO H.O. 100/89/99–100, Sampson's letter from Bordeaux, 24 July 1799; *Memoirs of William Sampson*, 55–195 for his own account of the time between October 1798 and the summer of 1799.

48 Ibid., 218; see ibid., 195–219 for Sampson's description of his stay in France; see PRO H.O. 100/104/249, Shee to Littlehales, 14 December 1801 relating to Sampson's petition.

Sampson 'reached Hamburg in the month of July'. Although the dates mentioned in his *Memoirs* are somewhat inconsistent, all the indications are that he was referring to the month of July 1802. As in the instance of Archibald Hamilton Rowan, there are no independent descriptions of Sampson's stay there, and one has to rely on his *Memoirs* alone. Since Sampson's statement of his Hamburg days shows a strong personal bias, his *Memoirs* have to be taken with a pinch of salt. His appraisal of the city, however, was devastating. 'I must say', he poured forth his displeasure at Hamburg, 'that of all the towns where it has been my fortune to be, this was the least agreeable. ... In this place, the very aspect of which is odious, there were few sources of enjoyment, and those expensive. From one or two respectable families, we received some attentions; but we soon found that retirement was our best prospect of comfort.' Together with his wife, who had joined her husband in the meantime, Sampson took up residence near Altona, on the banks of the Elbe, where he dedicated himself to 'the care and education of [his] children.' Suspecting that he might have to stay in Hamburg for a longer period of time, Sampson also made an attempt to learn German. He soon realised, however, that standard German was of no help to him in communicating with his fellow citizens. Alluding to the 'language of Hamburg and Altona', he stated that it 'is a most barbarous jargon, called plat Deüch [Plattdeutsch]', which indeed sounds odd even to German ears. Sampson's *Memoirs* show that the Irishman did not grow to like his place of refuge in the north of Germany; and he intensified his efforts to return to Ireland in the early years of the nineteenth century.[49] Even in his letters to the Irish authorities, Sampson gave vent to his bitterness about Hamburg. 'My affairs were not arranged for an emigration for life', he wrote to George Ponsonby in February 1806, 'in short, my enemies had a very good opportunity of gluttering their malice; for I was surrounded with their spies, of whom they have numbers every where, but more and more mischievous ones in Hamburg than in most places ... as I said before, no city was ever more infested with the little instruments of corruption and intrigue, noxious to society, and sometimes ruinous to those who use them.' Even though his judgement on Hamburg sounds slightly too malicious, Sampson was certainly not altogether wrong about the extent of espionage activities in the city. In early 1806, however, he was rescued from his unpleasant situation. He was permitted to leave Hamburg for England, but was still denied admittance to Ireland. After a short stopover in London, he decided to retire to the New World. Sampson landed at New York on 4 July 1806 and eventually died in America some thirty years later, in 1836.[50]

49 *Memoirs of William Sampson*, 219–23 for Sampson's statement of Hamburg.
50 Ibid., 237–9; see ibid., 224–66 for Sampson's petitions and the events leading up to his

In the early years of the nineteenth century, a number of United *émigrés* endeavoured to return to their native country. Some of the hotheads of the 1790s had lost their rebellious vigour after the failure of the rebellion. The lack of freedom in Ireland was preferable to the freedom of action abroad for men like Rowan, Sampson, Fitzgerald and Byrne, all of whom had worked so vehemently for the cause of Irish liberty. The realities of their exile in Hamburg, such as material deprivations, isolation and a certain kind of rootlessness, carried a lot of weight. As a matter of fact, it was the hardships of exile that induced many an Irish pariah to jettison his revolutionary plans. Moreover, the Irishmen never got to like their place of refuge, and they even displayed a strong aversion to Hamburg. As seen in the instance of the Hamburg exiles, the Irishmen were not destitute of benefactors in Ireland as well as England. Politicians of high standing, such as the conciliatory Lord Lieutenant of Ireland, Cornwallis, and the Irish Lord Chancellor, Fitzgibbon, gave their support to the awkward rebels of former days. As long as Britain was at war with France, the acknowledged ally of the United Irishmen, the governments in London and Dublin were not prepared to absorb the malcontents they had repudiated. After the Peace of Amiens, however, the British authorities held out the prospect of a return to England, but adhered to the refusal of entry to Ireland to subjects, 'whose national spirit of intrigue no change of fortune seems to have diminish'd, who if their presumptuous manners are resisted, employ every means they so well understand, to undermine and calumniate', as Sir George Rumbold put it in August 1802. After a visit from A.H. Rowan, the new English minister in Hamburg sent word to his superiors in London that 'other Banish'd Irish have since attempted to introduce themselves to my notice', but Rumbold firmly declared himself against taking back the Irishmen.[51] The preferential treatment of Rowan, however, does not represent the English government's approach to the handling of Irish refugees; and it must be assumed that he was permitted to return to Ireland only because he was a man of high social standing. United petitioners of lesser importance were less fortunate. Hamburg and especially Altona, however, were suitable places of refuge for United exiles, who had grown weary of politics. Moreover, the city continued to serve as a stepping stone for United agents, who emerged after the reconstruction of the Society in 1798–9. Although relatively little is known about the political activities of United Irishmen in the city between 1799 and 1802, we know for a certainty that all important missions to and from France during that period

---

departure for America. See Madden, *The United Irishmen*, 2nd ser., 2nd vol., 335–88 for Madden's account of Sampson's life.

51　PRO F.O. 33/22/140–3, Rumbold to Hawkesbury, 10 August 1802.

went through Hamburg. All the indications are that the city still accommodated some sort of a loose Irish organization ['Club irlandois'] at the turn of 1800–1, that meetings were held and that the Irish in Hamburg were in correspondence with their United brethren in Ireland as well as France.[52] Nevertheless, due to the changes in Hamburg following the events of 1798–9, things quietened down in the city in the early years of the nineteenth century.

52 Nat. Arch. 620/18ᴬ/14, 620/49/82, various pieces of intelligence from Hamburg, September 1800–January 1801.

CHAPTER 7

Farewell from Hamburg: from the Fort George Prisoners to the Return of Samuel Turner, 1802–3

The somewhat blurred overall picture of United activities in the years after the rebellion of 1798 changed in 1802. On both sides of the Irish Sea, the United movement suffered from a certain lack of a sense of direction until things were eventually put in motion in 1802. In the wake of the Peace of Amiens in March 1802, ending the European war which had hitherto determined the Society's fortunes, the release of the Fort George prisoners in June gave a new impetus to United affairs. The 'Despard Conspiracy' and 'Emmet's Rebellion' of July 1803 were closely connected to the release of the old leaders and the chain of events, which followed their arrival on the Continent. Although the shaky state of peace diminished United prospects of military assistance from France for the time being, it made easier the travel of Irish agents between Ireland and France. With Britain's navy no longer barring the way to French and Dutch ports, United travellers enjoyed a freedom of action, which had been undreamt of in times of the British sea-blockade. The usual pattern of United migration somewhat changed after 1802. With easier access, Hamburg ceased to serve as the focal point for United affairs between Ireland and France. Moreover, Sir George Rumbold, the new British minister in Hamburg since November 1801, paid little attention to United doings. Since Samuel Turner also stopped feeding the British government with information, the activity of the United Irishmen in Hamburg by 1803 is obscure.

I

After several years of relative tranquillity, the release of the Fort George prisoners breathed new life into the Society. United migration increased substantially in the following months, when numbers of agents were on the move between the Continent and the British Isles, but also between Ireland and England. The United men in Ireland were obviously at pains to fit in their efforts with those of their radical brethren on the British mainland. According to Roger Wells, 'there is no doubt that the leaders originally planned a co-ordinated thrust in Britain and Ireland.' Marianne Elliott too emphasises the importance of the link between the United men on both sides of the Irish Sea. Although Wells as well as Elliott concede that the overall picture of the English movement remains confused, there is enough evidence to prove a substantial degree of overlap between Irish and British developments. Especially in terms of personnel, both movements were closely connected. United men, such as William Putnam McCabe, the interminable traveller between France and the British Isles in the years after the Irish insurrection, or James Farrell who had come to the fore in the United Irish movement in 1798, turned up in England as well as in Ireland. Various Irish radicals, who paved the way for the 'Despard Conspiracy' in late 1802, were to play a decisive part in 'Emmet's Rebellion' several months later. However, without detracting from the importance of the Anglo–Irish dimension of United efforts, there is no need to go into details about the history of the English movement, since it has already been subject of extensive research in previous years. As in the instance of 'Emmet's Rebellion', the issue at stake will rather be the question of United migration subsequent to the release of the Fort George prisoners in 1802.[1]

Some two months before the treaty between Britain and France was finally concluded at Amiens, 'William Tennent, Robert Simms, Robert Hunter, William Dowdall, and William Steele Dickson, were once more restored to the liberty of breathing the air and treading the soil of our native land … ', as Dickson later described his release. Since they were ranked among the United leaders of lesser importance, they had been deemed worthy of government lenience; and unlike their fellow prisoners, who were to be refused permission to return to Ireland some five months later, the five United men from Ulster were allowed to proceed homewards. They were set free on 30 December 1801 and subsequently transported to Greenock, at the mouth of the Clyde. They were then shipped off to the Down coast, finally landing at Hollywood on 12 January 1802.[2] While Tennent, Simms, Hunter and Dickson appear to have refrained from resuming their old activities, William Dowdall soon set about re-establishing contacts with his United companions. In the following months,

1 Wells, *Insurrection*, 244. See ibid., 220–52, Elliott, *Partners in Revolution*, 282–97 and ibid., 'The "Despard Conspiracy" Reconsidered', *Past and Present*, 75 (1977), 46–61 on the Anglo–Irish dimension of United activities in the early years of the nineteenth century.
2 Madden, *The United Irishmen*, 2nd edn, 4th ser., 183, Dickson's narrative. See Baillie, W.D., 'William Steele Dickson, D.D. (1744–1824)', *Irish Booklore*, II (1976), 259 on the release of the Ulstermen.

he helped to smooth the way for a closer co-operation between the malcontents in Ireland and England. Due to the economic hardships of war torn Britain, popular disaffection had grown substantially in the early years of the nineteenth century. Especially manufacturing districts in Lancashire and Yorkshire witnessed an enormous increase of subversive clubs, though only loosely organised at best. It was largely thanks to the Irish element within the United movement in England that activities gathered momentum around mid-1802. Apart from Irish agents travelling through England, United Irish exiles resident in Britain, such as Patrick Finney, James Farrell, or John McNamara, were of crucial importance to the development which eventually led up to the shattering of the attempted coup in November.

When William Dowdall finally arrived in England in the summer of 1802, he must have found his United brethren in a state of agitation. Accompanied by William Putnam McCabe, he had left Ireland for England in July. While McCabe continued his journey to the Continent, Dowdall remained in London. Although he had been furnished with letters of recommendation to James Napper Tandy, the newly-released *éminence grise* of the United movement, he did not travel on to France. He stayed in London until September. After receiving a letter from McCabe, who had reached France in the meantime, he eventually returned to Ireland to prepare the ground for another Irish rising. In November, however, the tragic leader at the head of the Anglo–Irish conspiracy in London, Colonel Edward Marcus Despard, was arrested, together with some of his associates. Although United plans did not materialise, all the indications are that a revolt in England was to be an integral part of a more far-reaching scheme with uprisings in Britain and Ireland. Relatively little is known about the plans activities in support of which in England must have appeared convincing to Dowdall and his companions. Despite the failure of the 'Despard Conspiracy' in the following months, United preparations for another rising gathered steam.[3]

II

As in the instance of Dowdall's involvement in Despard's plot, events in Ireland in 1802–3 were closely connected with the fate of the Fort George prisoners. Some five months subsequent to the discharge of Dowdall and his four fellow prisoners, the remainder of the old leaders was set free. They had

3 PRO H.O. 100/112/158, 165–9, 381, 100/114/132, 227, Nat. Arch. 620/65/146, PRO P.C.I/3583 for Dowdall; see Wells, *Insurrection*, 220–48, Elliott, *Partners in Revolution*, 282–97 and idem, 'The "Despard Conspiracy" Reconsidered', *Past and Present*, 46–61 for the development on the mainland up to the 'Despard Conspiracy'.

been kept in custody until the peace agreement between Britain and France had finally removed government reservations about their release and the irritation of a spectacular return of the old United leaders; they were conveyed out of the country without loss of time. After leaving Fort George on board the *Ariadne* on 30 June 1802, they arrived at Cuxhaven, at the mouth of the Elbe, on 4 July. The following day, they took a boat upriver to Hamburg. On the passage to the free German city, animosities between Arthur O'Connor and Thomas Addis Emmet flared up again. While Emmet, like MacNeven, had been antagonistic towards O'Connor long before their arrest in 1798, they had put their disagreement aside for the duration of their confinement. The brittle truce, however, did not survive the summer of 1802; and if it had not been for their United companions, a duel could have terminated the life of one of them. Although their compatriots tried hard to settle the dispute, O'Connor and Emmet never again managed to patch up their relationship.[4]

Upon arriving at Hamburg, the exiled United leaders met with a warm welcome by Archibald Hamilton Rowan, who appears to have been well informed about their release. He later recorded in his *Autobiography* that he 'immediately wrote to them, offering them such services as I was capable of, in that country. Among the replies I received, I find one from Samuel Neilson,' and another one from T.A. Emmet. Neilson as well as Emmet showed themselves pleased about Rowan's gesture of goodwill, but they refrained from making use of his offer. While in Hamburg, Emmet commented on Rowan's letter on 8 July, answering him that

> Since I have shown it to Dowling, Chambers, and some others, with whom you were formerly connected in intimacy. They all desire me to assure you of their affection and esteem. We were in some measure apprised of your situation, and of the injury you might possibly sustain by holding intercourse with us; we therefore voluntarily deprived ourselves of the pleasure we should enjoy in your society, and declined calling on you directly on our arrival. For my part it would give me the utmost pain if your friendship towards me were to lead you into any embarrassment, or subject you to any misrepresentation on a point of such material importance to yourself and family.

4 Madden, *The United Irishmen*, 2nd ser., 1st vol., 300–5, Neilson's correspondence with his wife, May–July 1802; see ibid., 3rd ser., 2nd edn, 101–8, TCD MS. 873/557, MacDermot, 'Arthur O'Connor', *I.H.S.*, 62 and Elliott, *Partners in Revolution*, 323–4 for the quarrel between O'Connor and Emmet. See Emmet, T.A., *Ireland under English Rule*, 2nd vol. (New York, 1903), 259–328, Emmet's diary, 1803–4 for references to their relationship.

In their letters to Rowan, Emmet and Neilson declared themselves unwilling to resume their old activities. While this was apparently true for Neilson, it does not apply to Emmet who was to play a decisive part in the Society's fortunes in the following months. It is unclear why Emmet professed to withdraw from politics, but it must be assumed that, after staying in Hamburg, he did not get involved in United activities purely by chance and that he put on an innocent air in his letter to Rowan for reasons of secrecy. As early as July 1802, however, Emmet showed himself determined to leave Europe for the New World. 'I shall not go out big with expectation', Emmet tried to give reasons for his decision, 'and shall therefore, perhaps escape disappointment; but America, with all its disadvantages, opens to me the fairest field of honorable employment, and it possesses a charm in my eyes, which I look for in vain in this quarter of the globe.' It was not before long that the Irish party in Hamburg dispersed.[5]

In contrast to his colleagues on arriving in Hamburg, modesty was foreign to Arthur O'Connor's nature. He had lost no time in calling on Lady Pamela, the widow of his old comrade-in-arms, Lord Edward Fitzgerald, who had to listen to O'Connor 'weeping over memories of the past', as Frank MacDermot later poked gentle fun at the eccentric United leader. Soon afterwards, however, Arthur O'Connor left Hamburg. Accompanied by his fellow sufferer, John Chambers, he proceeded to Antwerp and Calais, but he had arrived in Paris by early 1803.[6] The remainder of the released United Irish scattered in the course of the following months. William James MacNeven went on a journey to Dresden, Prague and Switzerland, before he eventually travelled to Paris around October. There, he made contact with Talleyrand, the French Foreign Minister, in order to renew United–French negotiations on the Irish question. In time of peace, Talleyrand could hardly afford to enter into official negotiations with the United Irishmen, and thus assigned to one of his undercover agents the task of conferring with the Irishman. While French communications with MacNeven might be dismissed as a manoeuvre to tease the British secret service, they certainly indicate the shaky state of the peace between Britain and France. Since French authorities had not stopped flirting with the idea of launching an attack on the British Isles, the disaffected Irish could still be a trump card in the contest over supremacy in Europe. Although MacNeven's talks with the French came to naught at the close of 1802, it was not before long that sabre-rattling between Britain and France began again.[7]

5 *Autobiography of Archibald Hamilton Rowan*, 434–6 and 468–9, Rowan's account of the arrival of the state prisoners, including Neilson & Emmet's letters to Rowan, 12 & 8 July 1802.
6 MacDermot, 'Arthur O'Connor', *I.H.S.*, 61; see also Nat. Arch. 620/12/145, John Dunn to Farrell, Antwerp, 29 July 1802 and Madden, *The United Irishmen*, 2nd ser., 1st vol., 306.
7 Ibid., 2nd ser., 1st vol., 306, 2nd ser., 2nd vol., 221–2, 3rd ser., 2nd edn, 117–21; TCD

By the beginning of August, T.A. Emmet had left Hamburg. Together with Thomas Russell, John Swiney, Joseph Cormick and Hugh Wilson, all of whom had shared the same fate as Emmet at Fort George, he travelled on to Amsterdam, Rotterdam and Antwerp, before he stopped off at Brussels around September. Apart from Thomas Russell, who soon separated from his companions in order to proceed to Paris, Emmet and his friends stayed in Brussels until the following year, when all of them turned up in France. The remaining ex-state prisoners, namely Samuel Neilson, Joseph Cuthbert, George Cummings, John Sweetman, Edward Hudson and Matthew Dowling, were still reported to be in Hamburg by August 1802, but they appear to have left the city in the course of the following weeks. According to a letter, written by T.A. Emmet on 25 October 1802, Sweetman had gone to Lyons, and Dowling to Rotterdam. Little, however, is known about Cuthbert, Cummings and Hudson, and there is no clue as to the whereabouts of the three United men after the summer of 1802.[8]

It is easy to trace Samuel Neilson's moves after his discharge from Fort George. After arriving at Hamburg, he had taken up residence in Altona, at the house of Jakob Heusermann, Kleine Fischer-Straße 248, from where he eventually answered Rowan's letter on 12 July 1802. In the same way as Thomas Addis Emmet, Samuel Neilson was concerned about Rowan's safety. He paid attention 'to avoid the most remote possibility of implicating' him in anything that could endanger Rowan's application for pardon. Neilson had already made up his mind to keep away from politics in the future and to build up a new life for himself in America.

> In the New World, however, I hope to find the people as I ever found them at home, honest and sincere; I am not afraid of pushing my way among a people who, I may say, have sprung from ourselves. In the propagation of truth I know there is nothing but pain and trouble, and he who embarks in that cause with any other view will, I am confident, find himself mistaken.[9]

Tired of the difficulties that his involvement with the United Irishmen had created for him, Neilson separated from the men with whom he had spent

---

MS. 873/526 & 560 and Elliott, *Partners in Revolution*, 298–300 for MacNeven's activities after his release and France's attitude towards British disaffection in 1802–3.

8 TCD MS. 873/560, Emmet's letters from Brussels, dated 25 October and 8 November 1802; Madden, *The United Irishmen*, 2nd ser., 1st vol., 306, Samuel Neilson's account of the whereabouts of the released United leaders.

9 *Autobiography of Archibald Hamilton Rowan*, 435–6.

the last four years at Fort George. After a month in Hamburg and Altona, he set out for Ireland in order to meet his family before leaving for America. When he left Cuxhaven on board the *Providence* on 6 August 1802, he was accompanied by another United exile, Anthony McCann of Drogheda. The latter had fled Ireland in the summer of 1797 and was subsequently included in the Fugitive Act. Although there are vague references to McCann in various correspondence in the following years, it is virtually impossible to follow his trail after 1798. After taking part in Tandy's expedition, he had arrived at Hamburg in early November 1798, and though mostly residing in Hamburg appears to have left the city on several occasions. By 1802, he had become the business partner of Thomas Ridgeway, owner of the *Providence*, a smuggling vessel operating between Hamburg and the British Isles. In the early years of the nineteenth century, many United exiles appear to have enlisted the assistance of Ridgeway and McCann, and also Samuel Neilson fell back upon his old comrade-in-arms in August 1802.[10] According to a secret information, dated 20 August 1803, 'Ridgeway had landed him [McCann] and Neilson four miles from Dublin and that they went to Emmet's Country House.' In fact, Neilson only stayed in Dublin for a few days, as Leonard McNally reported to Dublin Castle on 22 September 1802. There, he met James Hope and Charles Teeling, two of the leading figures of the post-rebellion United Irishmen. Accompanied by Hope, Neilson set out for the North to visit his family. By October 1802, he had returned to Dublin, where he appears to have booked a passage to America. At any rate, he had reached New York by December, when he informed his wife about his arrival. He settled down at Poughkeepsie, a small town on the Hudson some eighty miles north of New York, but died as early as 29 August 1803. McCann, who was still rumoured to be in Ireland in the spring of 1803, had returned to Hamburg by mid-October 1802. He disappeared from the scene until the following summer, when British authorities became aware of him.[11]

United enthusiasm had begun to flag in the face of France's unfathomable attitude towards Ireland. Bonaparte's role as absolute dictator had caused the Irish radicals to be suspicious of French intentions. The 'distressing usurpation

10 Madden, *The United Irishmen*, 2nd ser., 1st vol., 306–7, Neilson's correspondence with his wife, August 1802; ibid., 2nd ser., 2nd vol., 521, McCann and the Fugitive Bill; Nat. Arch. 620/49/82, 620/12/143 and PRO F.O. 33/18/62, various reports on McCann, 1799–1802; see chapters 4 and 5 of this study on Anthony McCann in 1797–8.

11 Nat. Arch. 620/11/130/18 & 620/10/121/16, secret information, 20 August 1803 & McNally's letter, 22 September 1802; PRO H.O. 100/112/156–7, 165–9, 238, 241–2, 290–6, 100/114/189–91, Nat. Arch. 620/65/126, 620/11/160/26, 620/12/140, 620/14/198/5, PRONI T.2627/5/K/128 and Madden, *The United Irishmen*, 2nd ser., 1st vol., 306–36, various sources relating to Neilson, McCann and Ridgeway, 1802–3.

in France', as Samuel Neilson put it on 12 July 1802, might also happen to the Irish in the event of a French landing in Ireland.[12] Nevertheless, the United Irishmen were still hoping for French assistance in case the brittle peace between France and Britain would come to an end. In the second half of 1802, while silence reigned between England and France, the Irish radicals had to do without French promises of military aid. The release of the state prisoners eventually spurred on the movement's new principals, who had emerged in the wake of the Irish insurrection. The arrival of the men from Fort George at Hamburg was followed by months of busy United migration; and it seems as if the United Irishmen had been jolted out of their slumbers by their old leaders. While most of the released radicals did not take an active part in 'Emmet's Rebellion' of July 1803, the attempted coup for the most part originated in a circle of men associated with them: the United leaders on the Continent triggered off the chain of events which eventually led up to 'Emmet's Rebellion'.[13]

In the summer and autumn of 1802, Thomas Addis Emmet and his associates were at the hub of the development, which culminated in the tragic rebellion of 1803. In August, Emmet was reunited with his brother Robert in Amsterdam. Robert Emmet, who had remained on the Continent after his arrival at Hamburg in August 1800, accompanied his brother's party to Brussels, where the Irishmen eventually split up some time later. While it is unclear to what extent Thomas Addis exerted an influence on his younger brother, it must be assumed that his conversations with Robert were not merely of a personal nature. Robert's meetings with his brother did certainly not act as a curb on his radical development, but rather induced him to act with determination. Apart from visiting his older brother, Robert's revived enthusiasm must also be attributed to his encounter with Thomas Russell. 'Of all the leaders it was Russell who was most determined to renew preparations for another rebellion', and it was he, like Robert Emmet, who cleared off to Paris after separating from his companions in Brussels.[14] Some weeks later, Emmet packed his bags and started out for Ireland, and after a short stopover in Hamburg, reached his native country by October 1802.[15]

Two months later, Emmet was followed by one of the leading United Irish in Paris. In all probability, Emmet had run into William Hamilton while stay-

---

12 *Autobiography of Archibald Hamilton Rowan*, 435, Neilson to Rowan, 12 July 1802.
13 Elliott, *Partners in Revolution*, 297–302 on France and the United question, 1802–3.
14 Ibid., 281.
15 Madden, *The United Irishmen*, 3rd ser., 2nd vol., 209–12 and 3rd ser., 2nd edn, 291–2 & 317 on Robert Emmet's moves in the second half of 1802; Nat. Arch. 620/11/130/18, secret information, 20 August 1803, for his stopover in Hamburg.

ing in the French capital, and it was certainly no accident that both reunited in Ireland some time later. William Hamilton from Fermanagh, brother-in-law of Thomas Russell, however, who had arrived in France in the spring of 1798, reached London in December 1802. There, he met up with Thomas Russell's brother, John, but also with Edward Carolan, and John Byrne from Dundalk. After leaving Ireland in 1797, Byrne had turned up in France and Germany, before he eventually disappeared to England. At the close of 1802, he was on his way to Ireland to convey letters from James Tandy. At the beginning of January, Hamilton, Carolan and Byrne finally set out for Ireland, where Hamilton was meant to prepare the ground for another rising. He had been commissioned by his fellow exiles to sound out his United brethren about their intentions, and he seems to have been satisfied with what he found out when he left the country again in the following month.[16] Determined to rouse the Irish exiles into action, William Hamilton returned to the Continent in February 1803. In Brussels, he initiated Thomas Addis Emmet and William James MacNeven into recent plans, whereby the two United doyens were to proceed to Paris in order to head up the Irish group. Hamilton then set about mobilising his friends in France. Together with William Putnam McCabe, he tried to induce his countrymen 'to come to Ireland in order to assist in exciting another insurrection in this country.'[17] Accompanied by Michael Quigley and Brian McDermot, two of the lesser state prisoners included in the Banishment Act who had been released in the previous year, he departed from LeHavre towards the end of February 1803. After landing at Southampton, the Irishmen travelled on to Oxford. There, they were joined by John Byrne who had already been privy to Hamilton's first journey to Ireland in December. Via Birmingham and Liverpool, they eventually reached Dublin in early March. Some four weeks later, Thomas Russell, staying first at his brother's house in London, left for Ireland on 1 April. Under the name of Eager, he had applied to the respective authorities for a passport and had subsequently succeeded in making his way to Ireland without any difficulties. Although some sources suggest that he was accompanied by William Hamilton, it seems that the two United men travelled separately. By April 1803, however, the masterminds of the projected coup had congregated in Ireland.[18]

16 PRO H.O. 100/114/113 & 147, 100/115/13, P.C. I/3583, Nat. Arch. 620/13/168/1, 620/13/173, 620/11/138/40 and Elliott, *Partners in Revolution*, 302–3 on Hamilton's journey to Ireland. See chapter 4 of this survey on Hamilton and Byrne in 1797–8 and chapter 6 on Carolan.
17 Nat. Arch. 620/11/135, statement of Michael Quigley, 23 July 1803.
18 PRO H.O. 100/113/193–4, 100/114/113–6, 147, 201–3, 100/115/13, 37–47, 175–6, Nat. Arch. 620/64/2, 8, 9, 620/67/59, 620/11/135, 620/11/130/44, 620/12/141/35, 620/11/138/40 and PRO P.C.I/3583, various letters, reports and testimonies relating to the jour-

Robert Emmet and his associates proceeded with utmost caution in the spring of 1803. Since a rising in Dublin was to blaze a trail for the disaffected in other parts of Ireland, particular care was taken to strengthen the Society's position in the Irish capital. In various parts of the city, the United leaders created arms depots and caches, which were destined to serve as a starting point for a surprise attack on Dublin Castle. In co-operation with a selected group of local leaders, the insurrection was then to spread to the counties, where troops were to be levied at short notice. Since only a small number of confidants was initiated into United plans, little news of the Society's activities became public knowledge, and in the spring of 1803 Dublin Castle was mostly in the dark about the disaffected. There was no inkling of an imminent crisis before March, when Marsden informed Wickham that 'Emmet is in Ireland' and that 'a game will be played here.'[19] If it had not been for a number of United mishaps, Dublin Castle could have been taken completely unawares some months later. Their obsession with secrecy, however, while a benefit to the United Irishmen, also prevented them from getting a footing on the ground. In contrast to the mass radicalism of 1798, the United Irishmen of 1803 tried hard not to publicise their cause. The small cadre of United leaders rather counted on a ready response on the day from the French. A French landing in Ireland in particular would certainly rally the masses to their side. Although there was no sign of the French sending a fleet to Ireland in the spring of 1803, Robert Emmet still reckoned on assistance when he dispatched Pat Gallagher in May. The latter was instructed to 'communicate to none but' Thomas Addis Emmet who had settled down in Paris in the meantime. Upon reaching the French capital on 31 May, Gallagher informed Emmet about the state of affairs in Ireland as well as about United preparations for the rising. He made it clear to Emmet that 'a small and immediate force' should be sent to Ireland where the United men were on the verge of acting independently. Since time was ripe for action, France should not waste this opportunity.[20]

Although war was declared on 18 May 1803, the French were slow to react to Irish overtures. In the meantime, Bonaparte had gone over to challenging England in the north of Germany. After occupying Hanover in early

neys of Hamilton, Quigley, McDermot and Russell; see Nat. Arch 620/52/219, PRONI T.2627/5/K/83 and *Memoirs of Miles Byrne*, I, 341–52 on Quigley and McDermot. See Elliott, *Partners in Revolution*, 303–5 for another account of the Irishmen's moves between January and April 1803.

19 PRONI T.2627/5/K/96, Marsden to Wickham, 29 March 1803.
20 Emmet, *Ireland Under English Rule*, II, 266–7. See Elliott, *Partners in Revolution*, 302–6 on the United Irishmen's preparations for the rising in 1803.

June, he had captured Cuxhaven by the middle of the month. While his armies were approaching the gates of Hamburg and Bremen, the Irish question was pushed into the background.[21] As late as 19 July, the French War Minister assured T.A. Emmet of France's intention 'to do England all the harm we can ... ' Stating that 'we know nothing can do her so much as separating Ireland ... ', Berthier hinted at Ireland's importance for French war plans; but by the time French authorities had finally forced themselves to take a decision, Robert Emmet's attempted coup had failed. Owing to a number of unfortunate mishaps in the days before, Emmet had decided to launch his attack against Dublin Castle on 23 July in order to prevent the conspiracy from being uncovered. Since United preparations had been far from concluded, the premature Dublin rising had ended in disaster within hours. By October 1803, Robert Emmet as well as Thomas Russell had been captured and executed, and many United leaders in Ireland had been taken into custody. Following the events of 1803, the home movement disbanded. The failure of 'Emmet's Rebellion' broke the backbone of the Society in Ireland; and the United Irish leaders on the Continent never again managed to put new heart into United affairs at home.[22]

III

While things were coming to a head in Ireland, the United Irishmen in Hamburg received little attention in 1802–3. Although various Irish *émigrés* were still resident in the city, there is no mention of them in the Hamburg sources. Except for a handful of reports, Sir George Rumbold paid no attention to people like Fitzgerald, Byrne, Sampson, Rowan and Turner, and he did not even breathe a word about the arrival of the Fort George prisoners in the summer of 1802. Following the suppression of the rebellion in 1798, the governments in Dublin and London became complacent about their malcontent subjects. The Peace of Amiens, putting an end to the Franco–Irish alliance in 1802, reinforced this complacency. Thus, Emmet's attempt took both governments unawares; and if it had not been for the insufficiencies of United preparations, Britain's embarrassment would have been complete. Hamburg, a nerve centre for Britain's intelligence network on the Continent for a number of years, became an intelligence backwater by 1803.[23]

21 See PRO F.O. 33/23/121–88 for Rumbold's accounts of the French campaign, June 1803.
22 Emmet, *Ireland under English Rule*, II, 283, T.A. Emmet on his meeting with Berthier; see Elliott, *Partners in Revolution*, 306–22 on 'Emmet's Rebellion'.
23 See ibid., 317–20 for the governments' negligence of United activities.

Samuel Turner's fate is certainly indicative of British lack of interest in the surveillance of United activities. Whereas he had been the key man in Britain's continental espionage network until around the year 1800, he remained in the shadows in the early years of the nineteenth century. Despite his crucial involvement in the exposure of O'Connor, Napper Tandy, and their associates, the United Irishmen had not caught on to Turner by early 1799. According to Lelarge, a French–born informer in the service of the Senate, he was still in communication with important figures, such as Thomas Paine or General Clarke. Lelarge's report of February 1799 shows that Turner had succeeded in maintaining his cover as United contact in Hamburg. Moreover, he feigned deep sympathy towards Tandy and his unfortunate friends. After writing on behalf of the Hamburg prisoners on 15 April and 4 June 1799, he was not heard of until the following year.[24] Although it must be assumed that he was still in contact with Dublin and London, there is no mention of his name in public records before the summer of 1800, when he sent the authorities word of the mission of Thomas O'Meara and Edward Carolan. Some two months later, Under-Secretary King once again puzzled about Turner's whereabouts. In a letter, dated 9 October 1800, he informed Marsden that 'Richardson [=Turner] has not written lately, I imagine he is gone into the Country.'[25] It was not before long, however, that Turner reported back from Hamburg. On 19 December 1800, he wrote to the Foreign Office, going into details about the correspondence and connections of his fellow exiles in the city with radicals in France, where Irish *émigrés* had grown to be suspicious about the new government. Turner had received news from 'a brother democrat at Paris' that 'all hopes are given up of any good to their liberties under the reign of Bonaparte. At length they begin to look on Mr Pitt as not so great an enemy to the rights of Mankind.' Turner showed himself disgusted with French politics, but also ridiculed his countrymen. Once again, he gave vent to his mistrust of his 'catholic Brethren, whom I ... cry out as fellows who only wish to separate their country from England to give her up to the Dominion of the Priesthood.' At any rate, Turner was at pains to make useful contacts in order to sound out the Irish on the Continent. His letter shows that he still enjoyed the confidence of his compatriots and that he was entrusted with their secrets.[26] Some two months later, he was approached by an Irishman

24 Ham. Staats. Senat Cl. 1, Lit. Pb, Vol. 8c, Fasc. 2, Nr. 21, Lelarge's report on Roberts (Turner's alias), 16 February 1799; see Senat Cl. 1, Lit. Pb, Vol. 8d, Fasc. 15b1, Inv. 3 & 4, Turner's letters (Turner signed himself Roberts) of 15 April and 4 June 1799. See chapter 6 of this study on Turner and the Irish prisoners in Hamburg in 1799.

25 Nat. Arch. 620/18^A/14, King to Marsden, 9 October 1800; see chapter 6 of this study on Turner's involvement in the exposure of the mission of Carolan and O'Meara.

26 PRO F.O. 97/241, Turner's letter from Hamburg, 19 December 1800. Although the letter is not signed, there is no mistaking Turner's handwriting. Moreover, the envelope bears the

named Beamish, who had arrived in Hamburg from Cork in December 1800, about writing to the French government. According to the letter Turner eventually addressed to Talleyrand, 'this gentleman is now deputed by a great majority of the landed interest of his country and has requested me to make this representation to assure you that they, the people of property, feel such indignation against England and are so dissatisfied with their present political situation, that they are ready to co-operate with an efficient French force and break off all connection with their Tyrants for the purpose of forming a representative constitution and establishing its independence under the guarantee of France.' After throwing mud at the French in his information to the British Foreign Office some months before, Turner now functioned as a skilful petitioner on behalf of Beamish, and proved adroit at using the rhetoric of both parties most convincingly.[27]

In the following year, Turner's traces vanished, and it was not before the spring of 1802 that he turned up again. In a letter to Edward Cooke, Under-Secretary of State in the Irish Civil Department, he brought up the question of money on 18 May. After corresponding with Lord Castlereagh and Sir James Craufurd, both of whom had declared themselves in favour of Turner, he enquired about 'a pension of 300 pounds per annum the government has thought proper to bestow on me for information on Irish affairs.' Faced with a peace which seemed to make future employment redundant, he was now concerned with securing an ongoing recompense for his past services. 'Now that the war is over', he argued, 'and it is supposed all persons in my line are discharged, I make it a point to spend much more money than heretofore in order to do away any idea of my being employed and income diminished and it is for that reason I request your attention, and beg the honour of a line thro' Sir George [Rumbold] to say where the draft is to be put.' Turner did not lower his sights and put special emphasis on the fact that the government should not do without his valuable services. His letter sounds somewhat imperious, and yet, it is undeniable that he was uncertain about his future in Hamburg. Moreover, Turner seems to have lost a lot of the overcautiousness, which was one of the remarkable features of his early activities as a government spy. For the first time since his defection from the United Irishmen in 1797, he signed himself Samuel Turner, instead of using one of his aliases, namely Richardson or Roberts.[28]

signature 'Rd.son' [=Richardson=Turner]. See also Nat. Arch. 620/49/82, French intelligence from Hamburg, 11 November 1800 for an account of Turner's contacts.

27 PRO F.O. 33/21/60–7, Turner's petitions on behalf of Beamish, enclosed in Craufurd's letters of 13 & 17 February 1801; see also PRO H.O. 100/100/133–7 and 142–3 for Turner's employment.

28 Nat. Arch. OP/132/2, Turner to Cooke, Hamburg, 18 May 1802.

For the moment, the Irishman's persistence was crowned with success. He continued to reside in Hamburg, and money was made available for him. Turner was in favour with Sir George Rumbold, who did not choose to drop the Irish spy. On 24 August 1802, the English minister addressed a letter to Lord Hervey, one of the under-secretaries in the British Foreign Department, in which he picked up the question of Turner's services. 'This Roberts', he stated, 'still receives thro' my hands a considerable gratification, and the secret of his Employment appears to be consider'd of high moment. I conceiv'd that it wou'd have been imprudent, indeed improper on me to have discontinued the price of his discretion.' Although Rumbold tried to justify the expenditure of money on Turner, he was puzzled about how to employ him now the situation in Europe had calmed down.[29] While London was discussing Turner's claim for a pension, Rumbold did not know what to do with the Irishman. After functioning as Britain's top spy on the Continent for five years, and with the peace holding, Turner was allowed to leave his post in the late summer of 1802. At the time he departed from Hamburg, some of the United men on the Continent had already begun contemplating another rebellion in Ireland. Turner himself, however, later recorded the circumstances of his last months on the Continent:

> At this time Sir G. Rumbold saying nothing was to be done at Hamburg, sent Turner to Paris, there the government and rebel Irish had been set on their guard against him by some of the Irish gentlemen formerly in the confidence of Dublin Castle, now thro' pique and disappointment little better than the United Irish. In consequence a pretext was made of a quantity of Louis d'ors (which came thro' Sir Rumbold to Turner) being false, because said not to 've been coined in France. Turner was thrown for nine weeks into the concergerie and afterwards detained prisoner on parole eight months at Paris, when the government was forced to return him his money and after every exertion had been made but in vain to send him to the gallows, during this captivity he was forced to spend large sums in order to support the character he had always maintained on the continent, that of an independent Gentleman.[30]

In Paris, Turner's United brethren seem to have had a hunch that there was something not quite right about their countryman. Turner had been among

---

29 PRO F.O. 33/22/156–8, Rumbold to Lord Hervey, 24 August 1802.
30 Nat. Arch. 620/11/160/4, Turner's description of his life is enclosed in his letter to Wickham, dated 16 June 1803. Although the description itself is not signed, there is no mistaking Turner's handwriting.

the first United Irishmen to arrive on the Continent, but had remained aloof in Hamburg for the most part of his exile. Although he had always posed as an upright radical, he had managed to keep out of precarious affairs of any kind and had showed no inclination whatsoever to participate in any of the expeditions. Moreover, how could he keep up the lifestyle of an 'independent Gentlemen' while his fellow exiles were living on the verge of poverty? Considering these inconsistencies, it is hardly surprising that his compatriots in France began to be sceptical about Turner.

Turner's disatisfaction and discontent was evident in the spring of 1803. After meeting Turner in Paris, J. Talbot, formerly British chargé d'affaires in Switzerland, expressed his disgust at the Irishman's offensive behaviour in a letter to Wickham on 29 March 1803. 'A Mr Turner', he explained, 'I think he says he comes from Newry, and who subsequently lived at Hamburgh, where he says he was employed by the British Government offered his services as a spy shortly after our arrival, but he is such an impudent and suspicious looking fellow that we would have nothing to do with him. He talked of his intimacy with you, and was extremely clamorous about the arrears upon a pension which he says he has from England. I have since heard that this fellow has been holding very violent language.'[31] Turner was in serious trouble by the spring of 1803, when he received news that his father 'was rapidly declining'; and he did not find it hard to bring himself to leave Paris for his native Ireland.[32]

By June 1803, he had reached England. There, he tried to get in touch with various government officials, namely Lord Castlereagh, John King and Lord Pelham, in order to prepare the ground for his return to Ireland. Since his efforts were not immediately crowned with success, Turner also addressed a letter to the Irish Chief Secretary William Wickham on 16 June, in which he put his case. 'I've requested to be erased from the proscription as you know', he recorded his notions, 'and to be assured the continuation of the two hundred and fifty pounds per annum as heretofore from the British establishment if not further employed.'[33] Shortly after receiving Turner's letter, the Irish Chief Secretary conferred with the British Home Office, 'with a view of ascertaining whether Turner's attainder can be removed in any other way but by Act of Parliament so as to avoid attainder of Blood.' He explained that 'now that Turner has openly avowed his Connection with Government I think that no inconvenience can result from our avowing it ourselves but on the contrary, much good as it may tend very much to hold an example to others

31 PRONI T.2627/5/Y/2, J. Talbot to Wickham, Paris, 29 March 1803.
32 Nat. Arch. 620/11/160/4, Turner's description of his own life (See footnote 30 above).
33 Nat. Arch. 620/11/160/4, Turner to Wickham, 16 June 1803.

by convincing them that Government is not ungrateful in cases where Individuals have of their own accord stepped forward to its assistance.'[34] Wickham, however, was certainly not interested in denouncing Turner. His reference to open avowal and acknowledgement is more a reference to the complexities of securing what Turner wanted – the removal of his name from the list of the proscribed – and his readiness to pursue that course, despite its risks for Turner, than anything else. In a letter to the Irish Chief Secretary, dated 6 October 1803, Turner strongly emphasized that 'my counsel Mr Bell I would wish to keep in the dark as well as every other person as to my connexions with government. ... I would have waited on you myself with this but feared being looked on as a spy if I appeared so often at the Castle, a report that would do me as much harm as if I was still supposed a rebel.' Turner strove to institute a 'criminal process'. He explained to Wickham that 'my alledging I am not the person and the Crown confessing the fact, or error, will be sufficient,'[35] and set about taking the matter in hand himself. Shortly after writing to Wickham in early October, he started out for England in order to remove any obstacles in the way of his vindication. Apart from clearing up remaining misunderstandings, he was preoccupied with obtaining a decent reward for his services as a government spy. After conferring with John King and Lord Gosford, he had returned to Dublin by early November.[36] At any rate, Turner had succeeded in pushing ahead with his business. On 25 November 1803, he eventually appeared at the King's Bench 'to plead to the act of Attainder of 1798.' On showing proof of his absence from Ireland for upwards of a year prior to the outbreak of the insurrection, the attainder was reversed. After being discharged, Turner continued to reside in Dublin until his death in around 1810.[37]

The circumstances of Turner's return to Ireland are indicative of the cunning that distinguished him from all other government spies. As in the instance of his defection in 1797, he did not leave anything to chance. He finally managed to make a grand exit, 'preserving to the end the reputation of a patriot among the popular party in Ireland and enjoying the friendship of Daniel O'Connell.'[38] While a shadow of suspicion had fallen on him in

34 PRONI T.2627/5/K/162, Wickham to Marsden, 7 July 1803.
35 PRONI T.2627/5/Y/28, Turner to Wickham, 6 October 1803.
36 PRONI T.2627/5/Y/43, Turner to Wickham, 5 November 1803 and PRO H.O. 100/ 115/219, Turner to King, 6 November 1803.
37 *Faulkner's Dublin Journal*, 1 December 1803. I am grateful to Ruan O'Donnell for drawing my attention to this piece of information. See *Dictionary of National Biography*, XIX, 1282–3 on Turner's return to Dublin.
38 *Dictionary of National Biography*, XIX, 1283 on Turner's return to Dublin.

France in around 1802–3, it was only several years later that his treachery became known with all its implications. Nevertheless, Luke Cullen's account of Fitzgerald's stay in Hamburg seems to confirm that some suspicions of Turner existed from early on. 'Fitzgerald was often heard to say:', Cullen claimed, 'Who can place confidence in the professions of men, when such red-hot patriots as Turner and Duckett become the seething dogs of England?' Considering that it is impossible to give proof of Cullen's claim of what Fitzgerald actually said or believed, his account nevertheless confirms an awareness of Turner's true activities in around 1840, when Cullen wrote his account for Madden.[39] Around the same time, James Hope, one of the United leaders to pave the way for 'Emmet's Rebellion', accused Turner of betrayal in his autobiographical account for Madden's *The United Irishmen*. 'We had traitors in our camp from the beginning to the close of the career of our society', he complained. 'For years our agent in Hamburg (Mr Turner), ... [was] furnishing Pitt with all our secrets, foreign and domestic.'[40] At any rate, by the 1840s, Madden knew about Turner's treachery, some fifty years before W.J. Fitzpatrick applied himself to the problem in his *Secret Service under Pitt*.[41]

Turner had genuinely earned his reputation as a spy. The prudence with which he proceeded, the accuracy of his information, as well as his showing as a double agent made him stand out from other government informers, such as Leonard McNally, George Orr, or John Murphy. The latter had also been at one time or other members of the United men, but none of them had been as effective as Turner, who had succeeded in worming himself into the confidence of the British government, his United brethren, the French as well as Hamburg authorities. The effects of his activities went beyond the narrow confines of the north German city, enabling London and Dublin to gain an insight into the machinery of Irish radicalism as a whole. It was thanks to Turner that the British secret service gained a foothold in Hamburg, where he was at the hub of United affairs. It was due to his information that news of the Franco–Irish alliance became an open secret among the authorities. For instance, along with evidence coming in from other sources, Turner had left the government in Dublin in no doubt by the early months of 1798 of its need to act. It did so at several levels in March 1798, which was in effect the month of key government decisions on policy. In a concrete sense, however, Turner was comparatively uninformed, and passed on little if any precise information. Like the Irish abroad at large, he was in the dark about actual invasion plans, scale, dates or proposed places of landing. The value

39 TCD MS.1472/191, Cullen's version for Madden.
40 Madden, *The United Irishmen*, 3rd ser., 1st vol., 240.
41 Fitzpatrick, W.J., *Secret Service under Pitt* (London, 1892)

of his information lay in other regards. Firstly, he made it possible to make arrests of travellers, such as the four Hamburg prisoners, and intercept United Irish as well as French letters, thus helping to impede immensely the exchange of information between Ireland and France. Secondly, by backing the more extreme camp in Paris, Turner not only preserved his own credentials but added to the depth of the divide among the United Irishmen themselves, to say nothing of the harmful effects on United–French communications resulting from misunderstandings within the Society. In this way, Turner helped to undermine the Franco–Irish alliance and to counteract United efforts at home. The British authorities were well aware of Turner's importance on the Continent when they refused to give way to Irish demands for exploiting the spy's talents in open court in the early months of 1798. Employment of Turner as a witness would have involved giving up his use, as Camden wished, in order to prosecute individual United Irishmen and would certainly have done great harm to the British espionage network as a whole. It was simply out of the question for London to do without Turner whose letters were its most valuable source of information on the Continent. While only nineteen of his letters have survived in the archives of Dublin, Belfast, London and Hamburg, government reports in England and Ireland teem with references to Turner, indicating that the actual number of letters written by the spy exceeded the number of those that could be clearly assigned to his authorship. Since he sometimes failed to sign his letters or name his addressees, dividing his correspondence into categories proves to be difficult. Nevertheless, he started feeding Downshire with information in late 1797 and had sent four letters to the powerful magnate by December of the same year. Except for two originals signed under the alias of Richardson, Turner's intelligence of 1798 is devoid of any signatures, only existing in the form of copies. Regarding the tone of the letters, the chronological and logical context, all the indications are that the author was Turner. While Turner's letters of 1798, five in number, do not reveal any of the respective addressees, there are grounds for the supposition that they were in the first instance addressed to Downshire and/ or members of the British government before they were eventually copied for the internal use of various government sections in Ireland. Turner's importance seems to have decreased after 1798, since only five letters could be found, dating from the years between 1799 and 1801. He wrote them on behalf of the Hamburg prisoners (two letters) as well as an Irishman named Beamish (two letters), and only one letter to the British Foreign Office contained intelligence of some substance. Henceforward, Turner's correspondence almost exclusively dealt with the conditions of his return to Ireland. It was mostly addressed to members of the Irish government (Wickham: three letters/ Cooke: one letter), except for one letter to John King, the Under-Secretary of State in the British Home Department. Although it must be assumed that only a fraction of his correspondence has survived over the years, Turner's letters illustrate the development of his career as a government informer. By the time he made his farewell from Hamburg, British interest in United activities had petered out. Lulled into a sense of false security, the authorities believed themselves able to do without Turner's services. By 1802–3, the north German city had receded from a place in intelligence concerns; and if it had not been for 'Emmet's Rebellion', the authorities would have wandered off the subject of Hamburg altogether. Although Elliott claimed that 'intelligence channels on the United men abroad had all but dried up' after Turner's return to Ireland, radical life went on in Hamburg.[42]

Shaken out of their complacency, Dublin and London turned to United affairs again in the aftermath of 'Emmet's Rebellion'. The intensive investigations, which followed the failure of the attempted coup, also shed light on the question of Hamburg's role in Franco–Irish relations. Once again, the authorities had been made aware of the city's importance for United communications; and it was certainly no accident that they followed Thomas Ridgeway's trail some two weeks after the events of 23 July. London had got wind of the smuggler, who had helped Samuel Neilson to return to Ireland in the previous year. In early August 1803, he was reported to be on his way to Ireland, together with his United partner, Anthony McCann. When Ridgeway was eventually arrested in Drogheda around the middle of the month, the authorities were forced to realise that there was no clue as to the whereabouts of Anthony McCann. The latter had duped his watchdogs into believing that he accompanied Ridgeway to Ireland, but he in fact had secretly returned to Hamburg after going aboard the *Providence*.[43] It is unclear what happened to McCann in the two months following Ridgeway's arrest in August 1803, but it must be assumed that the English minister in Hamburg became aware of the Irishman. Although Ridgeway had certainly been a good catch, it was actually McCann whom he was after. At any rate, the United Irishman had softened up on the English by October. 'Mr McCann has waited on me', Rumbold informed his London superiors on 24, 'to request I would say a word in his favor. He represented himself as having abjured the errors that he says his youth and inexperience have involved him in.'[44] After six years of exile on the Continent, Anthony McCann obviously decided to change sides. His belated defection in the autumn of 1803, however, is somewhat baffling. Subsequent

42 Elliott, *Partners in Revolution*, 317.
43 PRO H.O. 100/112/156–7, 165–9, 238, 241–2, 290–6, 100/114/189–91 and Nat. Arch. 620/12/140 for the circumstances of the arrest of Thomas Ridgeway.
44 PRO F.O. 97/241, Rumbold to King, 24 October 1803.

to the departure from his native Ireland in the summer of 1797, he had been included in the Fugitive Act, had taken part in Tandy's expedition in 1798, had entered upon a career as a smuggler, before he eventually got cold feet as late as 1803. The Irish Under-Secretary Marsden was ready with an answer with regard to McCann's change of mind, when he conferred with the British Home Office some months later. 'The affairs of the Partnership [McCann-Ridgeway] have gone on very badly', he explained to Reginald Pole Carew, 'and Macan is certainly in distress, which may have induced him to tender his Services in the way he has done, and the reward which Turner has received, who was Macan's neighbour while in Ireland, and who for a long time resided at Hamburgh, may have encouraged Macan to adopt a similar course: Turner received a pension, and a pardon, and it is within Macan's power to earn both.' As a matter of fact, McCann was well acquainted with Turner, who had already feathered his own nest; and the latter's example had certainly not deterred McCann from acting likewise. Without thinking twice, London and Dublin agreed to take up McCann's offer. According to Marsden, 'It is His Excellency's opinion that it is highly desireable the services of Mr Macan should be made use of as his connection with the Disaffected Irish, and his long residence on the Continent make it as much to be presumed in his case, as it could be in that of any other person with whom a confidential intercourse has not existed, that he can be usefull.' By the beginning of 1804, Anthony McCann had taken on Turner's position as United spy in Hamburg.[45]

Despite the employment of McCann, United days in Hamburg were numbered by 1803. Subsequent to the Franco–British peace agreement, United travellers had begun to follow alternative paths, often using the direct route between Ireland and France or putting into Dutch ports. While the situation in Europe had eased off, many United migrants went unnoticed. 'Emmet's Rebellion' of July 1803 had eventually made it perfectly clear to the authorities that their own negligence could have cost them dear. But while Dublin and London began to take the United Irishmen seriously again, and a new agent was installed in Hamburg, the home movement ceased to be a grave threat to government. The United Society in Ireland never recovered the ground it had lost in 1803 and subsequently disintegrated in the following years. Since United affairs in Hamburg stood or fell by the situation in Ireland, the failure of Emmet's attempt constituted the swan song for Irish radicals resident in the north German city. Although individual United Irishmen frequented Hamburg in the following years, the United heydays in the city were over by 1803.

45 PRO H.O. 100/119/206–7, Marsden to Carew, 28 February 1804. See Nat. Arch. 620/11/130/18 on McCann's acquaintance with Turner.

Epilogue

Subsequent to 1803, United affairs drew to a close. While the home organization collapsed soon after the failure of 'Emmet's Rebellion', the Society's leadership in France still endeavoured to keep the United flag flying. The renewal of war in May and the creation of an Irish Legion in the late summer of 1803 temporarily revived the United fighting spirit, which had suffered substantially from Emmet's fiasco. Now that they had received some kind of an institutionalised platform for Irish affairs, the United Irishmen cherished hopes of benefitting from the hostilities between Britain and France. But before long they were forced to realise that being bound to the Irish Legion was detrimental to their plans for the liberation of Ireland. The Irish legionaries were subordinate to Bonaparte as the supreme commander of the French armies, which in turn meant a considerable curtailment of their individual freedom of action. While the Irish business merged into French military affairs, United negotiations lost much of their effects. Lacking an organized movement at home, the United Irishmen in France had little to show for it anyway, all the more as they were divided amongst themselves. Disagreements between Thomas Addis Emmet and Arthur O'Connor put a great strain on the radicals' negotiations with the French authorities. Bickering within the organization interfered with the Irishmen's bargaining position and eventually contributed to the Society's disintegration in the years subsequent to Robert Emmet's rising. Since French promises of sending a fleet to Ireland had not materialised, the Irishmen began to go separate ways. In October 1804, Thomas Addis Emmet emigrated to the New World, followed by some of his United brethren, namely William James MacNeven, Hugh Wilson and William Sampson, all of whom had abandoned hope of a French–backed revolution in their native country. By 1806, the United Irishmen on the Continent had stopped putting up a united front; the organization had ceased to exist.[1]

---

1 Elliott, *Partners in Revolution*, 323–64 on the United Irishmen subsequent to 'Emmet's Rebellion'.

By 1806, United tracks in Hamburg had disappeared. William Sampson had left the city by March in order to travel to England and eventually to America. By all accounts, Edward Fitzgerald and possibly also Garret Byrne still resided in Hamburg, although there are only vague signs of their presence. While various pieces of information suggest that Hamburg was frequented by United men subsequent to 1803, the organization itself was certainly in its final throes.[2] For seven eventful years, Hamburg had mirrored the development of the Franco–Irish alliance. Starting with Lord Edward and Arthur O'Connor's journey in 1796, the Society's agents headed for Hamburg; and until 1803, all important United missions to and from France followed in their footsteps. Drawing up a list of United arrivals in Hamburg is tantamount to enumerating the cream of the Society: Edward Lewins, Napper Tandy, William James MacNeven, Samuel Turner, Alexander Lowry, Bartholomew Teeling, John Tennent, Revd Arthur MacMahon, James Quigley, William Duckett, William Bailey, William Hamilton, Thomas Burgess, Anthony McCann, William and Thomas Corbet, Bartholomew Blackwell, Hervey M. Morres, William Putnam McCabe, George Palmer, Thomas O'Meara, Edward Carolan, Robert and Thomas Addis Emmet, Malachy Delaney, Garret Byrne, Edward Fitzgerald, Archibald Hamilton Rowan, William Sampson, Samuel Neilson, John Chambers, Thomas Russell, John Swiney, Joseph Cormick, Hugh Wilson, John Sweetman, Matthew Dowling, Joseph Cuthbert, George Cummings, Edward Hudson ... All of them and many others resided in or passed through Hamburg at some stage between 1796 and 1803. Hamburg was *the* undisputed point of convergence for the United Irishmen on their way to or from France, to say nothing of the city's importance as a centre for United correspondence between Ireland and the Continent.

United affairs in Hamburg stood or fell with conditions within the Society. Considering that only Lord Edward and Arthur O'Connor established contact with the French authorities in the year following Tone's arrival on the Continent, the Irishmen's communications with France started sluggishly in 1796. As seen in the instance of Lord Edward, O'Connor, Lewins, MacNeven and their meetings with Reinhard, Hamburg did not merely serve as a Continental point of departure for the Irishmen's missions, but offered opportunities to enter directly into negotiations with the French. Often enough, Reinhard exceeded his powers by pursuing an Irish policy independent of his superiors in Paris, a fact which was eventually to prove his undoing later. It was not until the summer of 1797 that United affairs in Hamburg were really set in motion. Starting with the flight of the Ulster leaders, United numbers

2 Nat. Arch. 620/14/188/23, 620/14/198/4, various pieces of information relating to Hamburg, 1805–6.

in the city rose steadily in the year leading up to the rebellion. This clearly reflected heightening tensions in Ireland as well as the state of agitation within the movement. Analogous to this gain in numbers, British secret service activities concerning Hamburg were on the increase from the time of Turner's employment in mid–1797. Roused by alarming reports on United activities in the city, Dublin and London turned towards Hamburg. Subsequent to the Irish rebellion and the failure of the French expeditions, United arrivals peaked in the second half of 1798; and it was certainly no remarkable coincidence that the arrest of Tandy and his three friends occurred at that particular time. Thus, radical migration to Hamburg, like the degree of British interference in the city, reached their climax in 1798–9. Thereafter, United numbers as well as British vigilance declined. In the face of the set-backs of the previous years, the post-rebellion United Irishmen tightened their security after 1798, thus lulling the authorities into a false sense of security. While fewer radicals headed for Hamburg, the British government failed to take the United Irishmen seriously, not seeing that they had not abandoned their plans of a French–assisted revolution in Ireland. Astonishingly, Dublin and London were not aware of the flurry of activity which followed the state prisoners' arrival on the Continent in 1802; and it was not until shortly before Emmet's attempt that the authorities began to pay attention to United moves again. At any rate, the events of 1803 sealed the fate of the United Irishmen in Hamburg once and for all.

The activities of the United Irishmen in Hamburg constitute a remarkable overlap of German and Irish history, all the more as there was no such thing as a tradition of Irishmen in Hamburg prior to the 1790s. It was made possible by a combination of various events, such as the French Revolution and its effects on Irish radical thought (and on Europe as a whole!), the United Irishmen's association with the French, the coalition wars, the English sea-blockade of the French and the Dutch coast, and Hamburg's socio-economic and political-geographical situation at the time of the French Revolution. The interconnection of all these factors created the conditions for United activities in Hamburg. Although we must not lose sight of the fact that the Irishmen's connections with Hamburg represent a brief interlude in Irish history, the north German city was of vital importance for United–French communications. United presence in Hamburg was a unique occurrence, limited from the point of view of time, and yet, it had repercussions on the development of Irish nationalism in the 1790s and 1800s. For a number of years, the correspondence of the Irish and British authorities teemed with references to Hamburg, which had become synonymous with United trouble-making by the end of the eighteenth century. The city served as the most important outpost of the Franco–Irish alliance and also enabled the British intelligence service to have its finger on the pulse of Irish radicalism. While people like Sir James Craufurd, Samuel Turner, or even William Duckett have hitherto been viewed as a concomitant of the Irishmen's involvement with the French, their activities were part and parcel of the development of United affairs as a whole. Due to events, such as Tandy's arrest, the Duckett episode, and Turner's betrayal of his radical brethren, United matters took on a different complexion. To view Irish radicalism without paying heed to events in Hamburg is almost impossible. Surprisingly, the United Irishmen mostly passed unnoticed as far as the Hamburg authorities are concerned, and except for the Tandy episode, their activities in the city do not find expression in German historical investigations. This is why it is imperative to rescue them from oblivion.

Bibliography

PRIMARY SOURCES: MANUSCRIPTS

Belfast

Public Record Office of Northern Ireland

D.272	McCance Papers
D.607	Downshire MSS.
D.714	Cleland MSS.
D.3030	Castlereagh Papers
T.739	Proclamations, 1797
T.759 & 823	Transcripts of various documents relating to Archibald Hamilton Rowan, 1792–1805
T.755/IV–V	Pelham Papers (copy of Addl. MSS. 33103 & 33104, original in British Library)
T.2627/5	Wickham Papers (copy of MS. 38M49, original in Hampshire County Record Office)
T.3229	Sneyd Papers

Dublin
Trinity College

Manuscripts:

MSS.869/1–10	Sirr Papers
MS.873	Madden Papers
MS.1472	Luke Cullen Papers
MSS.1762–3	Pratt (Camden) Papers, 1795–7 (copy of MS.U. 840, original in Kent County Record Office)
MS.5967	Corbet Papers
MSS.7253–6	Hope MSS.

Microfilm:

Mic.50–59	Pratt (Camden) Papers (MS.U.840, original in Kent County Record Office)

National Archives

Manuscripts:
620/1–67   Rebellion Papers
1015–1026,
3001–3686   State Of The Country Papers (first and second series),
                    1796–1804
M.5892A   Miscellaneous Papers Of Garrett Byrne

National Library

Manuscripts:
MSS.8822   Blackwell MSS.
MSS.13665   Letters Of William Duckett

Microfilm:
pos.198   Selected Manuscripts Of Irish Interest From The Archives
                    Nationales, Paris
pos.210   Life Of William Duckett
pos.755–757   Pelham Papers (Addl. MSS. 33101, 33113–4, 33118, 33120,
                    original in British Library)

Hamburg

Staatsarchiv

Kämmerei:
Kämm.I, Nr.214,
Band 155   Wedde-Rechnung de Anno 1797
Kämm.I, Nr.214,
Band 158   Wedde-Rechnung de Anno 1800
Kämm.I, Nr.225   Fremdenschoßbücher, Bd.2, 1793–1811

Senat:

Cl.1, Lit.Pb, Vol.8c, Fasc.2, Nr.21
                    Dem Prätor erstattete Berichte des Franzosen Lelarge über
                    die in Hamburg sich aufhaltenden französischen Emigranten,
                    1796–1800
Cl.1, Lit.Pb, Vol.8d, Fasc.15b1, Inv. 1–24
                    Acta, die arretierten Irländer Napper Tandy et Consorten,
                    betreffend
Cl.7, Lit.Db, Nr.20, Vol.1, Fasc.3
                    Schoßregister der im Fremden-kontrakt stehenden Personen,
                    1724, 1799, 1801

Wedde:
Wedde I, Nr.29,
Band 78   Hochzeitenprotokoll de Anno 1797

London

Public Record Office

Admiralty:
Adm.I/3974–3975   Intelligence, 1782–1810
Adm.I/6033–6034   Intelligence, 1796–1801
Adm.I/3991   Letters relating to Ireland

Chatham Papers:
PRO 30/8/
323–327   Letters relating to Ireland, 1767–1805

Cornwallis Papers:
PRO 30/11/263   Irish Affairs
PRO 30/11/270   Letters from important people, 1781–1807

Foreign Office:
F.O. 27/51–54,
56, 58   Letters, papers, advices and intelligence, France, 1796– 1801
F.O. 29/16   Army in Germany, January–November 1798
F.O. 33/12–25   Hamburg, 1796–1804
F.O. 97/240–242   Hamburg, supplementary, 1781–1810

Home Office:
H.O. 69/26–30   Letters of Prince of Bouillon
H.O. 100/60–120   Ireland, 1796–1804

Privy Council:
P.C. I/23/A.38   London Corresponding Society, 1794–6
P.C. I/34/A.90   Treason, 1796
P.C. I/37/A.114   Miscellaneous, 1797
P.C. I/38/A.122–3 Miscellaneous, 1797, including
  and P.C. I/40/
  A.129–32   Mutiny at the Nore, Corresponding Societies
P.C. I/40/A.133   Miscellaneous, January 1798, including Corresponding
                   Societies
P.C. I/41/A.136–9 Miscellaneous, Corresponding Societies,
  and P.C. I/42/   Treason, Sedition, 1798
  A.140–4
P.C. I/43/A.147   Miscellaneous, June–September 1798, including Mutiny at
                   the Nore
P.C. I/43/A.150   Corresponding Societies, Treason, October–December 1798

P.C. I/43/A.152–3   Corresponding Societies, United Irishmen, 1799
P.C. I/44/A.155   Corresponding Societies, Ireland, April 1799
P.C. I/44/A.158–9   Corresponding Societies, Irish prisoners, United
and A.161   Englishmen, May–October 1799
P.C. I/45/A.164   Corresponding Societies, Secret information, Irish
                     prisoners, November–December 1799
P.C. I/3117   Corresponding Societies, Treason, 1797–1806
P.C. I/3473
and 3514   Corresponding Societies, Treason, State prisoners, 1800
P.C. I/3526, 3528,   Miscellaneous, 1801, including Corresponding
and 3535   Societies, Treason, State prisoners
P.C. I/3536a and
3552–3   Treason, State prisoners, Despard's conspiracy, 1802
P.C. I/3564 and   Miscellaneous, 1803, including Secret information,
3581–3   Secret societies, Irish insurrection

War Office:
W.O.I/396–397   Intelligence, various agents on the Continent, 1793– 1803
W.O.I/612   Correspondence from the Lord Lieutenant of Ireland,
                     1794–1808
W.O.I/778   Irish Militia
W.O.I/921–924   Letters of Prince of Bouillon
W.O.I 8/9   Out letters to Ireland, 1796–1803

PRIMARY SOURCES: PRINTED

Newspapers

Altonaer Addreß-Comtoir Nachrichten
Hamburgische Addreß-Comtoir Nachrichten
Hamburgischer Correspondent
Hamburgische Neue Zeitung
Hamburgischer Relations-Courier

Contemporary Works And Pamphlets

*Einige Bemerkungen über die unter dem Titel: Betrachtungen eines Hamburger Bürgers
    über die Inhaftierung einiger Irländer allhier, erschienene Schrift (Hamburg, 1798)*
Betrachtung eines Hamburger Bürgers über die Verhaftung einiger Irländer allhier
    (Hamburg, 1798)
The Correspondence of Edmund Burke, ed. Thomas W. Copeland (et al.), vols VI–IX
    (Chicago, 1967–70)

The Works of the Right Hon. Edmund Burke, ed. Henry Rogers, vol. I (London, 1841)

Burke, Edmund, *Irish Affairs*, ed. Matthew Arnold (London, Melbourne, Auckland, Johannesburg, 1988)

Büsch, Johann Georg, *Versuch einer Geschichte der Hamburgischen Handlung, nebst zwei kleineren Schriften eines verwandten Inhalts* (Hamburg, 1797)

Memoirs of Miles Byrne, ed. his widow, 3 vols (Paris, New York, 1863)

Memoirs and Correspondence of Viscount Castlereagh, Second Marquess of Londonderry, ed. Charles Vane, 3rd Marquess of Londonderry, 12 vols (1848– 54), I–IV

Correspondence of Charles, First marquis Cornwallis, ed. Charles Ross, 3 vols (London, 1859)

Emmet, Thomas Addis, *Ireland Under English Rule*, 2 vols (New York, 1903)

The Later Correspondence of George III, ed. A. Aspinall, vols I–III (Cambridge, 1962–7)

Neues Hamburger und Altonaer Address-Buch, 1796–1803 (Hamburg, 1796–1803)

Historical Manuscripts Commission, *Report on the Manuscripts of J.B. Fortescue, Esq., preserved at Dropmore*, IV–VI (London, 1905–8)

MacNeven, William James, *Pieces of Irish History* (New York, 1807)

Journals of the House of Commons of England, vol. 54: 1798–99

Journals of the House of Commons of Ireland [Appendices], vols XVI–XIX: 1797– 1800 (Dublin, 1800)

Journals of the House of Lords of Ireland, vol. VIII: 1798–1800 (Dublin, 1800)

Autobiography of Archibald Hamilton Rowan, ed. W.H. Drummond (Dublin, 1840)

Memoirs of William Sampson (New York, 1807)

Life of Theobald Wolfe Tone, ed. his son William T.W. Tone, 2 vols (Washington, 1826)

The Correspondence of the Right Honourable William Wickham, ed. his grandson W. Wickham, 2 vols (London, 1870)

SECONDARY SOURCES

Alter, Peter, *Nationalismus* (Frankfurt a.M., 1985)

Anderson, Benedict, *Die Erfindung der Nation. Zur Karriere eines erfolgreichen Konzepts*, german edn (Frankfurt a.M., New York, 1988)

Baillie, W.D., 'William Steele Dickson, D.D. (1744–1824)', *Irish Booklore*, II (1976), 238–267

Bartlett, Thomas, *The Fall and Rise of the Irish Nation: the Catholic Question, 1690–1830* (Savage, Md., 1992)

—— & Hayton, D.W., eds, *Penal Era and Golden Age. Essays in Irish History, 1690–1800* (Belfast, 1979)

Baylen, Joseph & Gossman, Norbert J., eds, *Biographical Dictionary of Modern British Radicals, Vol. I: 1770–1830* (Sussex, New Jersey, 1979)

Beckett, J.C., *The Anglo–Irish Tradition* (London, 1976)

——, *The Making of Modern Ireland, 1603–1923* (London, 1966)

Biro, Sydney Seymour, *The German Policy of Revolutionary France*, 2 vols (Mass., 1957)

Blanning, T.C.W., *The French Revolution in Germany* (Oxford, 1983)

Böhme, H., *Frankfurt und Hamburg. Des Deutschen Reiches Silber- und Goldloch und die allerenglichste Stadt des Kontinents* (Frankfurt a.M., 1968)

Boyce, D. George, *Nationalism in Ireland* (Dublin, 1982)

Campbell, Gerald, *Edward and Pamela Fitzgerald* (London, 1904)

Canavan, Anthony, *Frontier Town. An Illustrated History of Newry* (Belfast, 1989)

Corish, Patrick J., ed., *Radicals, Rebels & Establishments*, Historical Studies XV (Belfast, 1985)

Coughlan, Rupert J., *Napper Tandy* (Dublin, 1977)

Cox, Walter, 'James Bartholomew Blackwell', *Cox's Irish Magazin and Monthly Asylum for Neglected Biography* (January 1809), 32–4

Cronin, Sean, *Irish Nationalism. A History of its Roots and Ideology* (Dublin, 1980)

Cullen, L.M., *An Economic History of Ireland Since 1660* (London, 1972)

Curtin, Nancy J., *The United Irishmen. Popular Politics in Ulster and Dublin 1791–1798* (Oxford, 1994)

Dann, Otto & Dinwiddy, John, eds, *Nationalism in the Age of the French Revolution* (London, 1988)

Deutsch, Karl W., *Nationalism and Social Communication. An Inquiry Into the Foundations of Nationality*, 2nd edn (Cambridge/Mass. & London, 1962)

Dickson, David, *New Foundations: Ireland 1660–1800* (Dublin, 1987)

——, Keogh, Dáire and Whelan, Kevin, eds, *The United Irishmen: Republicanism, Radicalism and Rebellion* (Dublin, 1993)

Droz, Jacques, *L'Allemagne et la Révolution Française* (Paris, 1949)

Dugan, James, *The Great Mutiny* (London, 1966)

Elliott, Marianne, 'The "Despard Conspiracy" Reconsidered', *Past and Present*, 75 (May 1977), 46–61

——, *Partners in Revolution. The United Irishmen and France* (New Haven, London, 1982)

——, *Wolfe Tone. Prophet of Irish Independence* (New Haven, London, 1989)

Emsley, Clive, 'The Home Office and its Sources of Information and Investigation 1791–1801', *English Historical Revue*, XCIV (July 1979), 532–561

Farrell, Brian, ed., *The Irish Parliamentary Tradition* (Dublin, 1973)

Fitzpatrick, W.J., *Secret Service Under Pitt* (London, 1892)

Foster, R.F., *Modern Ireland 1600–1972* (London, 1988)

Froude, James Anthony, *The English in Ireland in the Eighteenth Century*, vol. III (London, 1881)

Garvin, Tom, *The Evolution of Irish Nationalist Politics* (Dublin, 1981)

Gooch, George Peabody, *Germany and the French Revolution* (London, 1920)

Goodwin, Albert, *The Friends of Liberty: The English Democratic Movement in the Age of the French Revolution* (London, 1979)

Gough, Hugh & Dickson, David, eds, *Ireland and the French Revolution* (Dublin, 1990)

Grab, Walter, *Demokratische Strömungen in Hamburg und Schleswig-Holstein zur Zeit der Ersten Französischen Republik* (Hamburg, 1966)

Greaves, C. Desmond, *Theobald Wolfe Tone and the Irish Nation* (Dublin, 1991)

Guillon, Edouard, *La France et l'Irlande Pendant la Révolution* (Paris, 1888)

Hannigan, Ken & Nolan, William, eds, *Wicklow: History & Society. Interdisciplinary Essays on the History of an Irish County* (Dublin, 1994)

Harder, Karl Wilhelm, *Die Auslieferung der vier politischen Flüchtlinge Napper Tandy, Blackwell, Morres (Morris) und George Peters im Jahre 1799 von Hamburg an Großbritannien unter Widerspruch von Frankreich* (Leipzig, 1857)

Harkensee, Heinrich, *Beiträge zur Geschichte der Emigranten in Hamburg, I: Das Französische Theater, II., Madame de Genlis* (Hamburg, 1896 & 1900)

Hausschild-Thiessen, Renate, 'Hamburg und die Wende vom 18. zum 19. Jahrhundert', *Hamburgische Geschichts- und Heimatblätter* IX, 8 (December, 1974), 181–208

Hayes, Richard, *Biographical Dictionary of Irishmen in France* (Dublin, 1949)

——, *Ireland and the Irishmen in the French Revolution* (Dublin, 1932)

Healy, F.J., ed., 'A Famous Franco–Irish Soldier: General William Corbet', *Journal of the Ivernian Society*, III (1910–11), 239–244

Hitzigrath, Heinrich, *Hamburg und die Kontinentalsperre* (Hamburg, 1900)

Jeannin, Pierre, *Gekräuselt, gepudert, mit untadeliger Anmut. Hamburg und die Französische Revolution* (Hamburg, 1977)

Jochmann, Werner & Loose, Hans-Dieter, eds, *Hamburg. Geschichte der Stadt und ihrer Bewohner* (Hamburg, 1982)

Johnston, Edith M., *Great Britain and Ireland 1760–1800. A Study in Political Administration*, 2nd edn (Westport/Conn., 1978)

Kee, Robert, *The Green Flag. A History of Irish Nationalism* (London, 1972)

Kopitzsch, Franklin, *Grundzüge einer Sozialgeschichte der Aufklärung in Hamburg und Altona*, 2nd edn (Hamburg, 1990)

——, *Hamburg zwischen Hauptrezeß und Franzosenzeit – Bemerkungen zur Verfassung, Verwaltung und Sozialstruktur*, in: Rausch, Wilhelm, ed., *Die Städte Mittel-europas im 17. und 18. Jahrhundert* (Linz/Donau, 1981)

Laufenberg, H., *Hamburg und die Französische Revolution* (Hamburg, 1913)

Lecky, W.E.H., *A History of Ireland in the Eighteenth Century*, vols III–IV, New Impression (London, 1913)

Lesch, Bruno, *Jan Anders Jägerhorn. Patriot Och Världsborgare Separatist Och Emigrant* (Helsingfors, 1941)

Lescure, M. de, *Rivarol et la Société Francaise Pendant la Révolution et l'émigration* (Paris, 1883)

Lindemann, Mary, *Patriots and Paupers. Hamburg, 1712–1830* (New York, Oxford, 1990)

Lyons, F.S.L., *Ireland Since the Famine*, 10th edn (London, 1987)

MacDermot, Frank, 'Arthur O'Connor', *Irish Historical Studies*, XV (1966), 48–69

Madden, R.R., *The United Irishmen. Their Lives and Times*, 3 ser., 7 vols (London, 1842–6), and revised edn, 4 vols (London, 1857–1860)

Maguire, W.A., 'Arthur McMahon, United Irishman and French Soldier', *Irish Sword*, IX (1969–70), 207–215

Malcomson, A.P.W., *John Foster. The Politics of Anglo–Irish Ascendancy* (Oxford, 1978)

McDowell, R.B., *Ireland in the Age of Imperialism and Revolution*, 2nd edn (Oxford, 1991)

McEvoy, Brendan, 'Father James Quigley', *Seanchas Ardmhacha*, V (1970), 247–259

Metscher, Priscilla, *Republicanism and Socialism in Ireland: A Study in the Relationship of Politics and Ideology from the United Irishmen to James Connolly* (Frankfurt a.M., Bern, New York, 1986)

Mettgenberg, Wolfgang, *James Napper Tandy. Ein Beitrag zur Geschichte des Auslieferungsrechts* (München, Leipzig, 1918)

Mitchell, Harvey, *The Underground War Against Revolutionary France. The Missions of William Wickham 1794–1800* (Oxford, 1965)

Moody, T.W. & Vaughan, W.E., eds, *A New History of Ireland, IV, Eighteenth- Century Ireland, 1690–1800* (Oxford, 1986)

Moore, Thomas, *The Life and Times of Lord Edward Fitzgerald*, 2nd edn (Dublin, London, 1909)

Ní Chinnéide, Síle, *Napper Tandy and the European Crises of 1798–1803*, O'Donnel Lecture (Galway, 1962)

Pakenham, Thomas, *The Year of Liberty*, 11th edn (London, 1978)

Palmer, R.R., *The Age of Democratic Revolution*, 2 vols (London, 1959 and 1964)

Piper, P., *Altona und die Fremden, insbesondere die Emigranten, vor hundert Jahren* (Altona, 1914)

Pringle, D.G., *One Island, Two Nations ? A Political-Geographical Analysis of the National Conflict in Ireland* (Letchworth, 1985)

Roebuck, Peter, *Plantation to Partition. Essays in Ulster History in Honour of J.L. McCracken* (Belfast, 1981)

Schramm, Percy Ernst, *Hamburg. Ein Sonderfall in der Geschichte Deutschlands* (Hamburg, 1964)

Schultze, Ernst, 'Englands Spionage gegen Irland', *Deutsche Strafrechts-Zeitung*, III (1916), 223–9

Servières, Georges, 'Un Épisode de l'Expédition d'Irlande. L'Extradition et la Mise en Liberté de Napper Tandy (1798–1802)', *Revue Historique*, XCIII (1907), 46–73

Sillem, W., 'Conrad Johann Matthiessen', *Mitteilungen des Vereins für Hamburgische Geschichte*, 11 & 12 (November & December 1891), 303–12 & 319–25

Smith, A.W., 'Irish Rebels and English Radicals, 1798–1820', *Past and Present*, 7 (April 1955), 78–85

Smyth, Jim, *The Men of No Property. Irish Radicals and Popular Politics in the Late Eighteenth Century* (Dublin, 1992)

Sutherland, D.M.G., *France 1789–1815. Revolution and Counter-revolution*, 2nd edn (London, 1988)

Stephen, Leslie & Lee, Sidney, eds, *The Dictionary of National Biography* (London, since 1917)

Swords, Liam, *The Green Cockade. The Irish in the French Revolution 1798–1815* (Dublin, 1989)

Thompson, E.P., *The Making of the English Working Class*, 3rd edn (London, 1980)

VanBrock, F.W., 'Captain McSheehy's Mission', *Irish Sword*, X (1972), 215– 228

——, 'A Memoir of 1798', *Irish Sword*, IX (1969–70), 192–206

Wells, Roger, *Insurrection. The British Experience 1795–1803*, 2nd edn (Gloucester, 1986)

Whelan, Kevin, *The Tree of Liberty: Radicalism, Catholicism and the Construction of Irish Identity 1760–1830* (Cork, 1996)

——, ed., *Wexford: History and Society* (Dublin, 1987)

Williams, T. Desmond, ed., *Secret Societies in Ireland* (Dublin, New York, 1973)

Wohlwill, Adolf, *Georg Kerner. Ein deutsches Lebensbild aus dem Zeitalter der Französischen Revolution* (Hamburg, Leipzig, 1886)

——, *Neuere Geschichte der Freien und Hansestadt Hamburg, insbesondere von 1789 bis 1825* (Gotha, 1914)

——, *Hamburgische Beiträge zur Geschichte der Jahre 1798 und 1799* (Hamburg, 1883)

——, *Reinhard als Französischer Gesandter in Hamburg und Die Neutralitäts-bestrebungen der Hansestädte in den Jahren 1795–1797* (Hamburg, 1875)

——, 'Die Verhaftung Napper Tandy's und die Conflicte Hamburg's mit den Großmächten 1798–1800, nach den Acten des Geh. Staatsarchivs in Berlin', *Mitteilungen des Vereins für hamburgische Geschichte*, I (1878), 33–6

Index